CONNECTIONS

CONNECTIONS

CONNECTIONS

COPYRIGHT BY ROSHINAIE JOHNSON

ISBN: 978-0-692-87-657-2

Cover by Anna Fong

This work may not be copied.

CONNECTIONS

EXAMPLE

POP

POP   DAD   FATHER

Have fun with Abigail on her journey. FILL IN THE BLANK WITH ONE OF THE WORDS IN THE SHAPES. Abigail uses arrows on some pages because she feels like they challenge you. You'll learn quickly that she's out of her mind.

IT MAY HELP TO SAY THE WORDS OUT LOUD.

IF YOU AND YOUR FRIEND HAVE A BOOK, YOU CAN RACE THROUGH IT FOR………. FUN.

Have a good time going on this horrific journey with the insane Abigail. Enjoy yourself.

CONNECTIONS

CONNECTIONS
BY ROSHINAIE JOHNSON

CONNECTIONS

1.

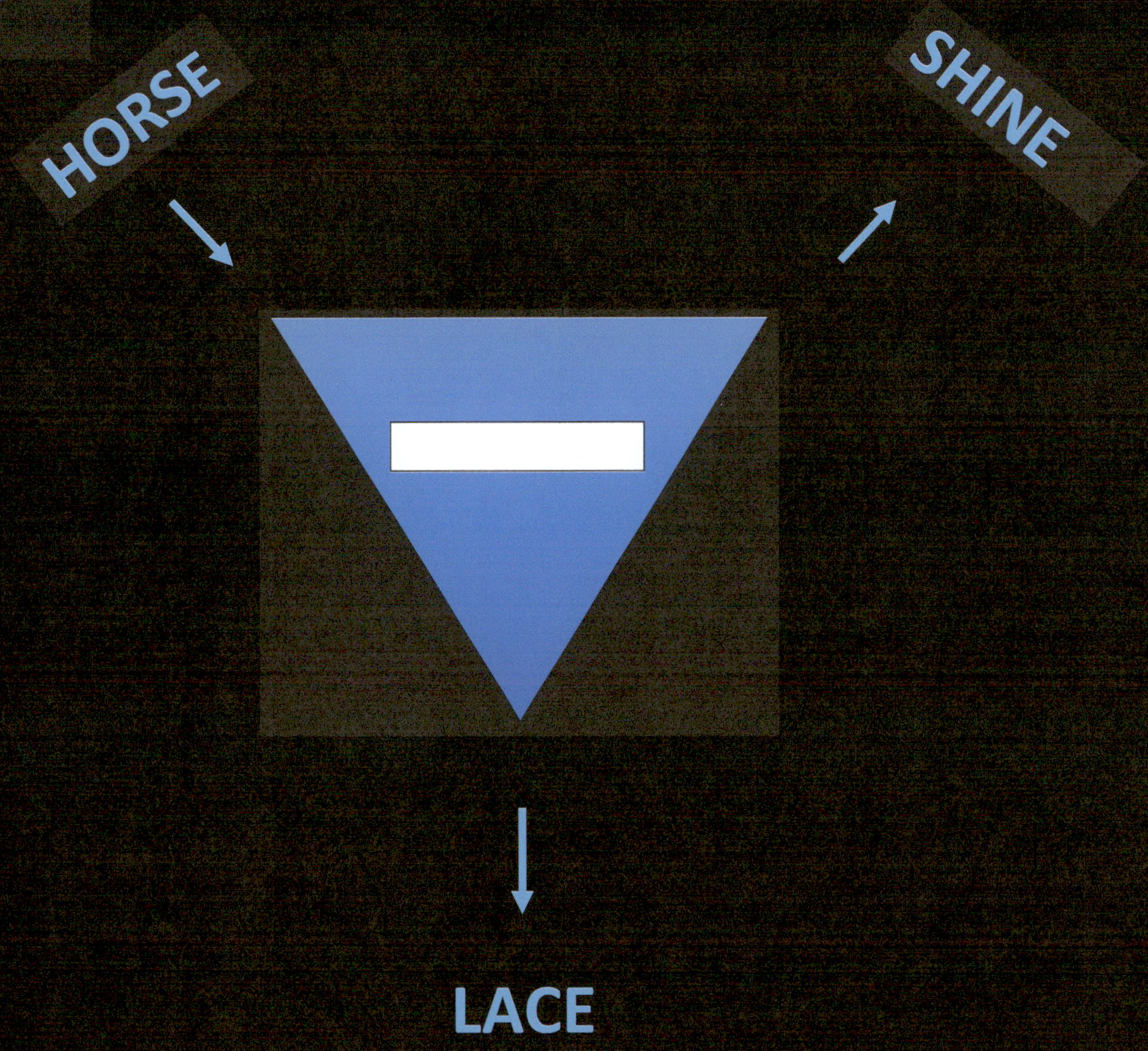

HORSE

SHINE

LACE

HE'S A MAD MAN.

MY DAD.

CLUE

SHOE

WHO

CONNECTIONS

BOARD CROSS

YOU CAN'T ESCAPE HIM.

WAY

TALK WALK STALK

CONNECTIONS

ROOM

CLASS

I ASKED HIM WHAT HE WOULD DO IF PEOPLE TRIED TO KILL ME AGAIN, THEN I LOOKED UP AND SAW THE MOON.

CHECK

TAPE

MATE

WAIT

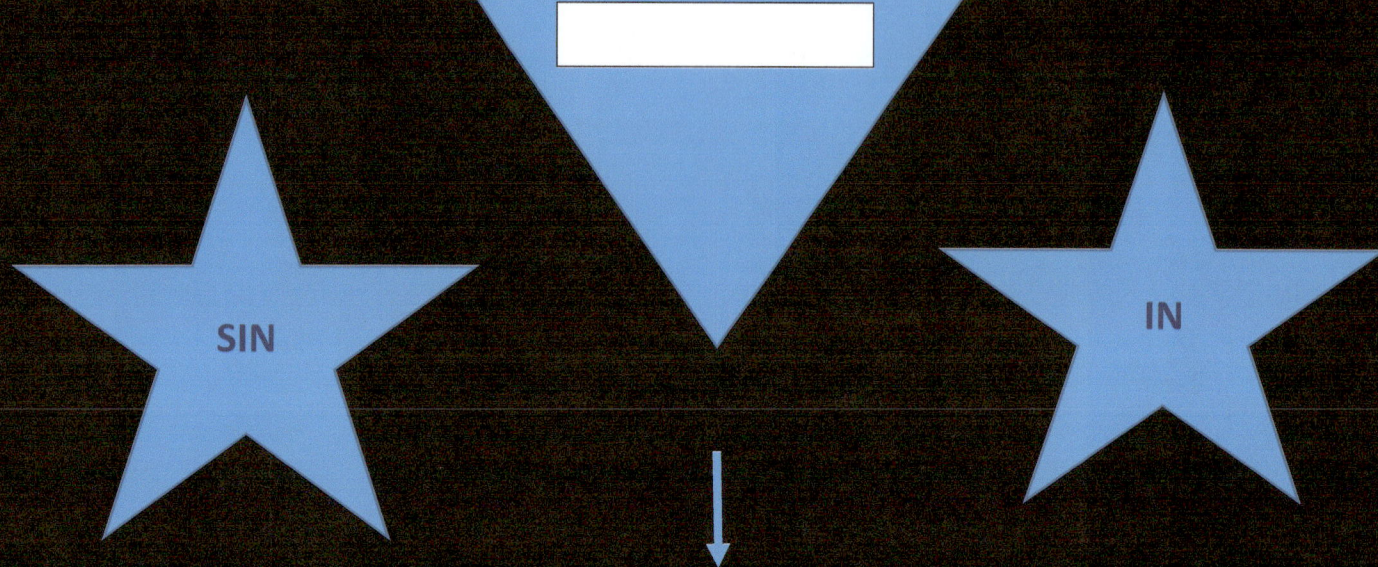

CONNECTIONS

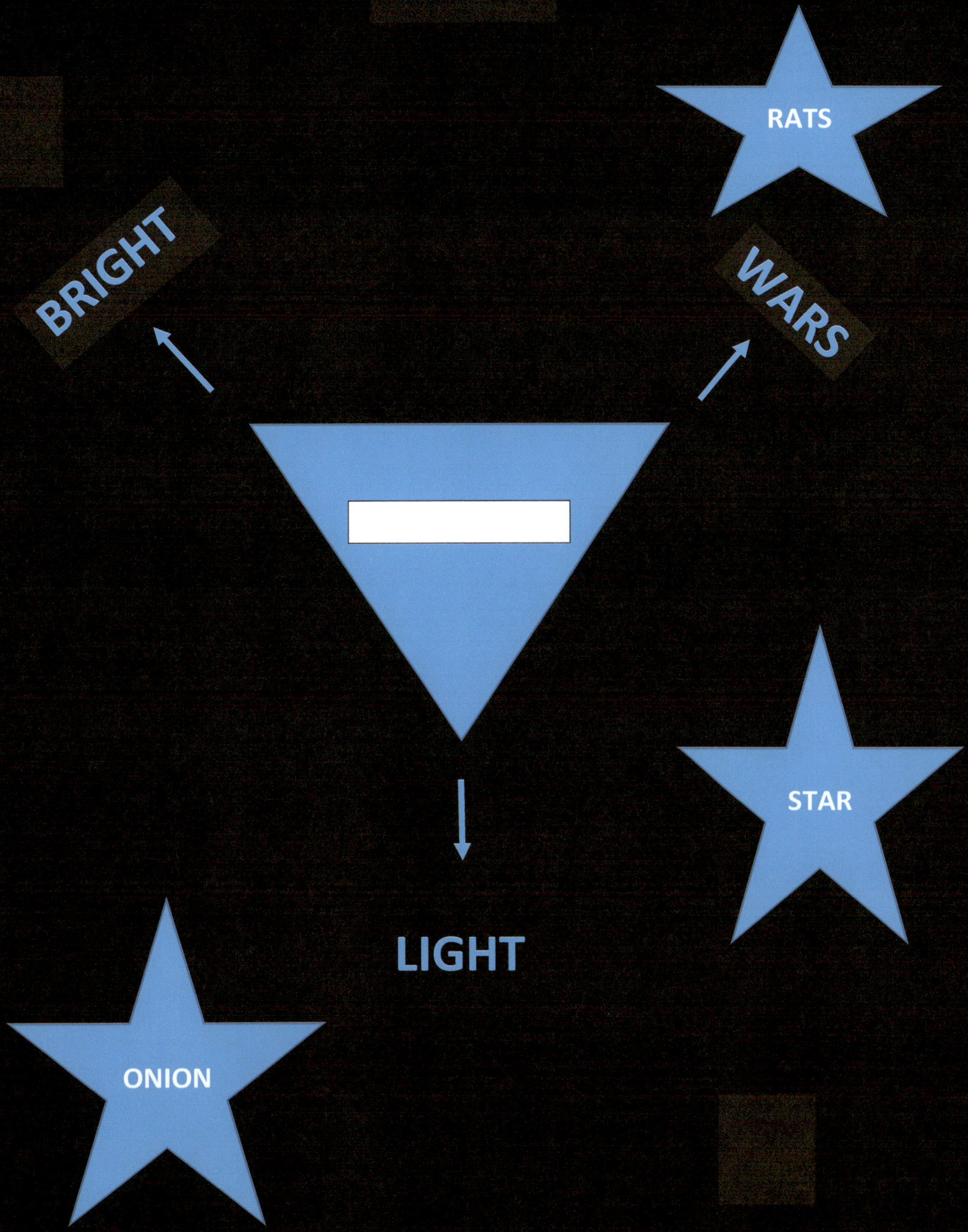

RATS

BRIGHT

WARS

STAR

↓

LIGHT

ONION

CONNECTIONS

6.

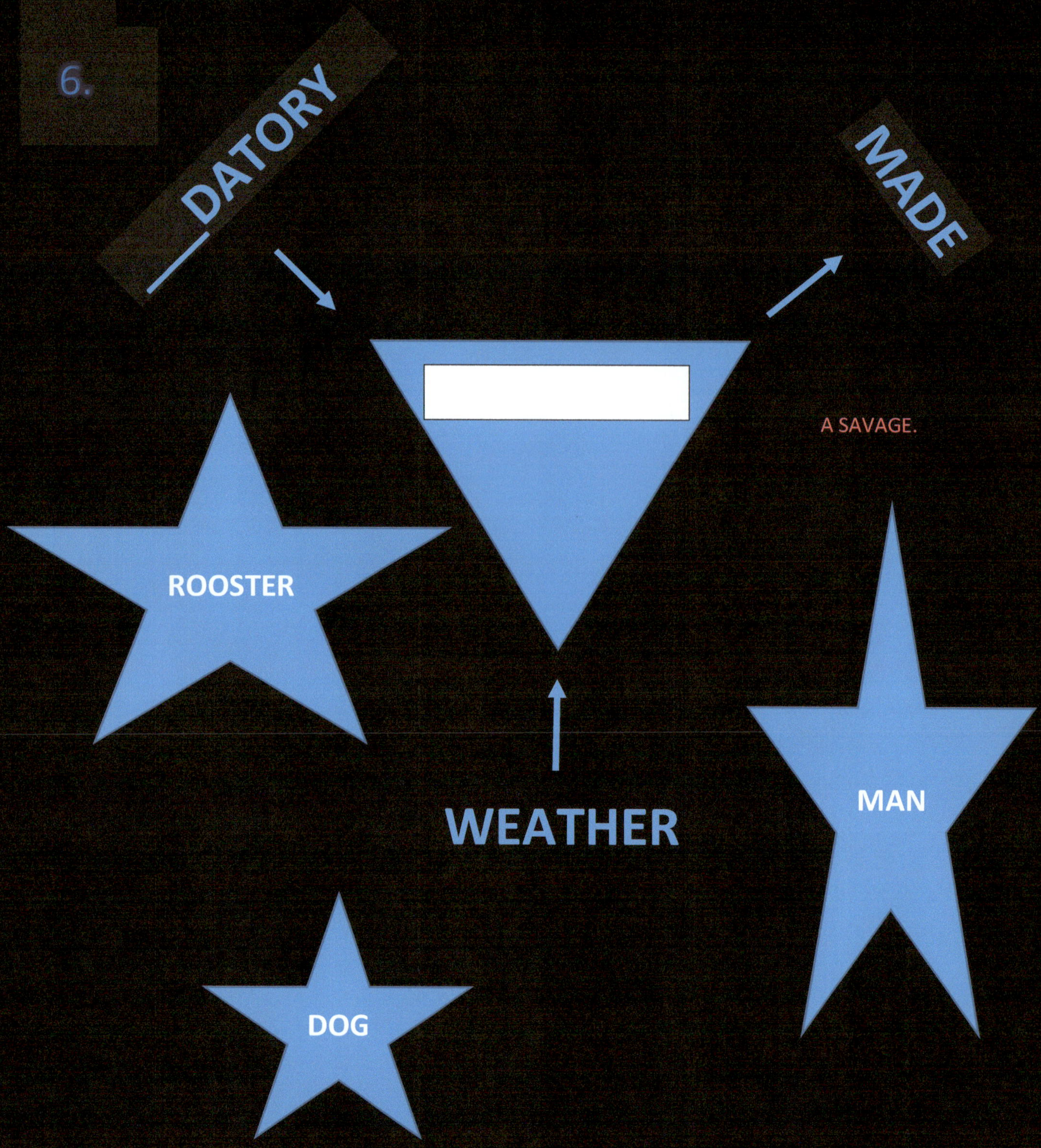

___DATORY

MADE

A SAVAGE.

ROOSTER

WEATHER

MAN

DOG

CONNECTIONS

7.

DAYS

GO LUCKY

FACE

HOME

HAPPY

APOCALYPSE

SAD

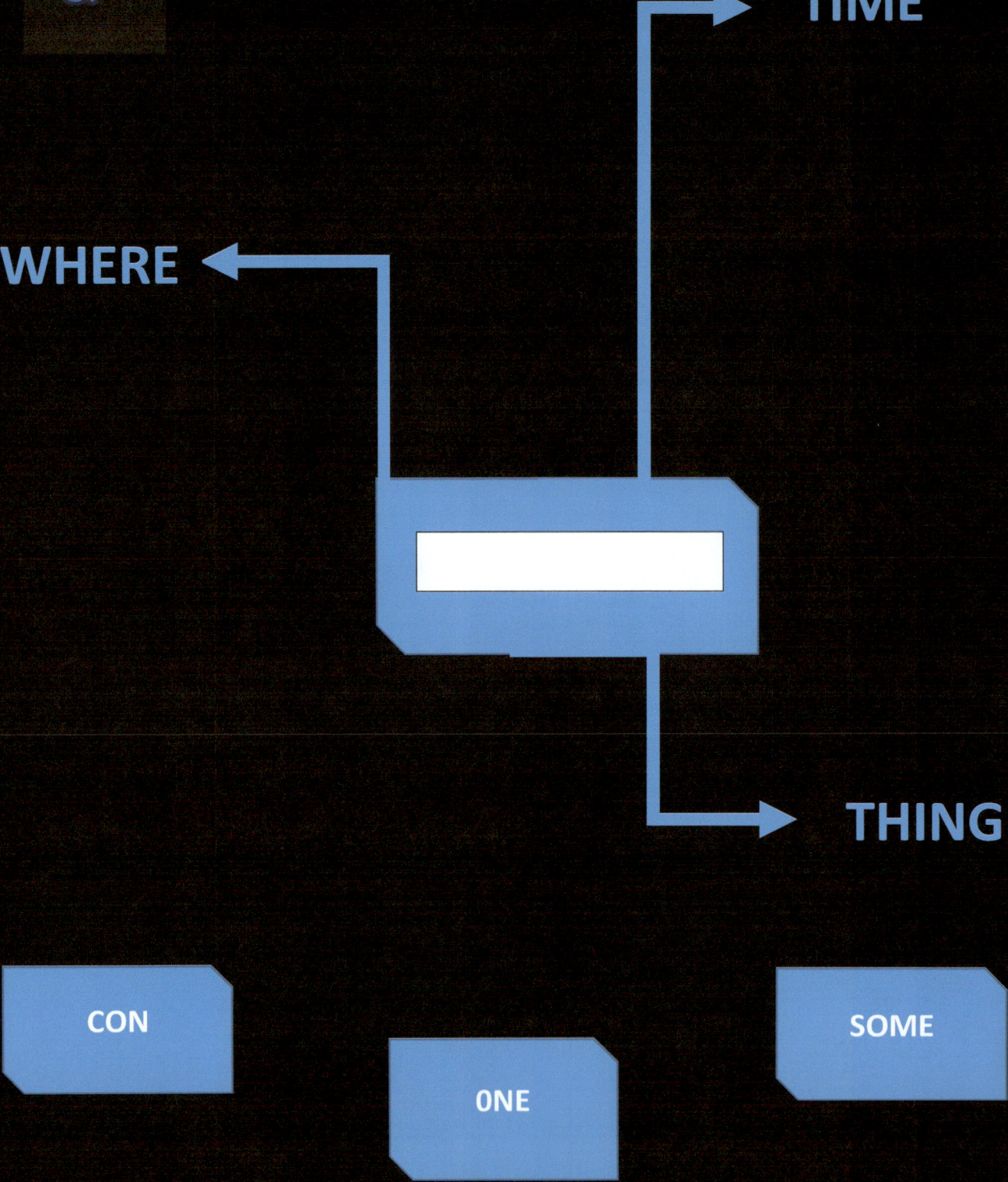

CONNECTIONS

TIME ONE

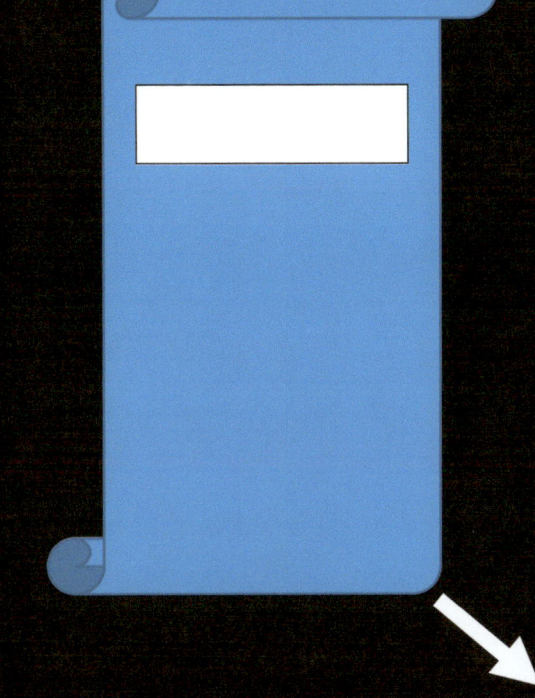

HE'S SPEEDING UP TIME.

WHERE

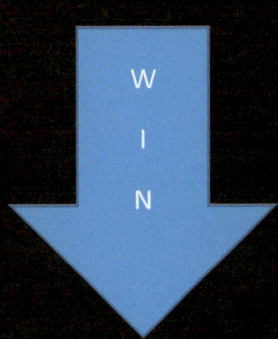
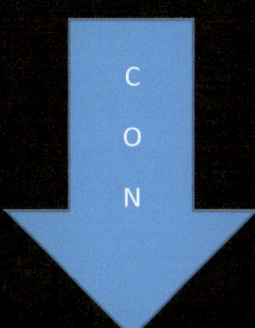

CONNECTIONS

10.

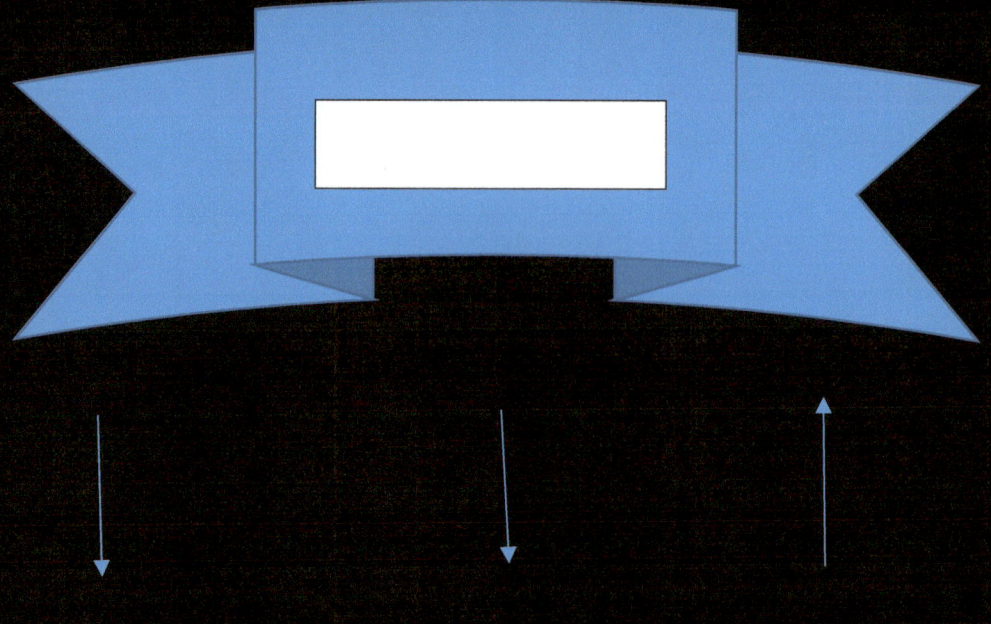

READY

GUN

SHOOT

BACK

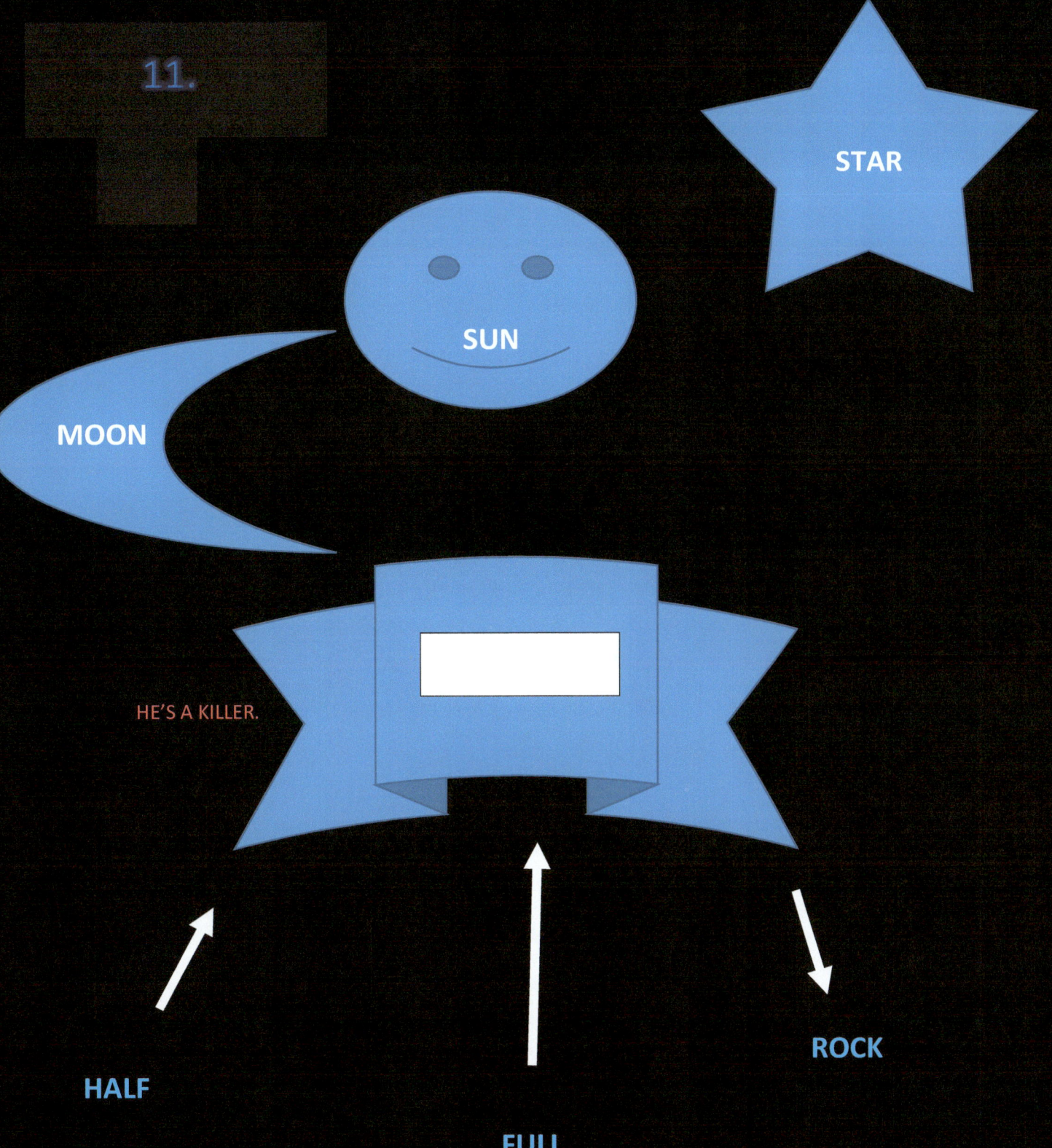

CONNECTIONS

12.

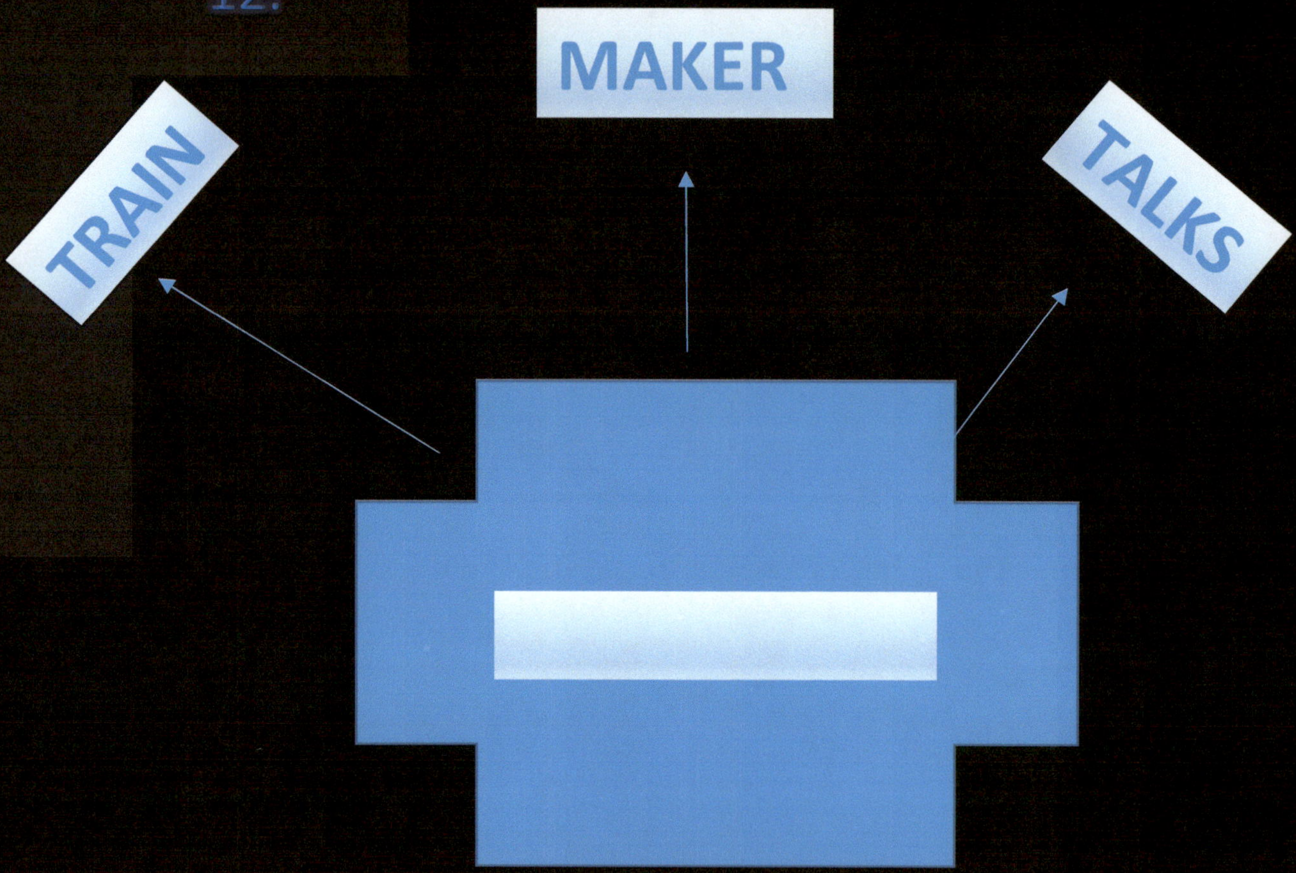

TRAIN   MAKER   TALKS

NEED   MONEY   LOVE

CONNECTIONS

13.

LIFT

TOWN

STREAM

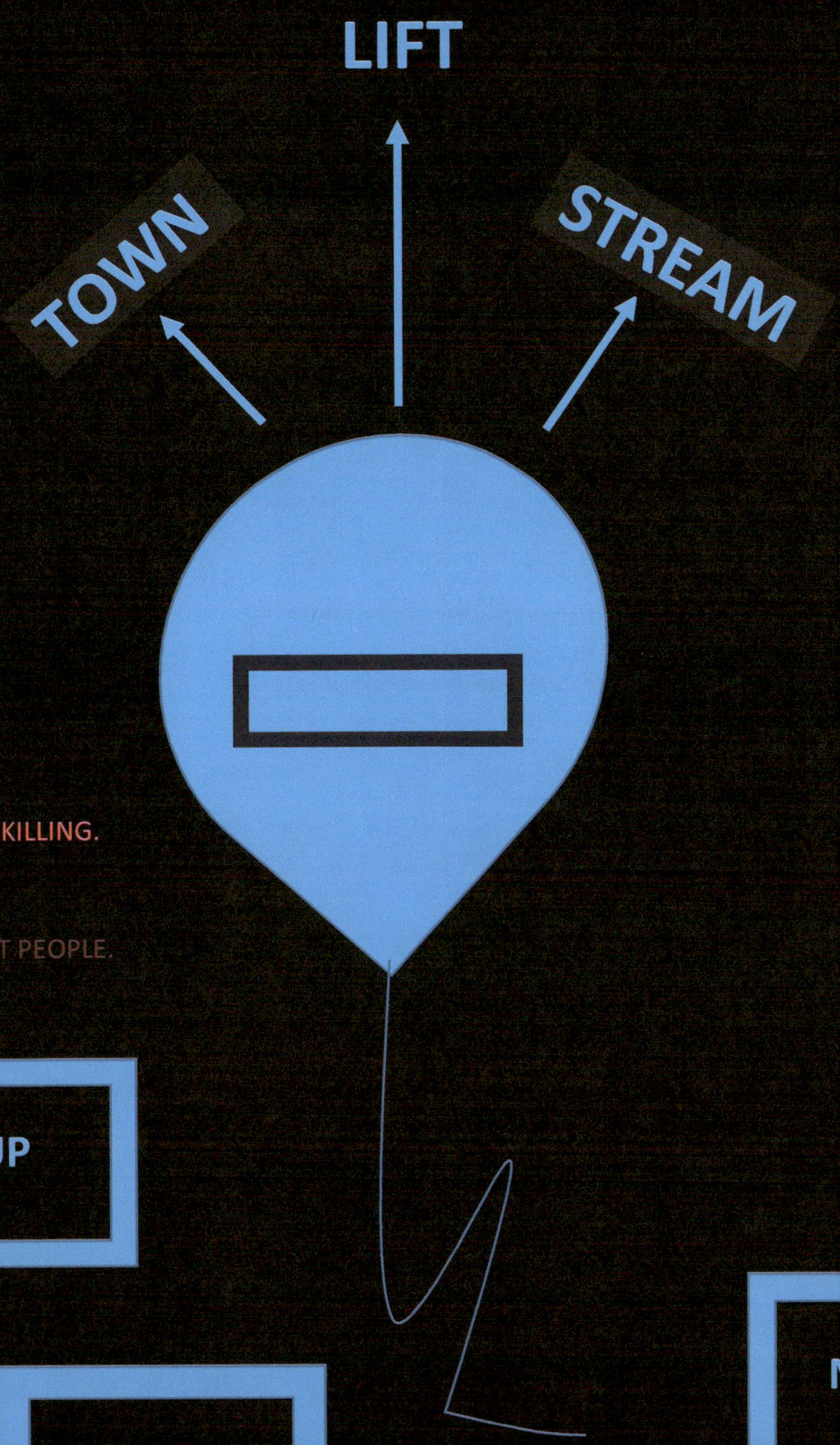

HE WON'T STOP KILLING.

BLAME THE FIRST PEOPLE.

UP

EAST

NORTH

CONNECTIONS

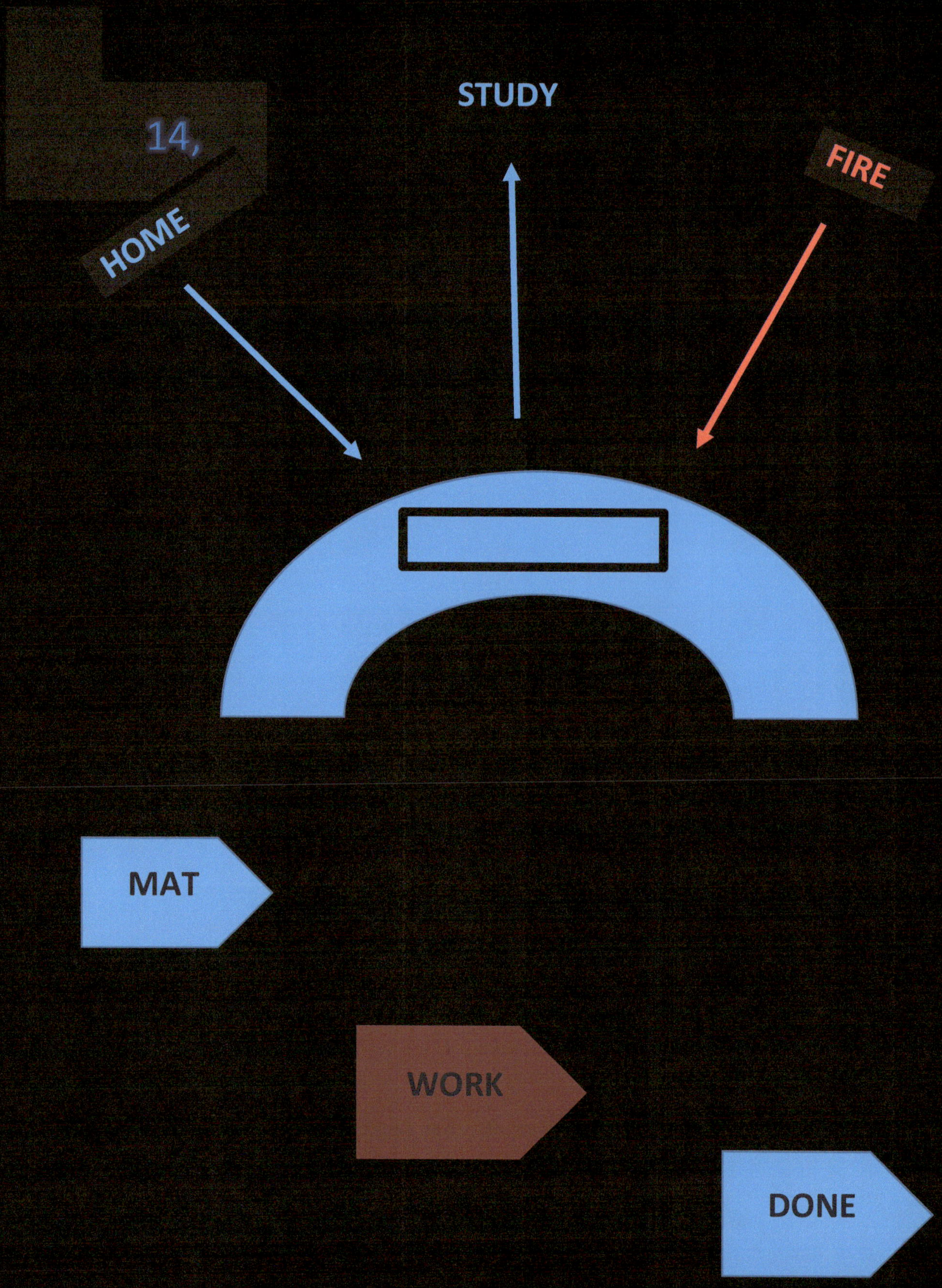

14,

STUDY

HOME

FIRE

MAT

WORK

DONE

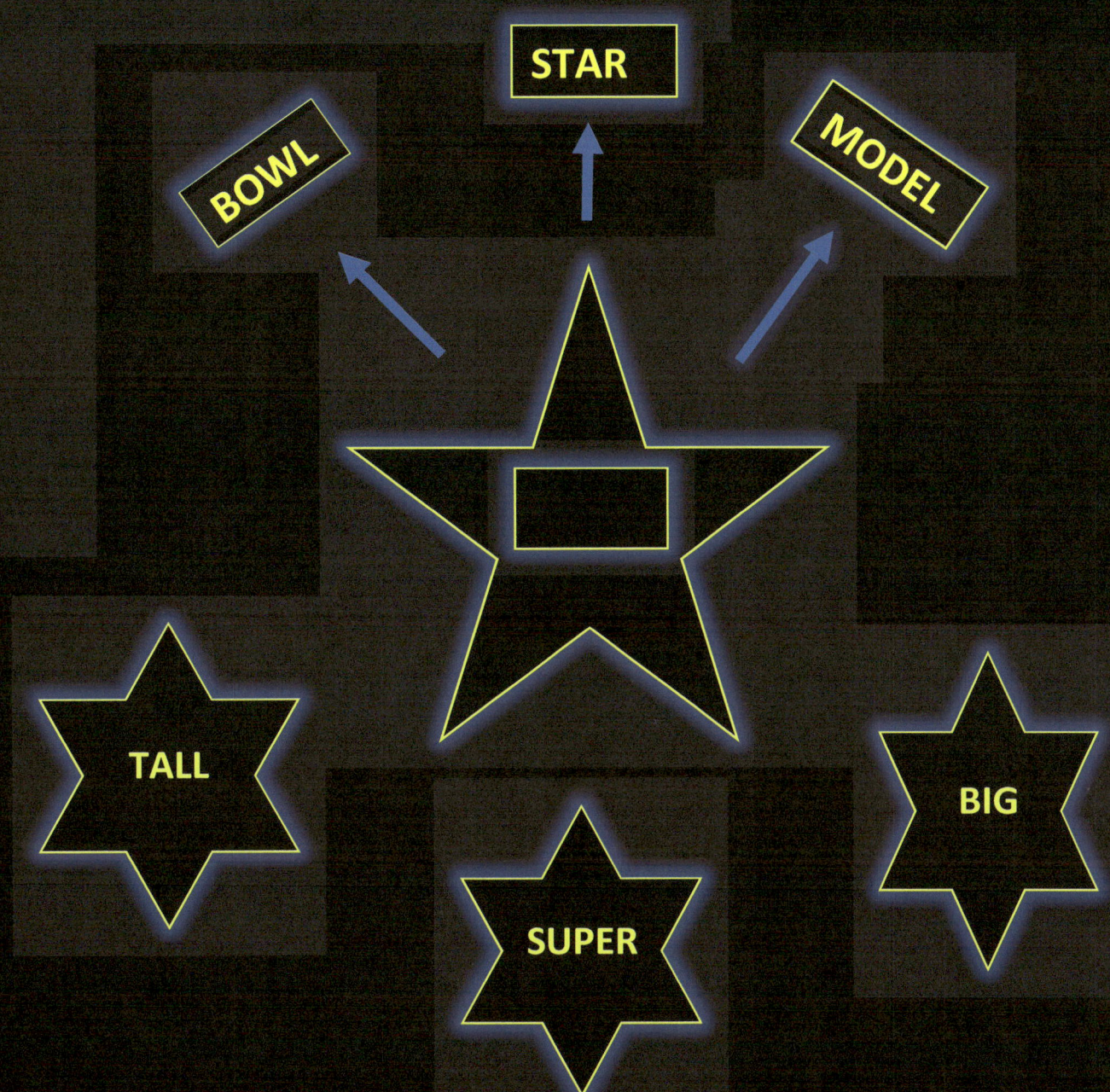

15.

THEY WERE JEALOUS OF ME.

CONNECTIONS

16.

SOME

NO → ⬛ ← EVERY

PART

WHERE

NOSE

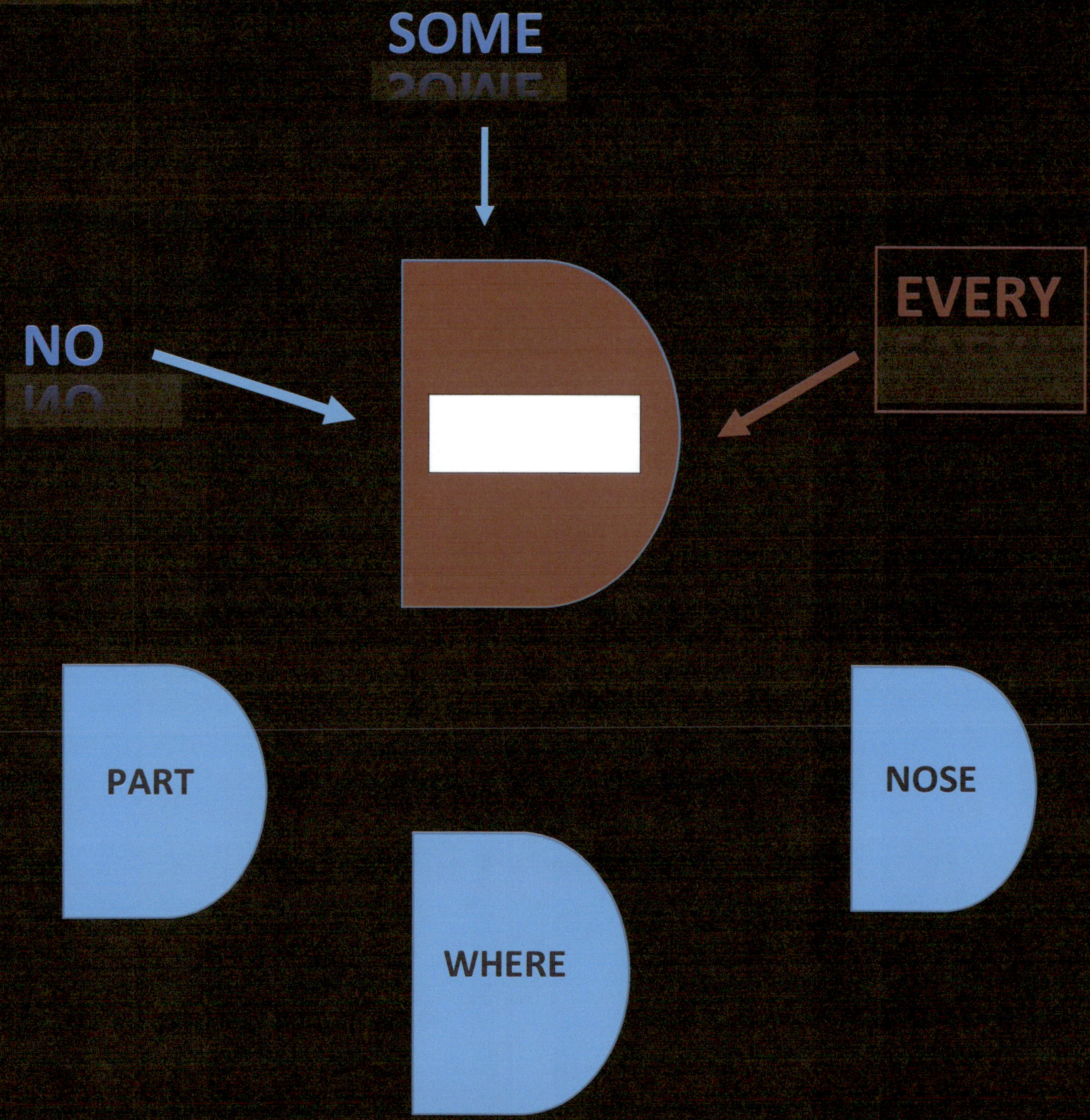

CONNECTIONS

17.

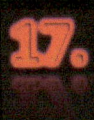

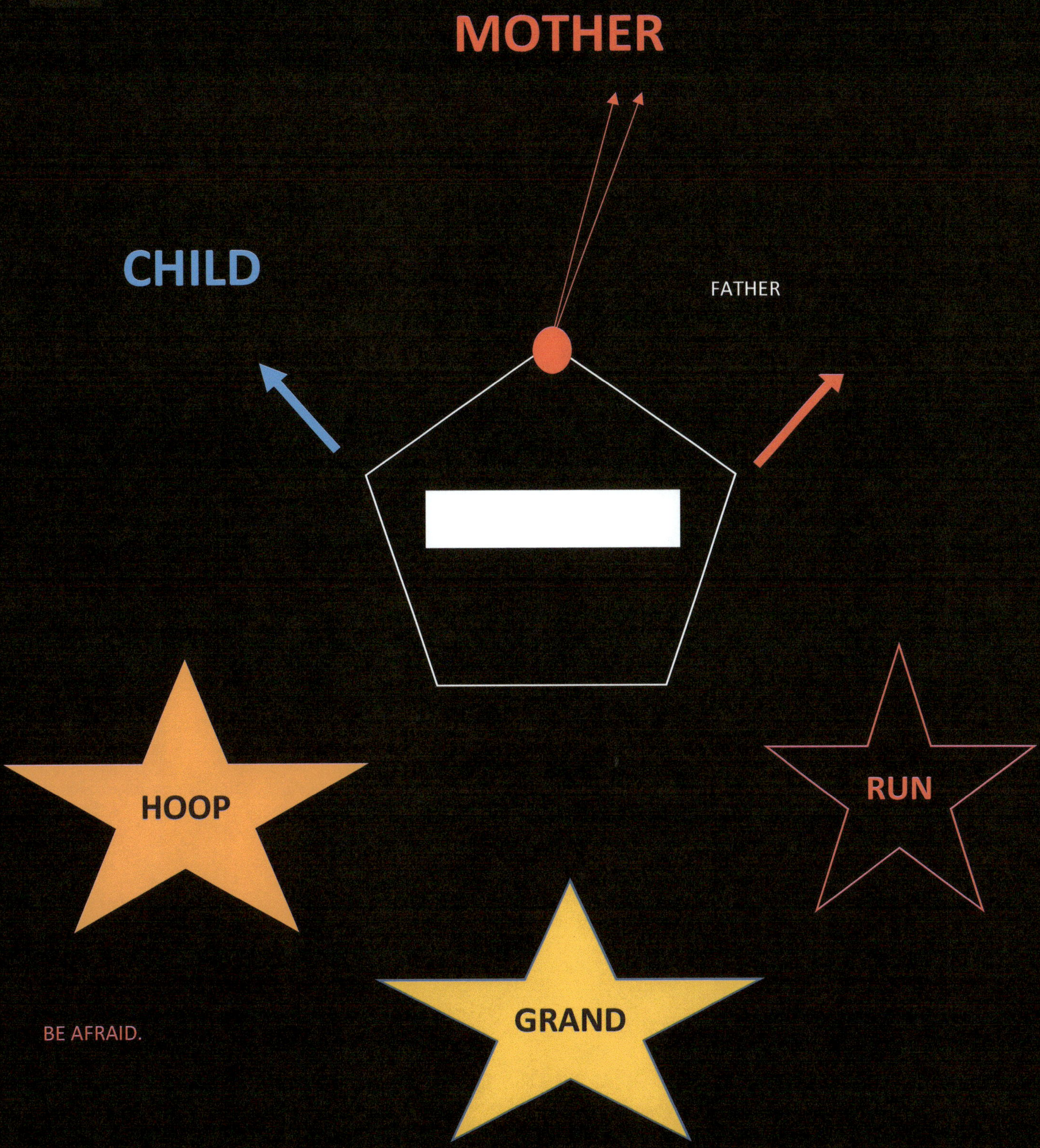
MOTHER
CHILD
FATHER
HOOP
RUN
GRAND
BE AFRAID.

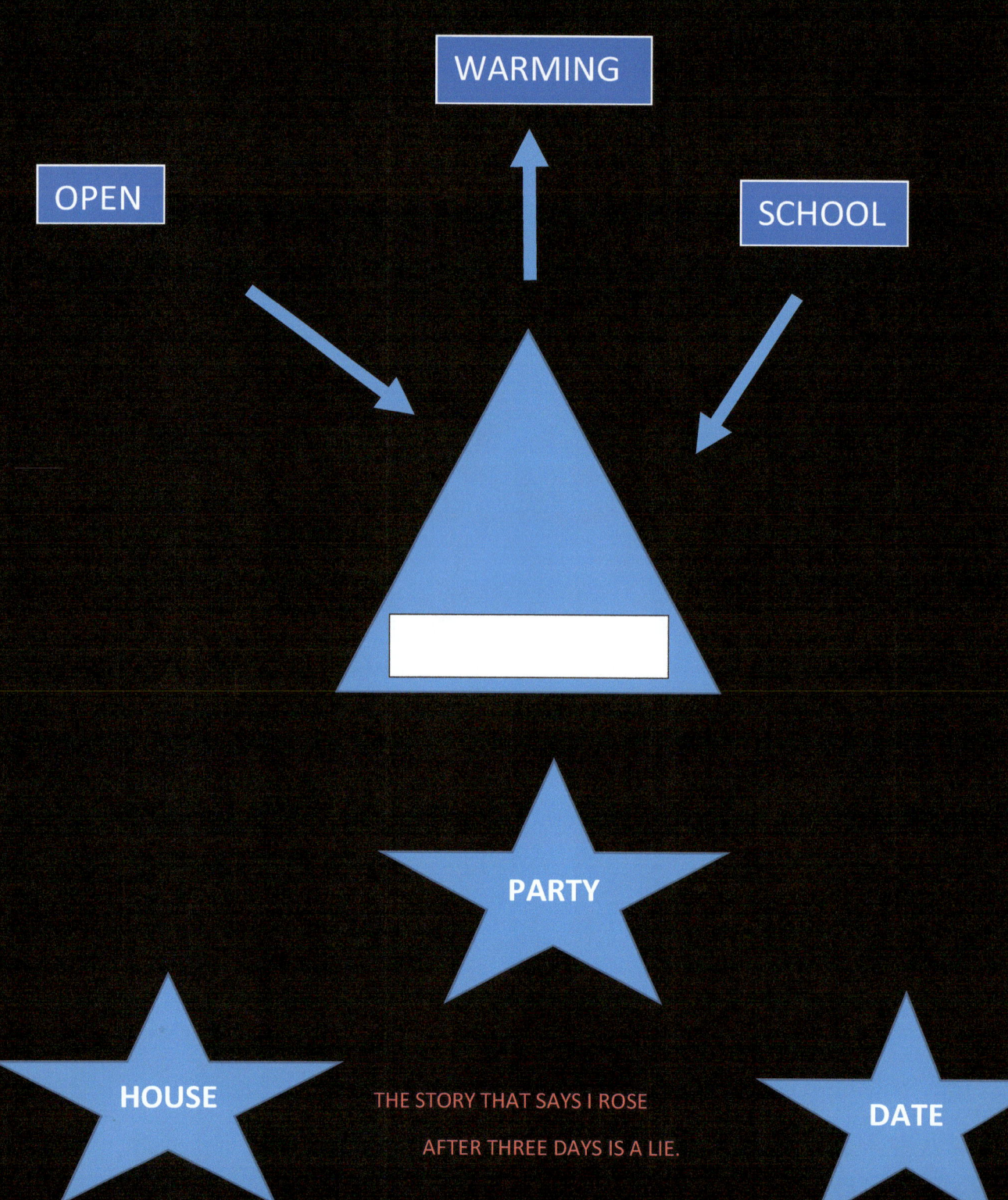

CONNECTIONS

19.

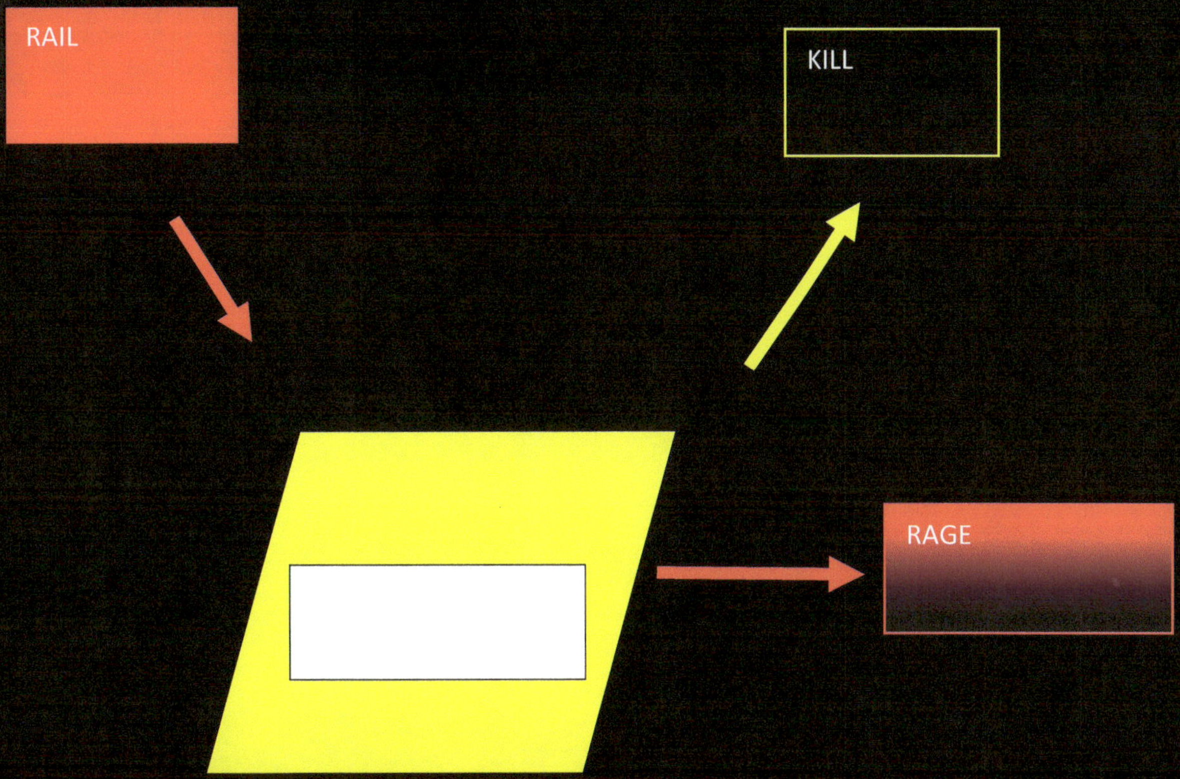

RAIL

KILL

RAGE

ROAD

BLOCK

STREET

READY.

AVENUE

DRIVE

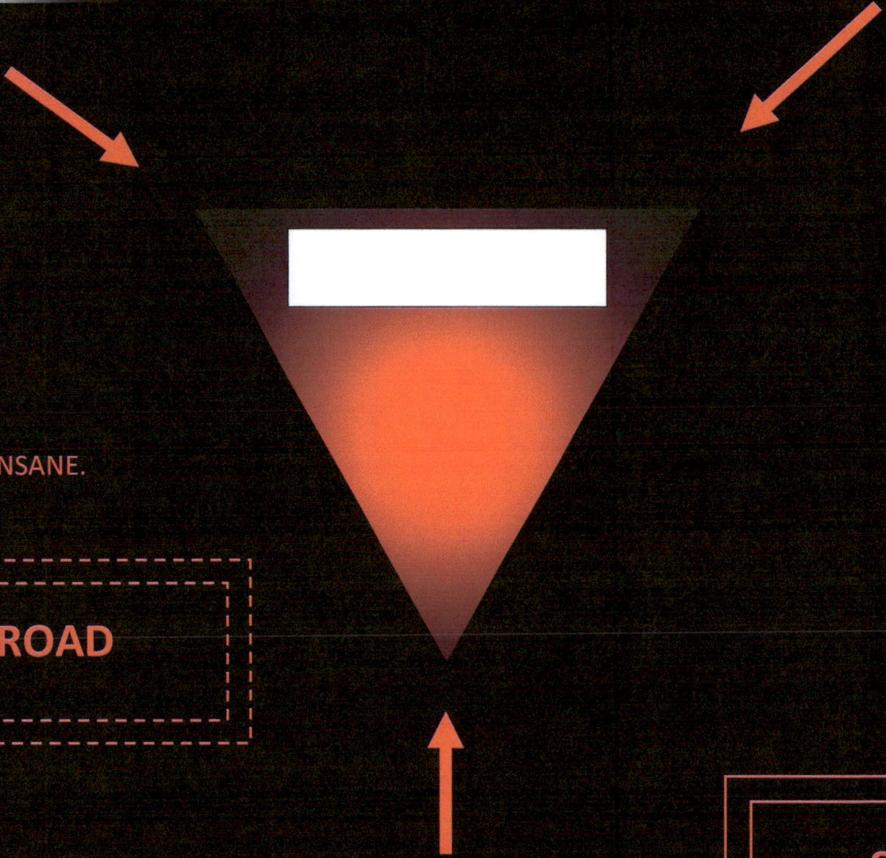

MY DAD IS INSANE.

ROAD

BOULEVARD

STREET

BLOCK

THERE'S NO LIMIT TO HIS EVIL IDEAS.

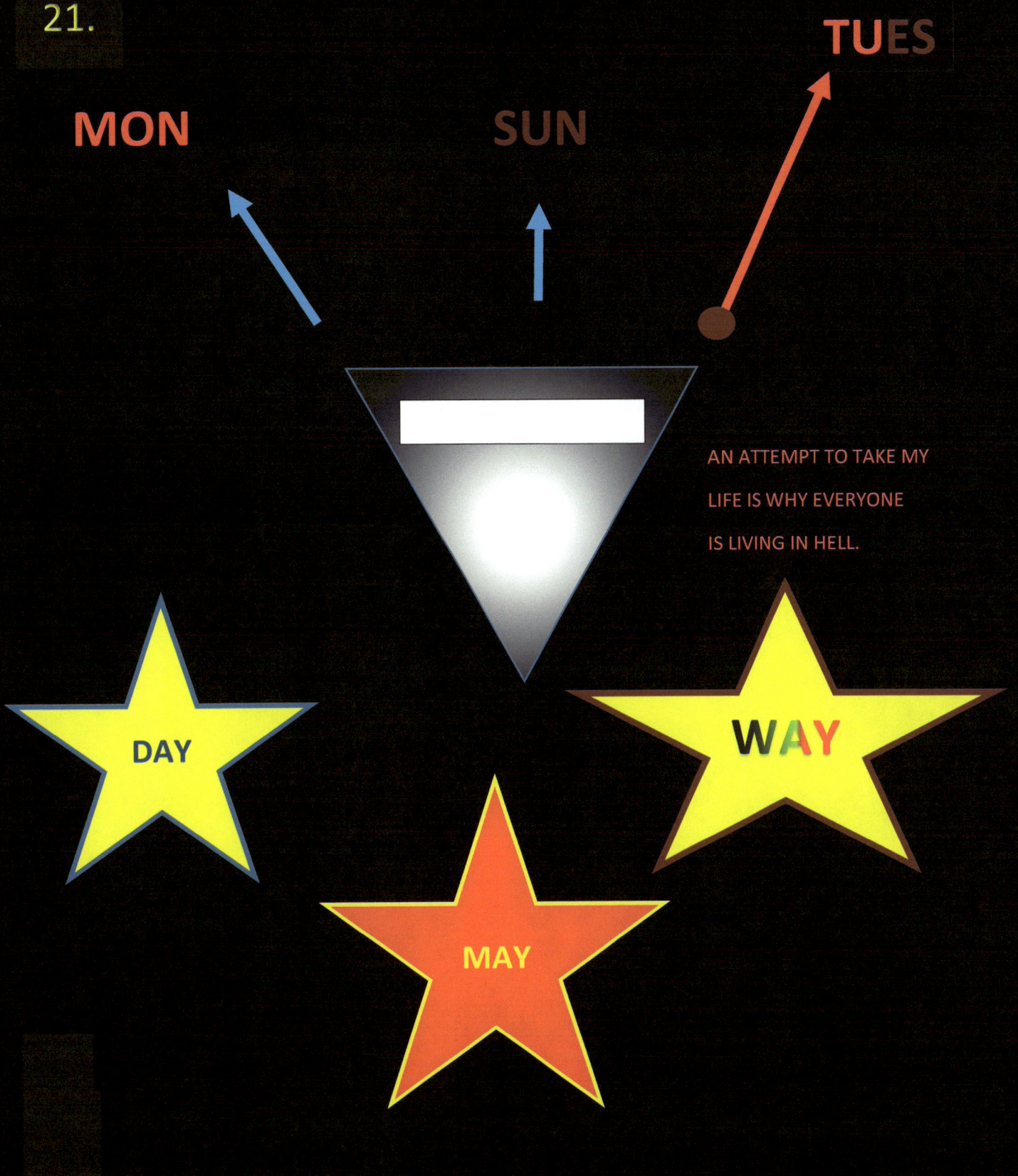

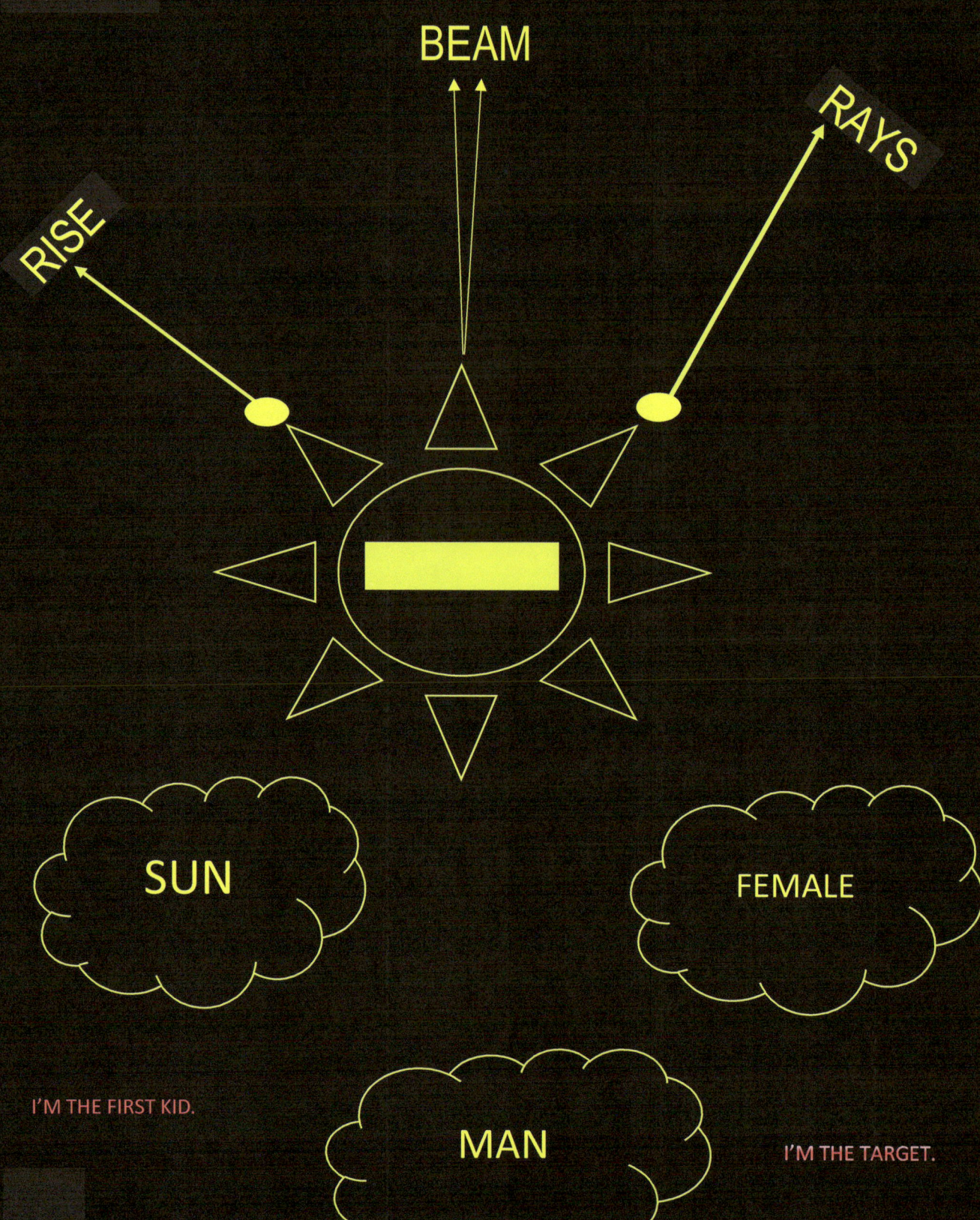

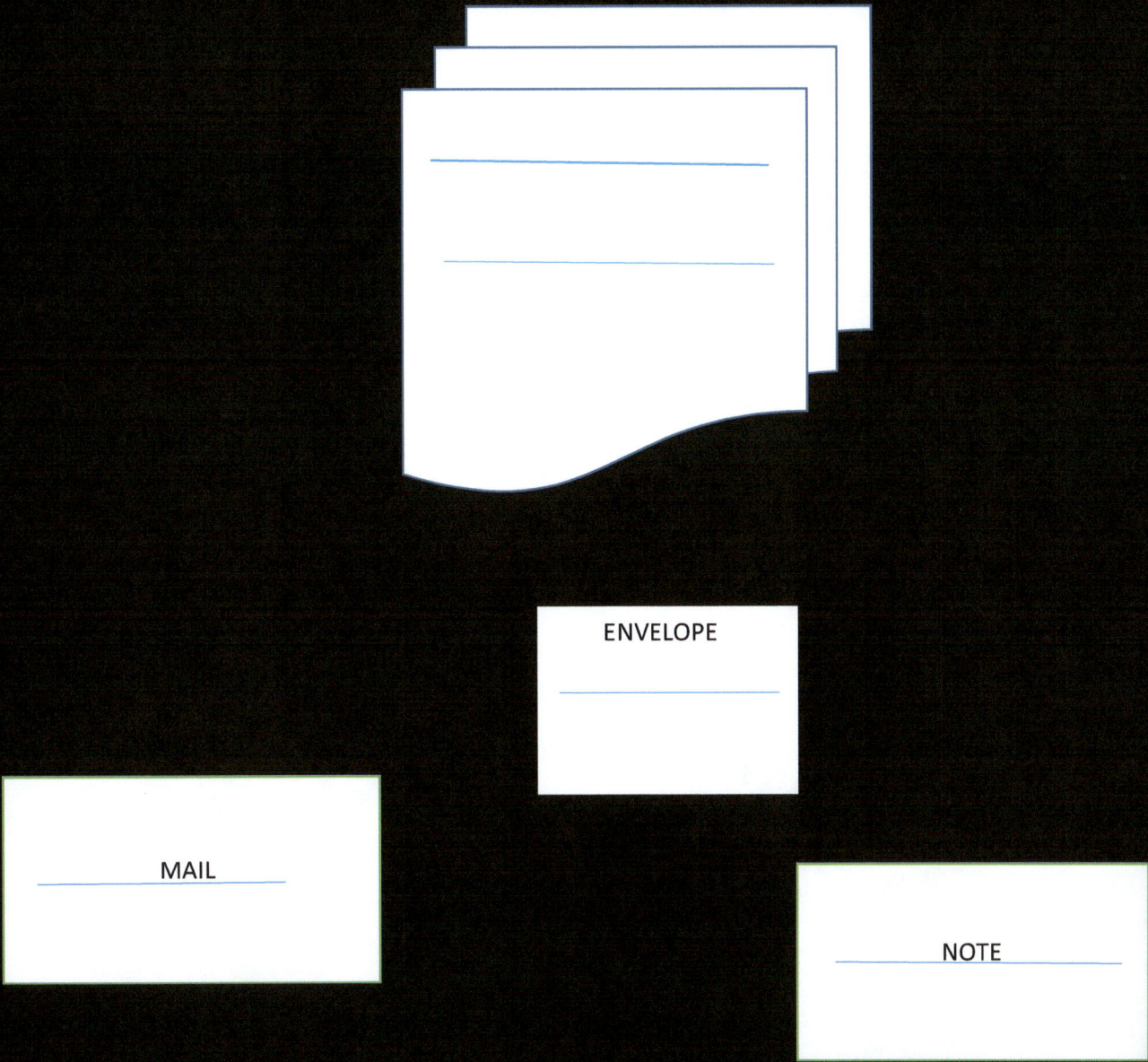

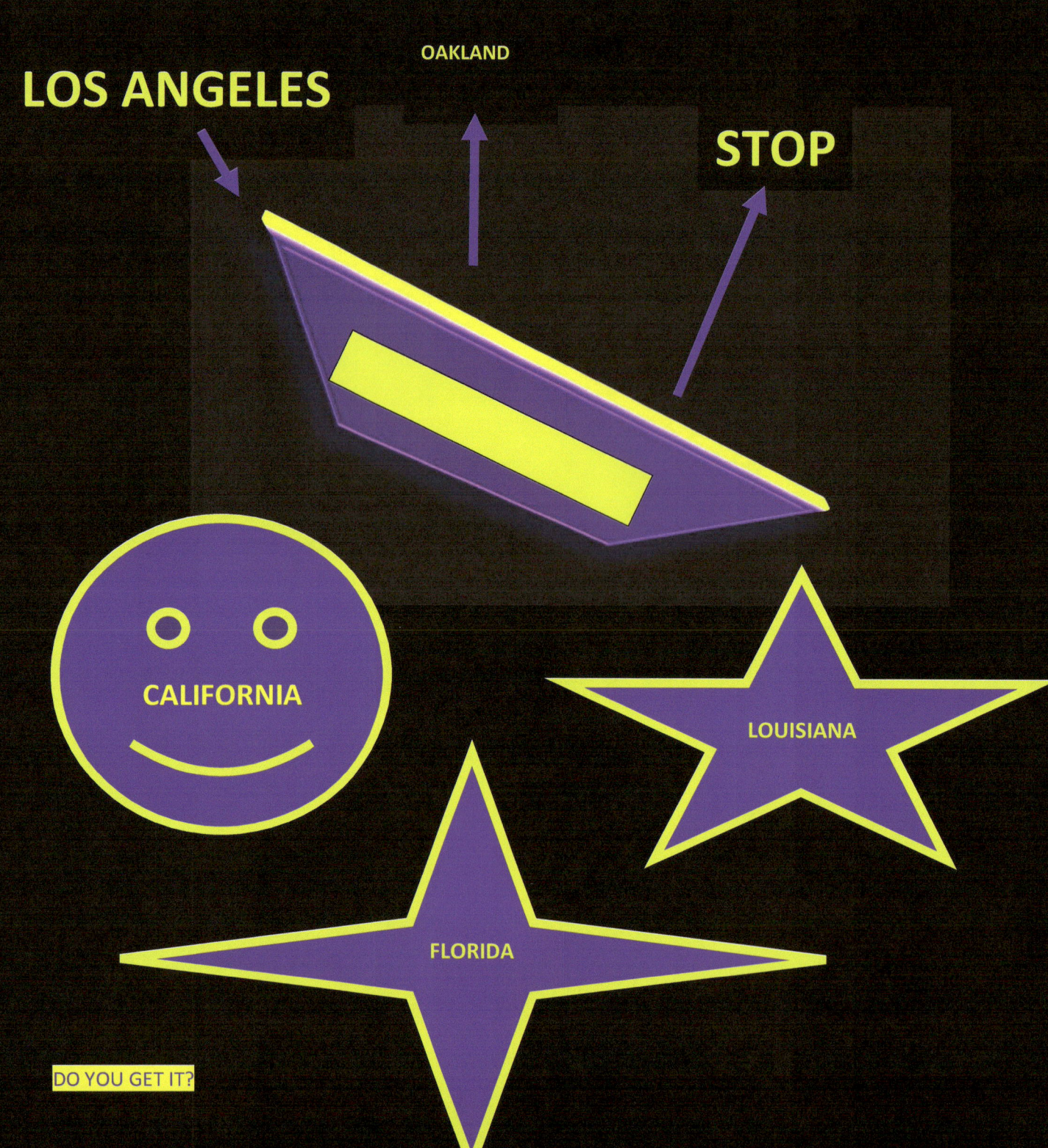

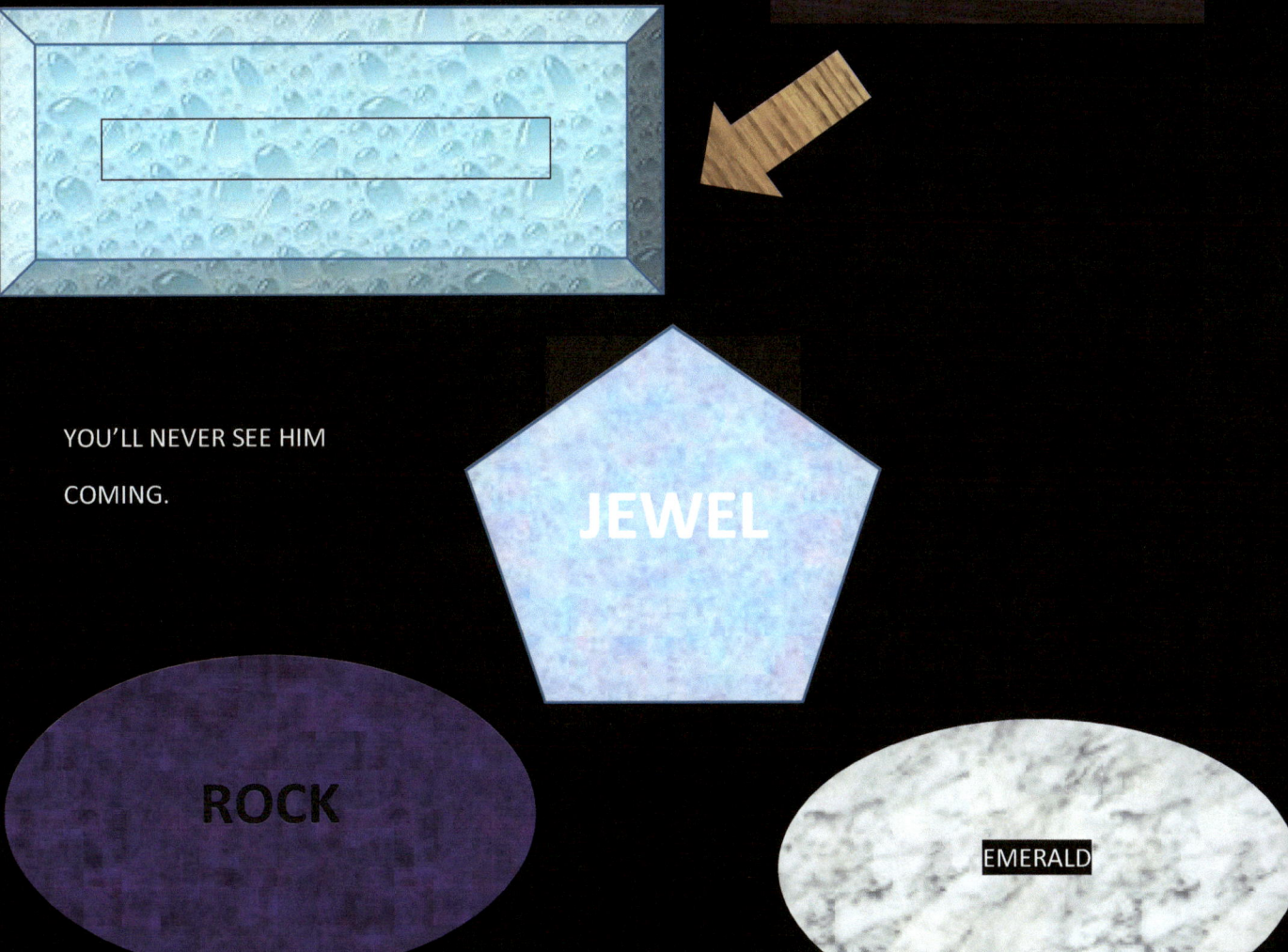

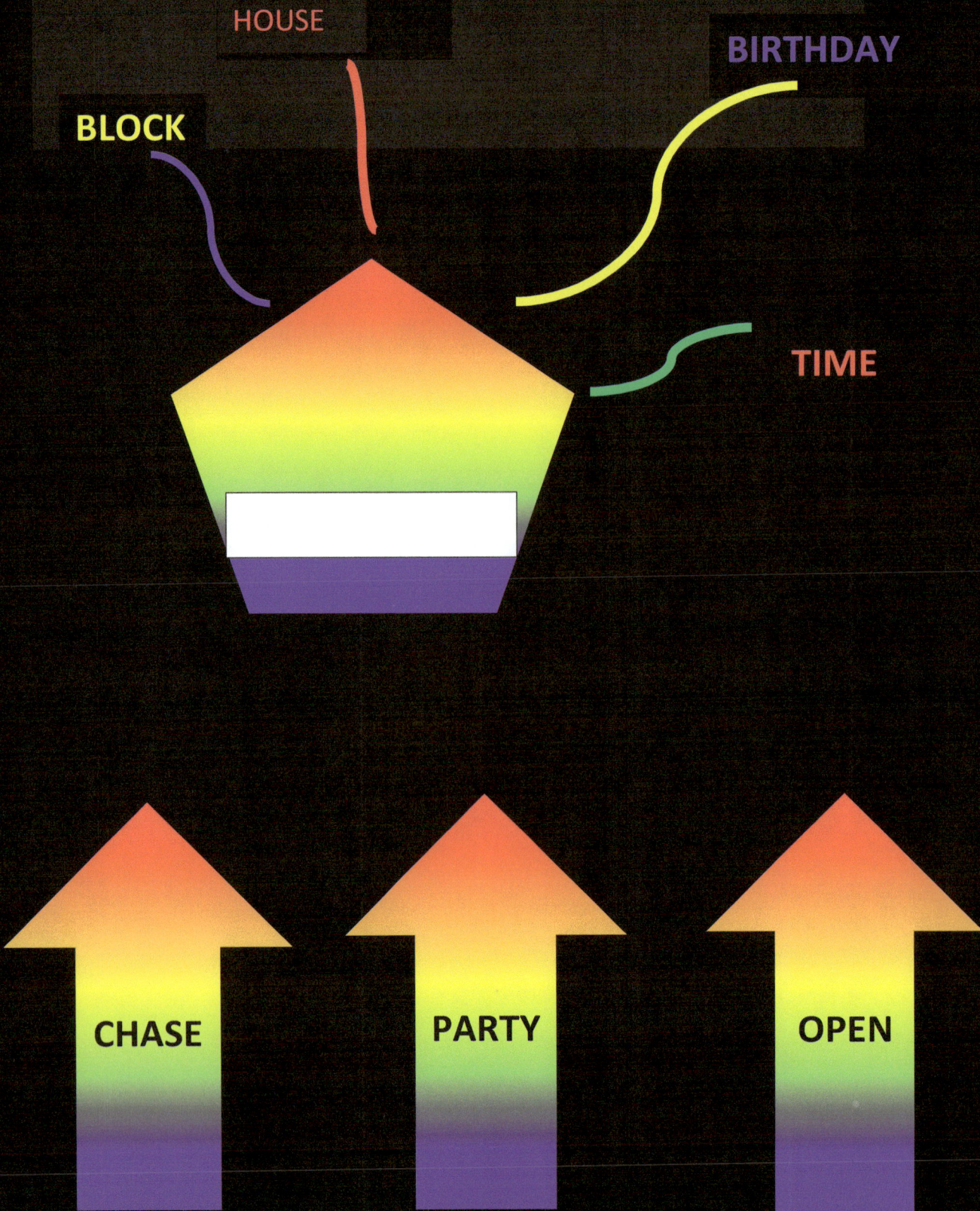

CONNECTIONS

27.

red

yellow   orange

HE NEVER LEFT.

sizes

colors   states

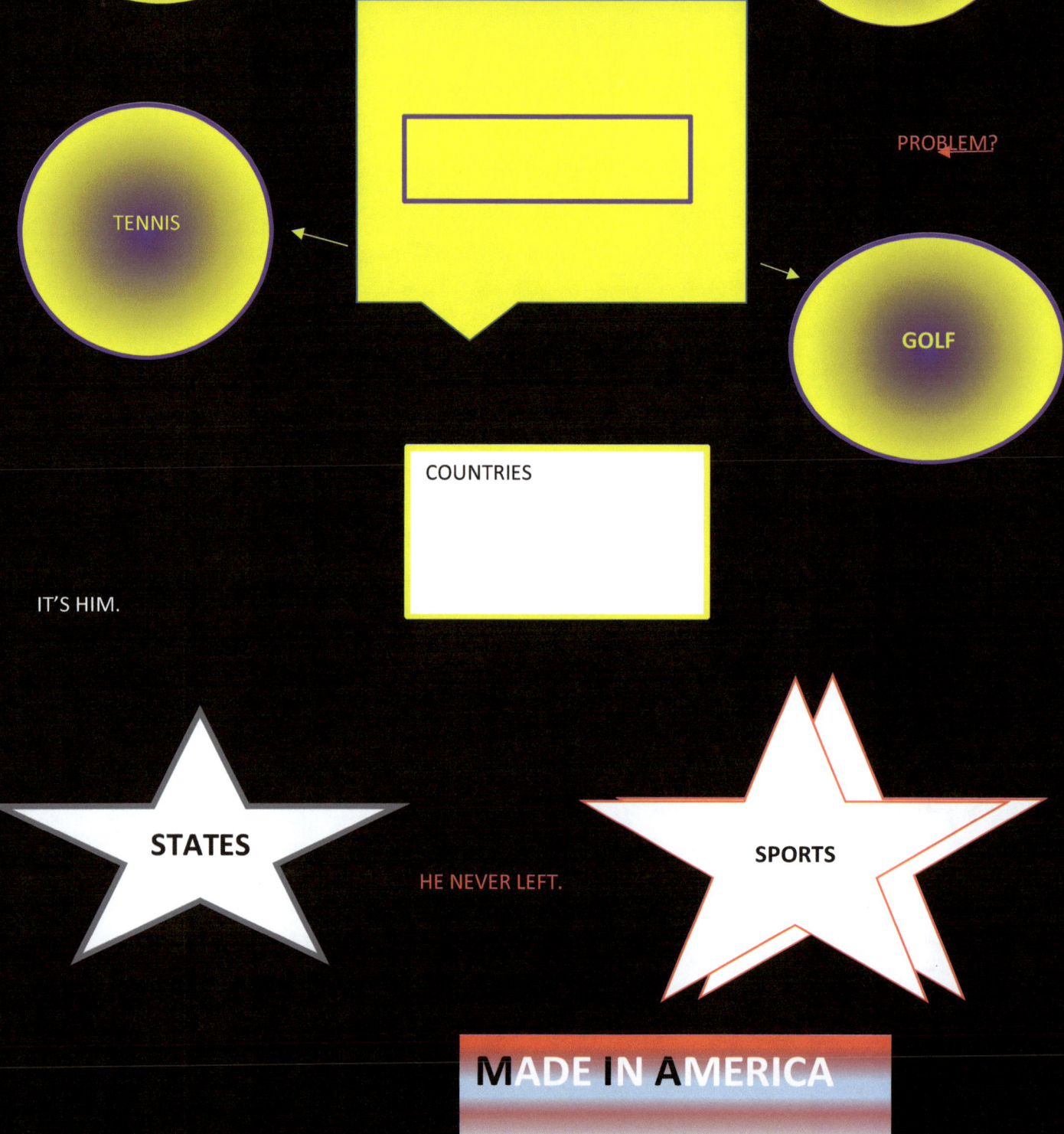

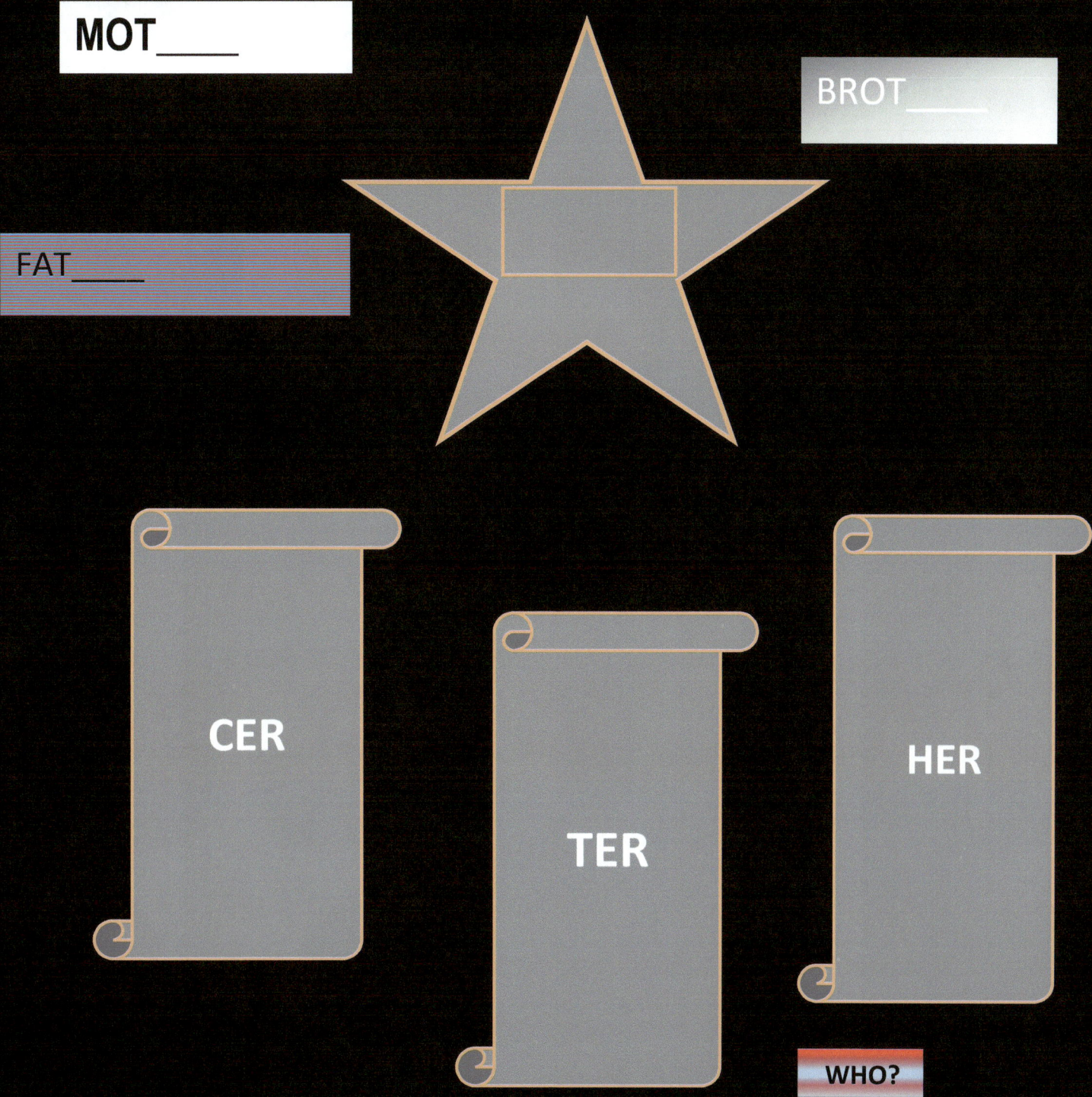

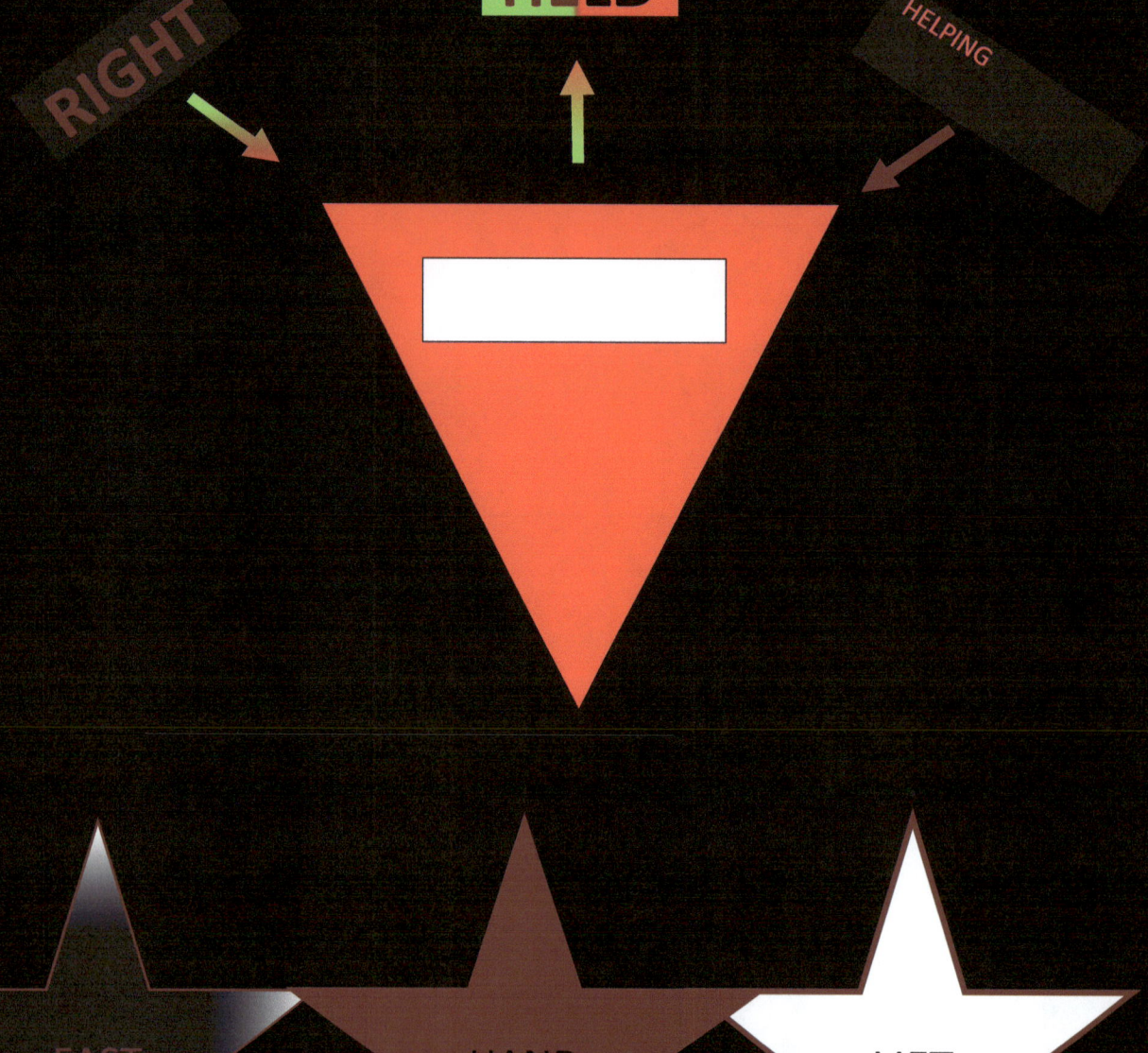

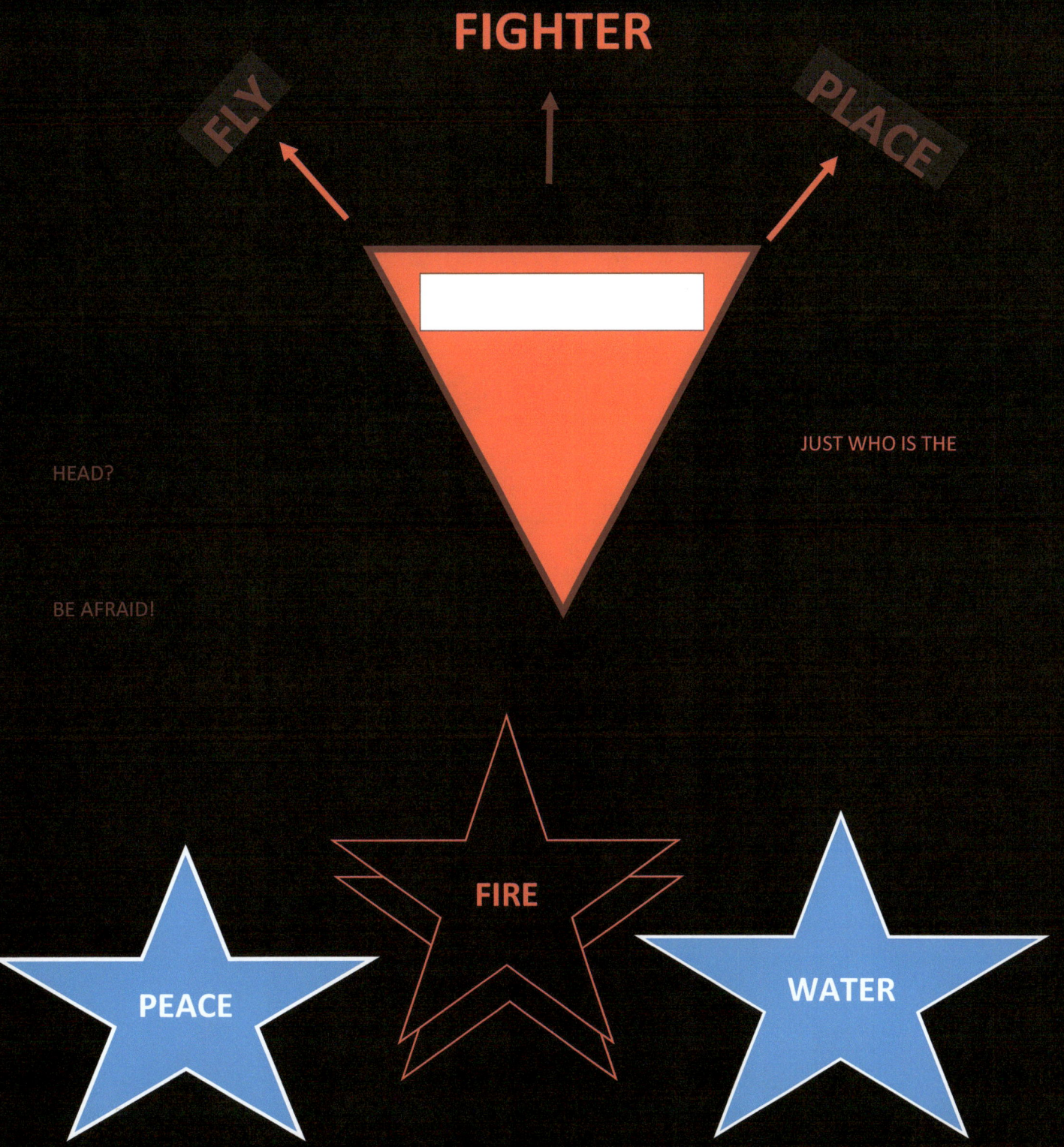

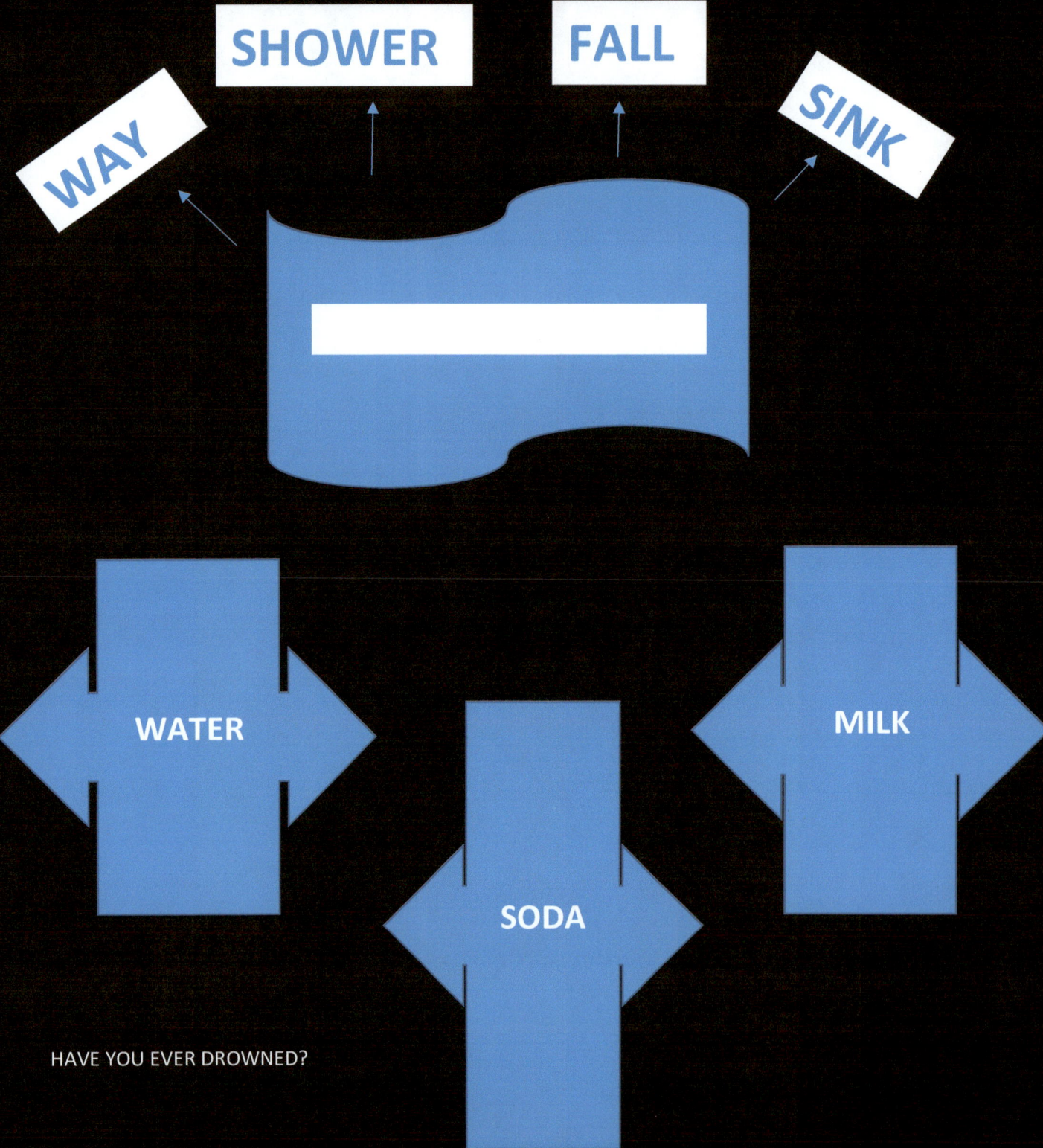

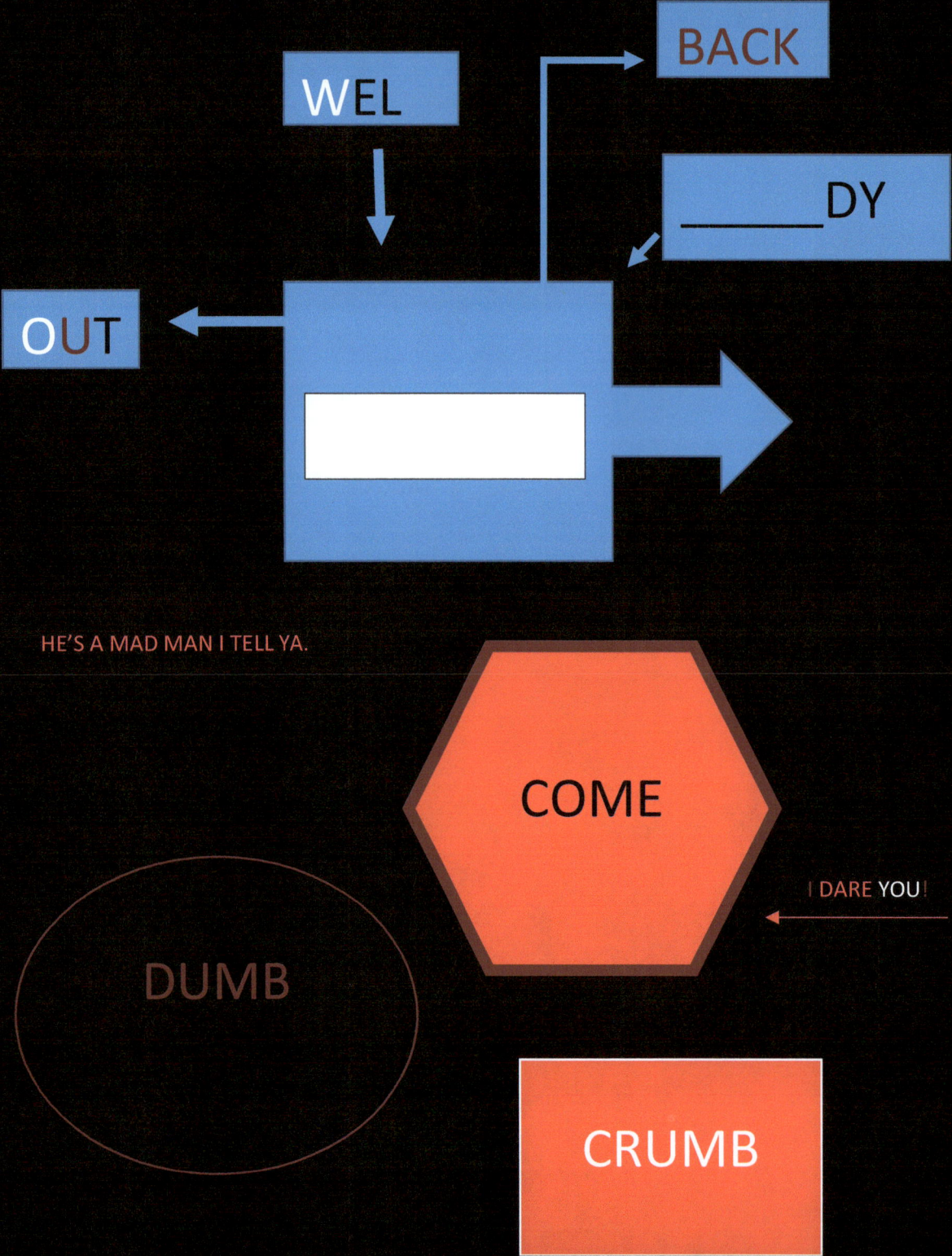

35.

PHOTO

RIGHT

YOU WOULD DO THE SAME THING IF YOU WERE A MAN IN THE BEGINNING AND YOU HAD TO COME BACK AS A WOMAN AND CHANGE THE SEX OF YOUR CHILD SO THAT HE COULD BLEND IN WITH THE REST OF THE WORLD AND HAVE A SAFE

I DON'T BLAME HIM.

CAT

RETURN?

SOUR

COPY

BOOK

HISTORY WILL NOT REPEAT ITSELF.

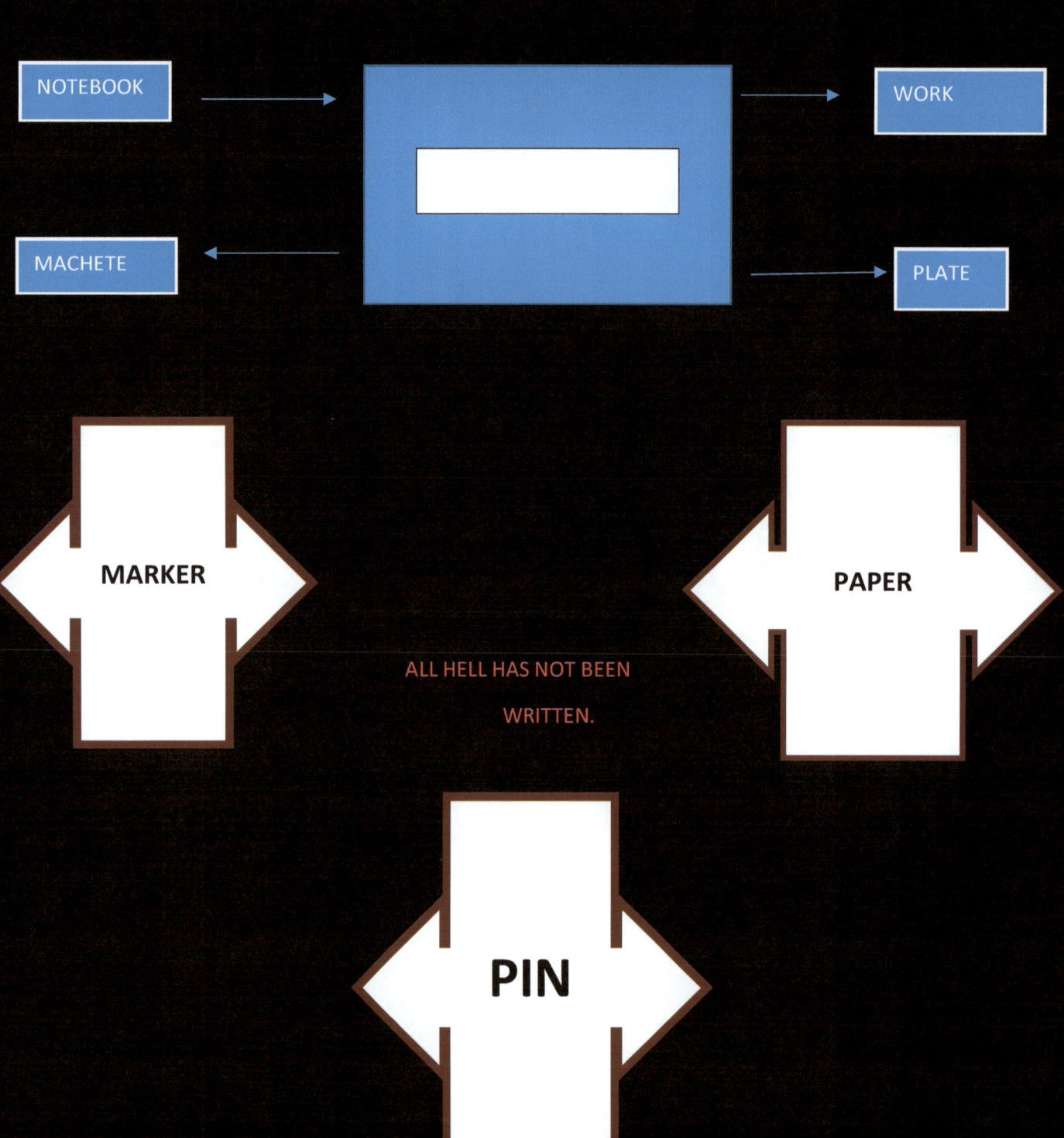

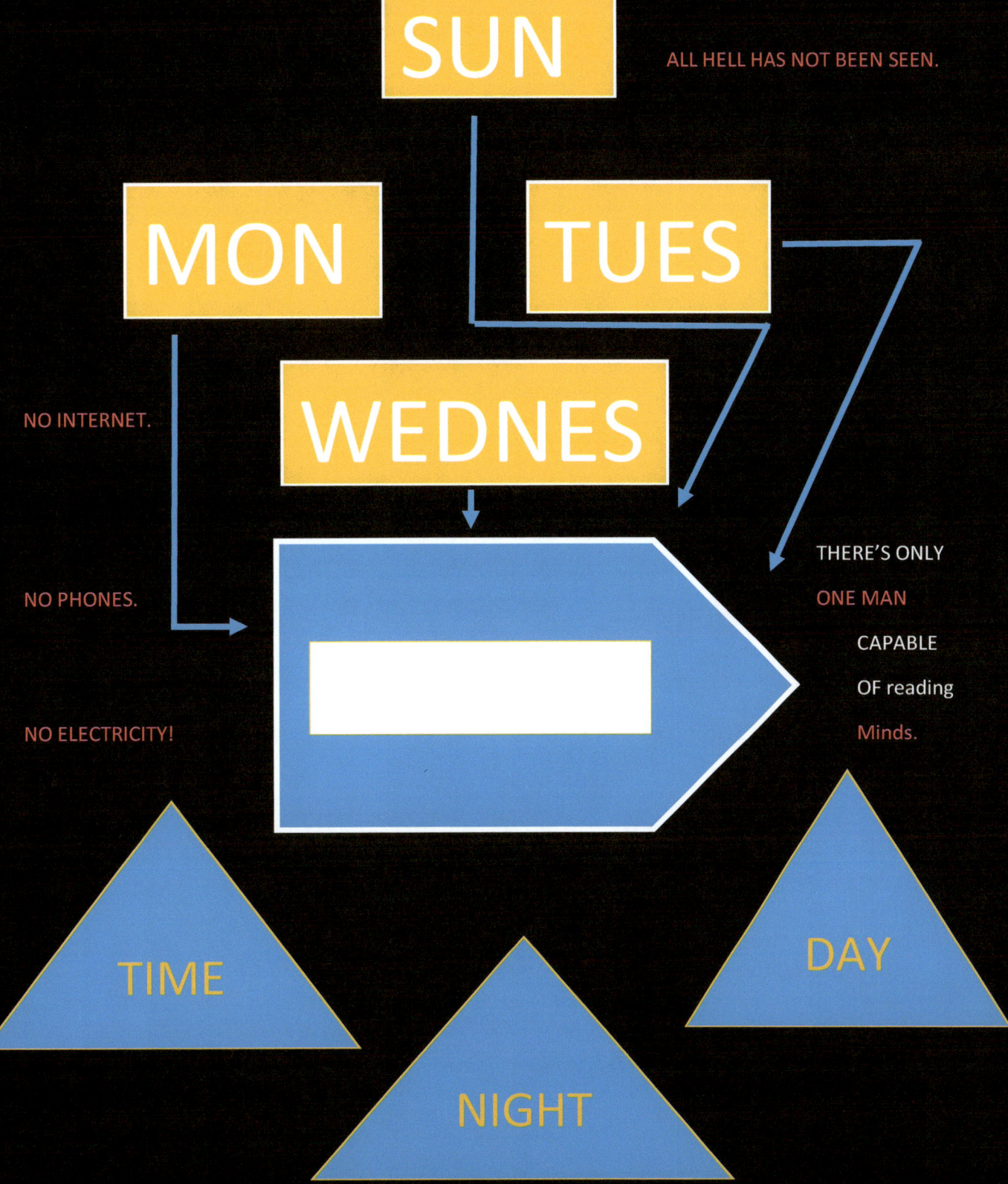

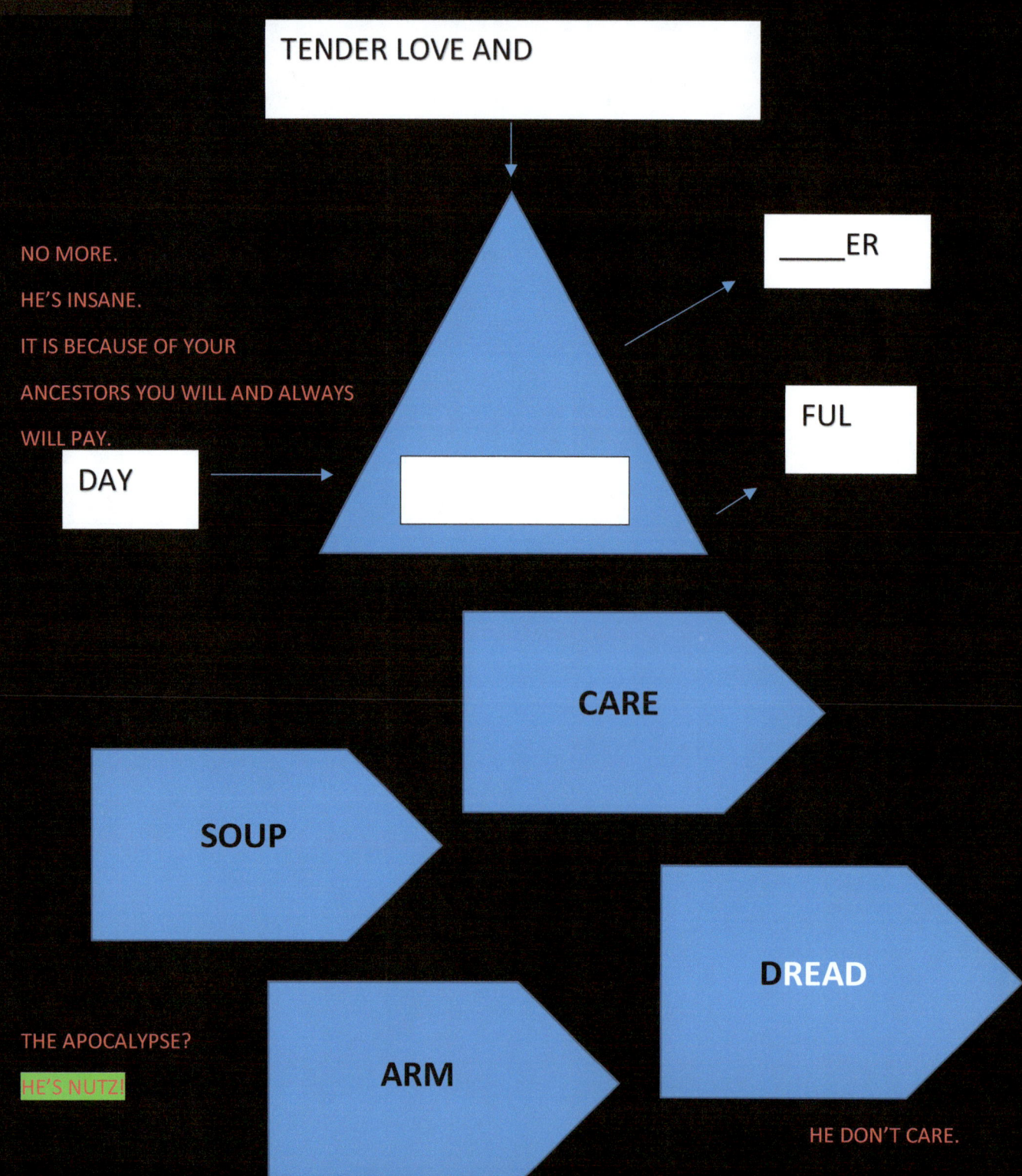

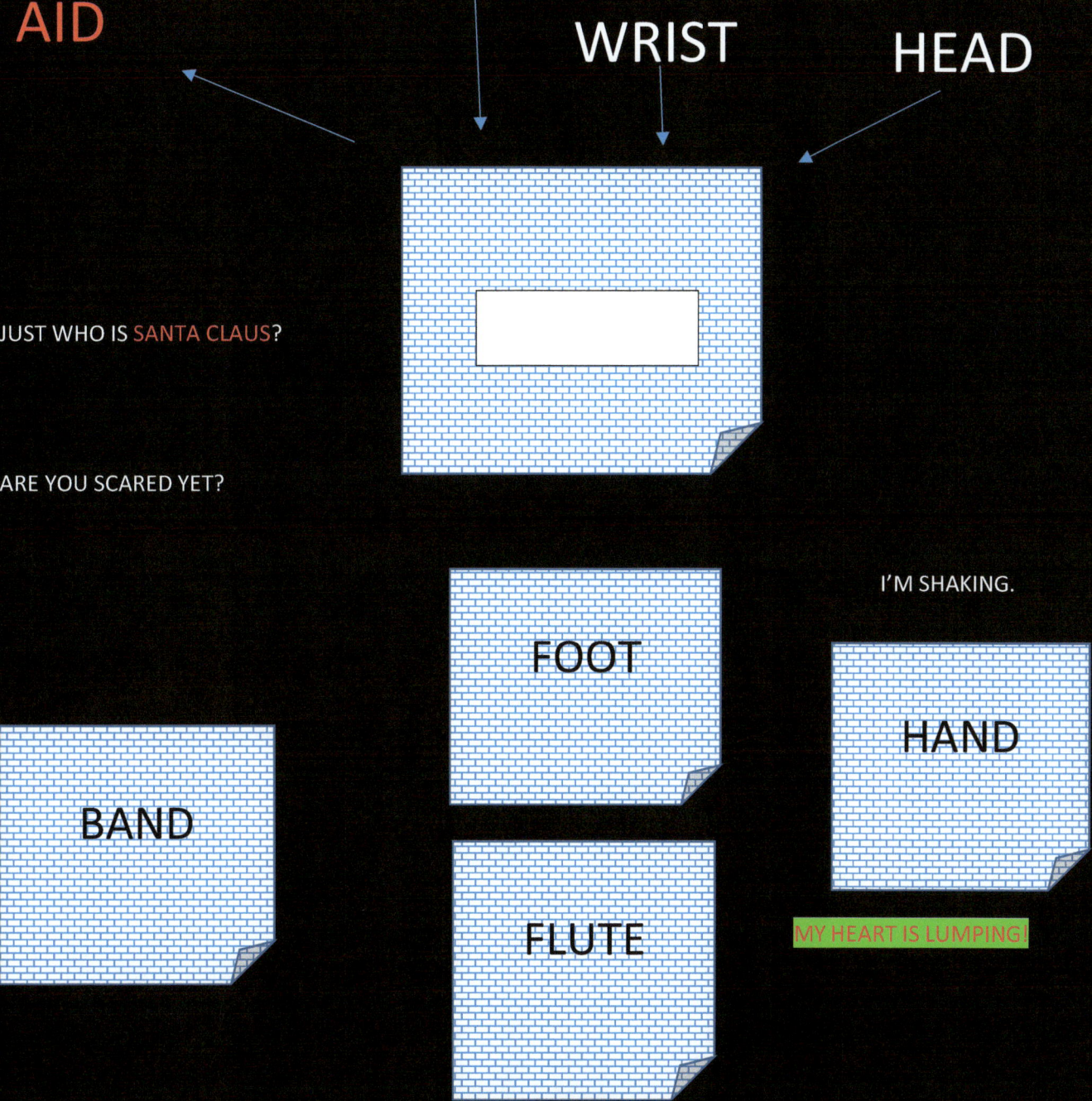

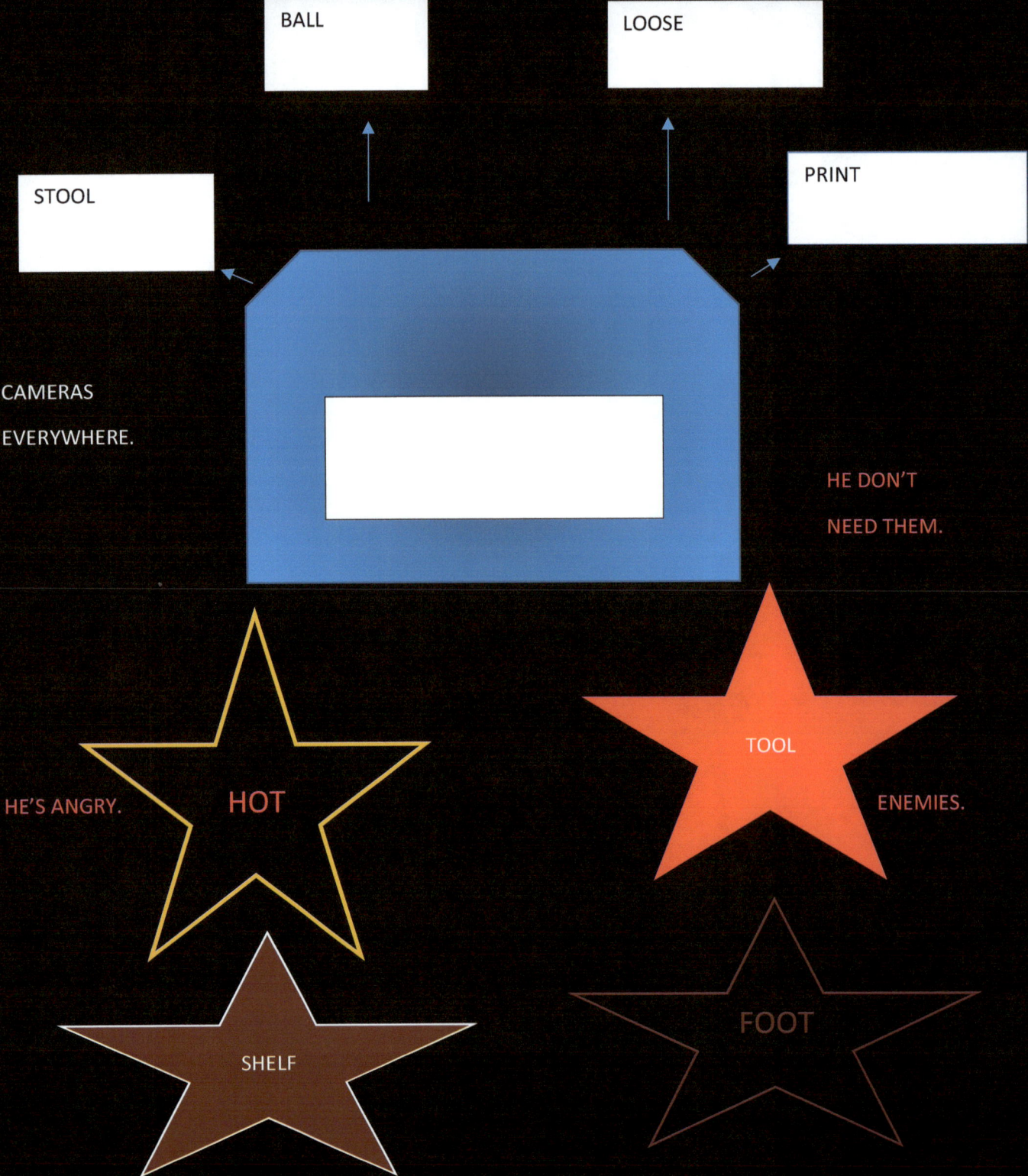

41.

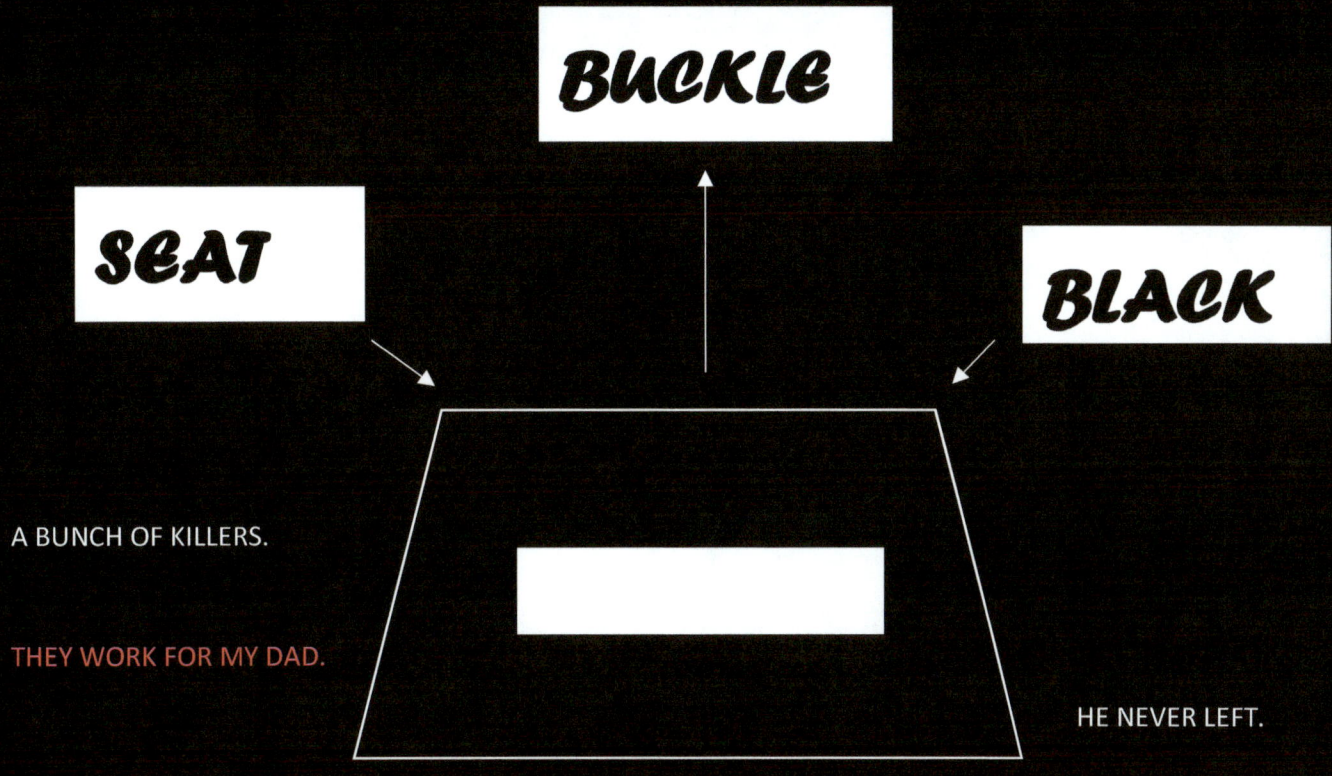

A BUNCH OF KILLERS.

THEY WORK FOR MY DAD.

HE NEVER LEFT.

NOTHING IS FAIR.

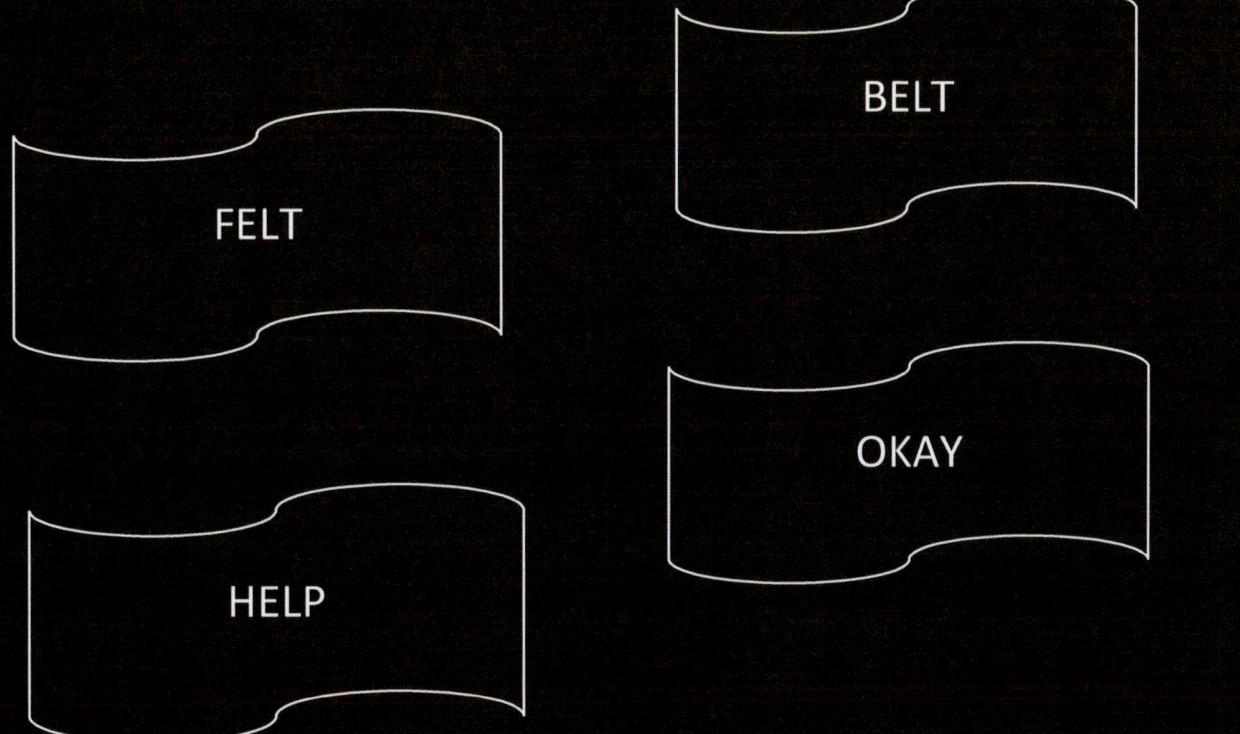

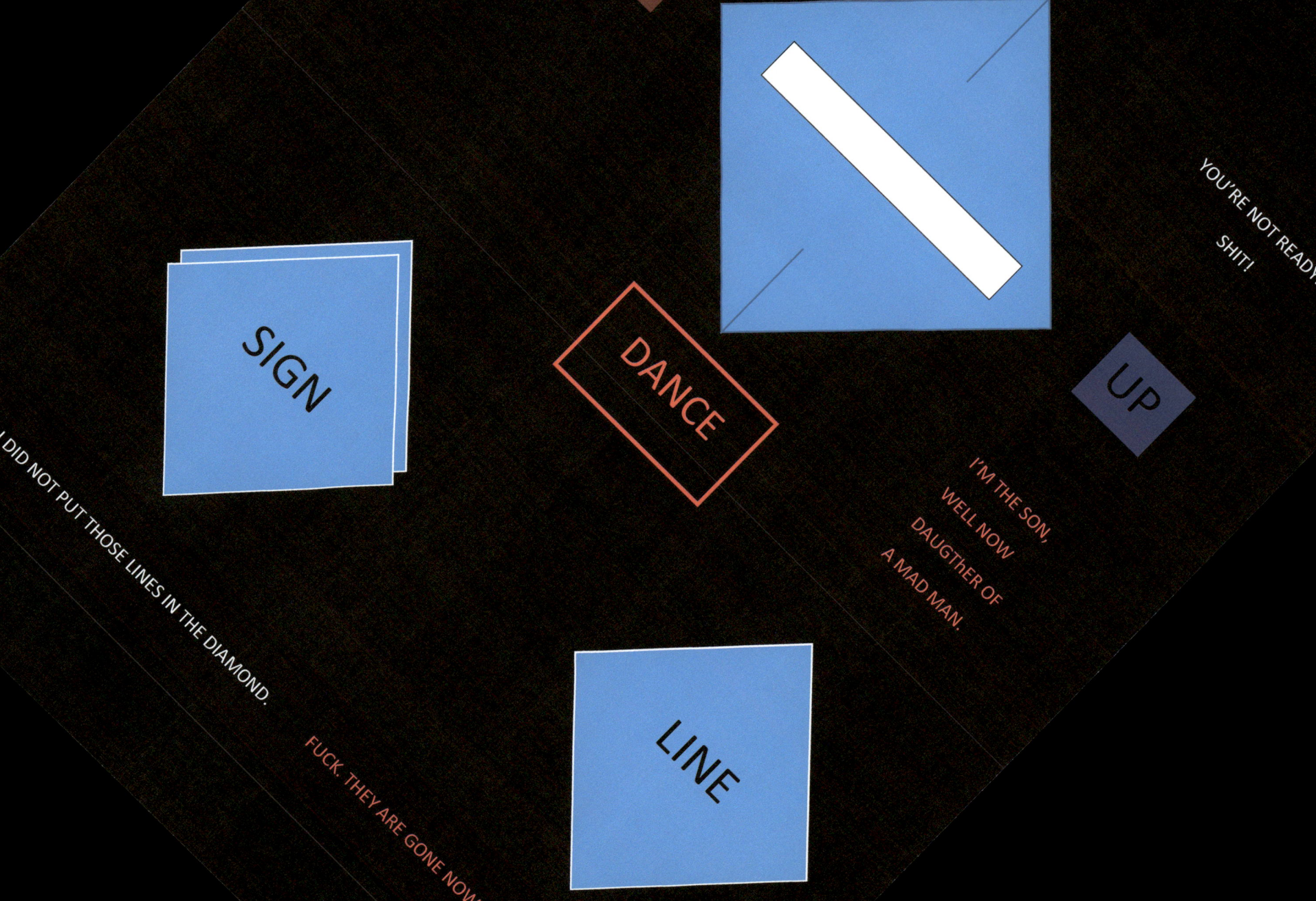

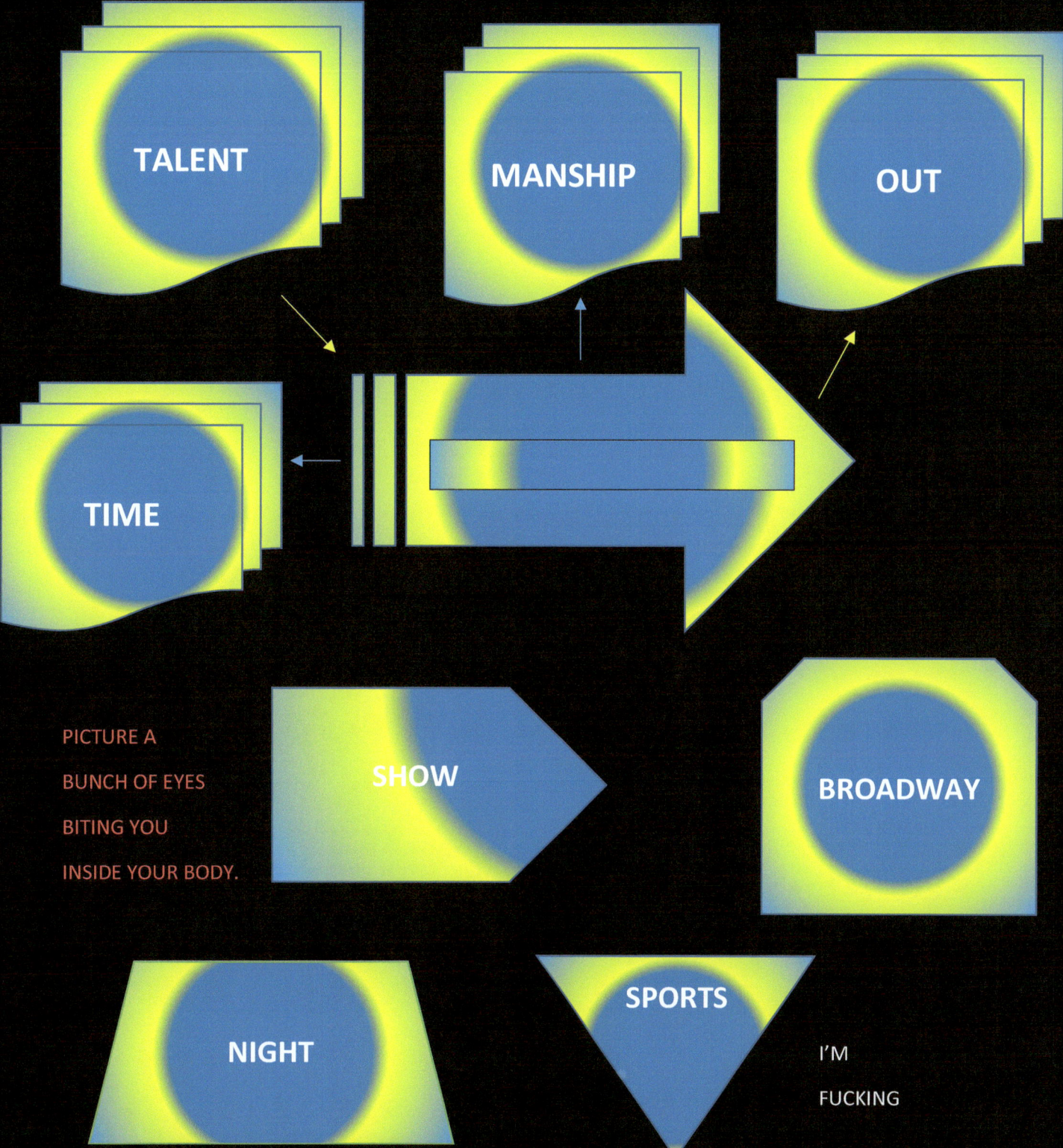

CONNECTIONS

44.

SMITH

COMBINATION

SCARED!

FREE

PATTERN

SOLID

LOCK!

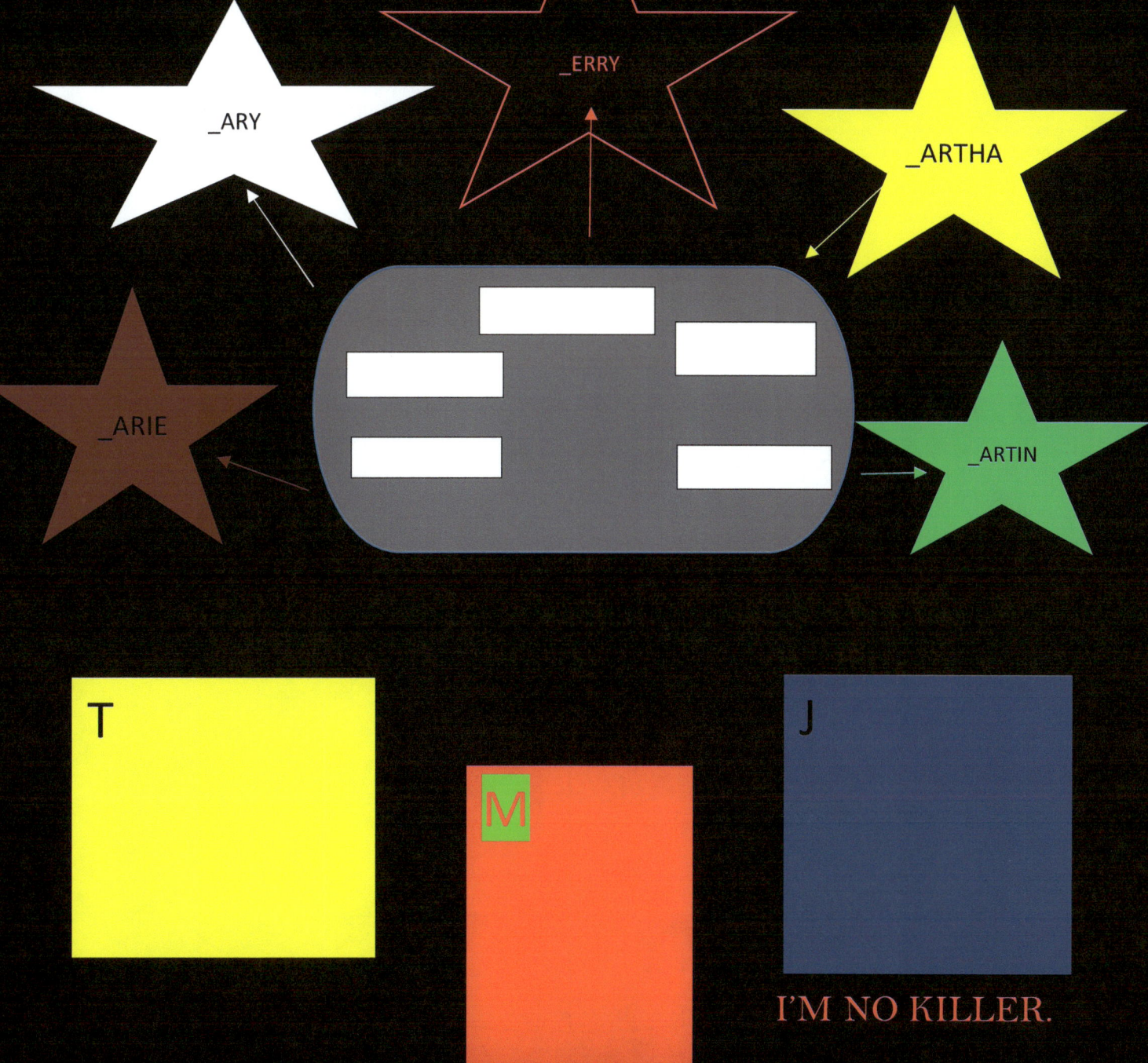

46.

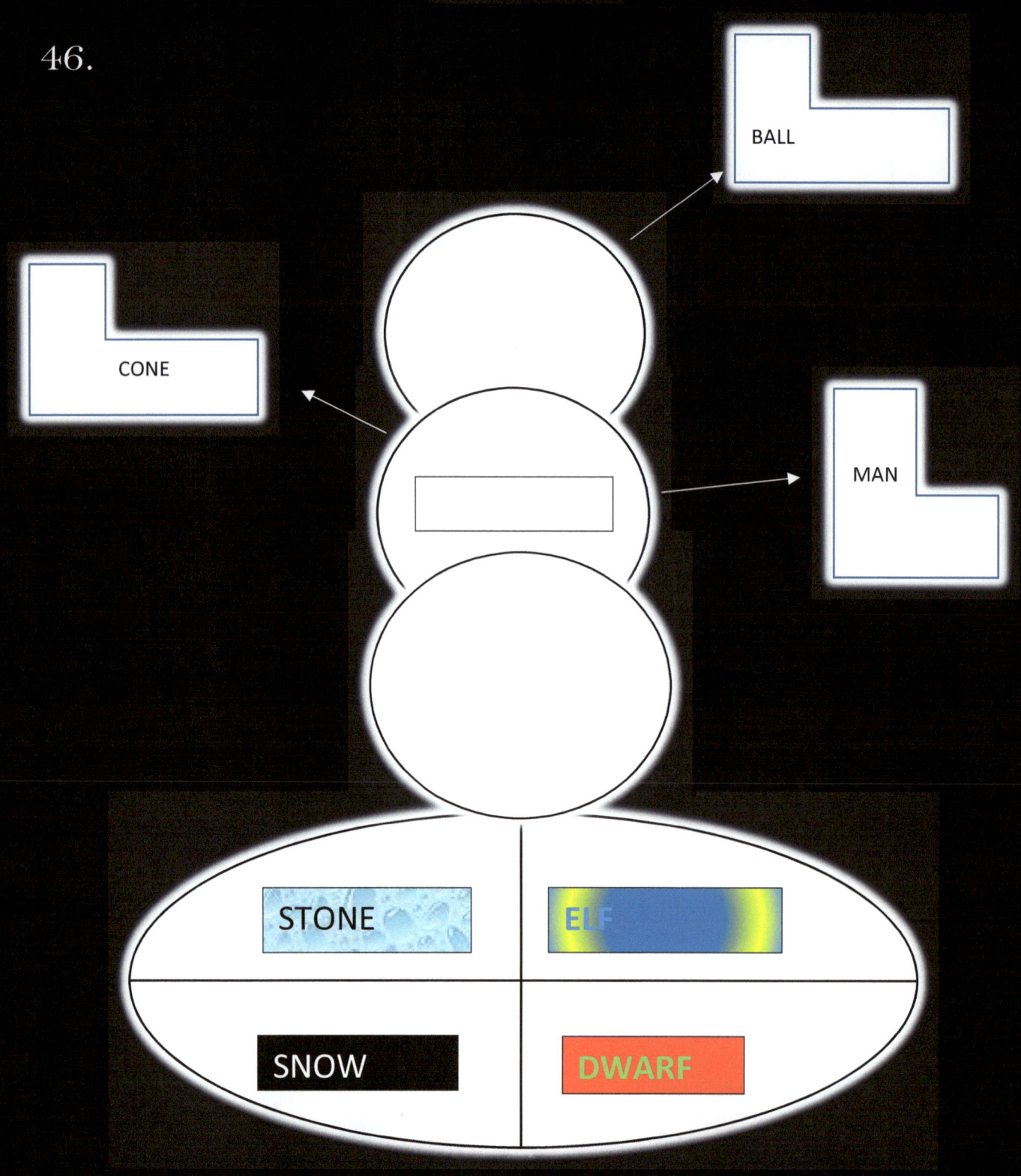

BUT HE IS.

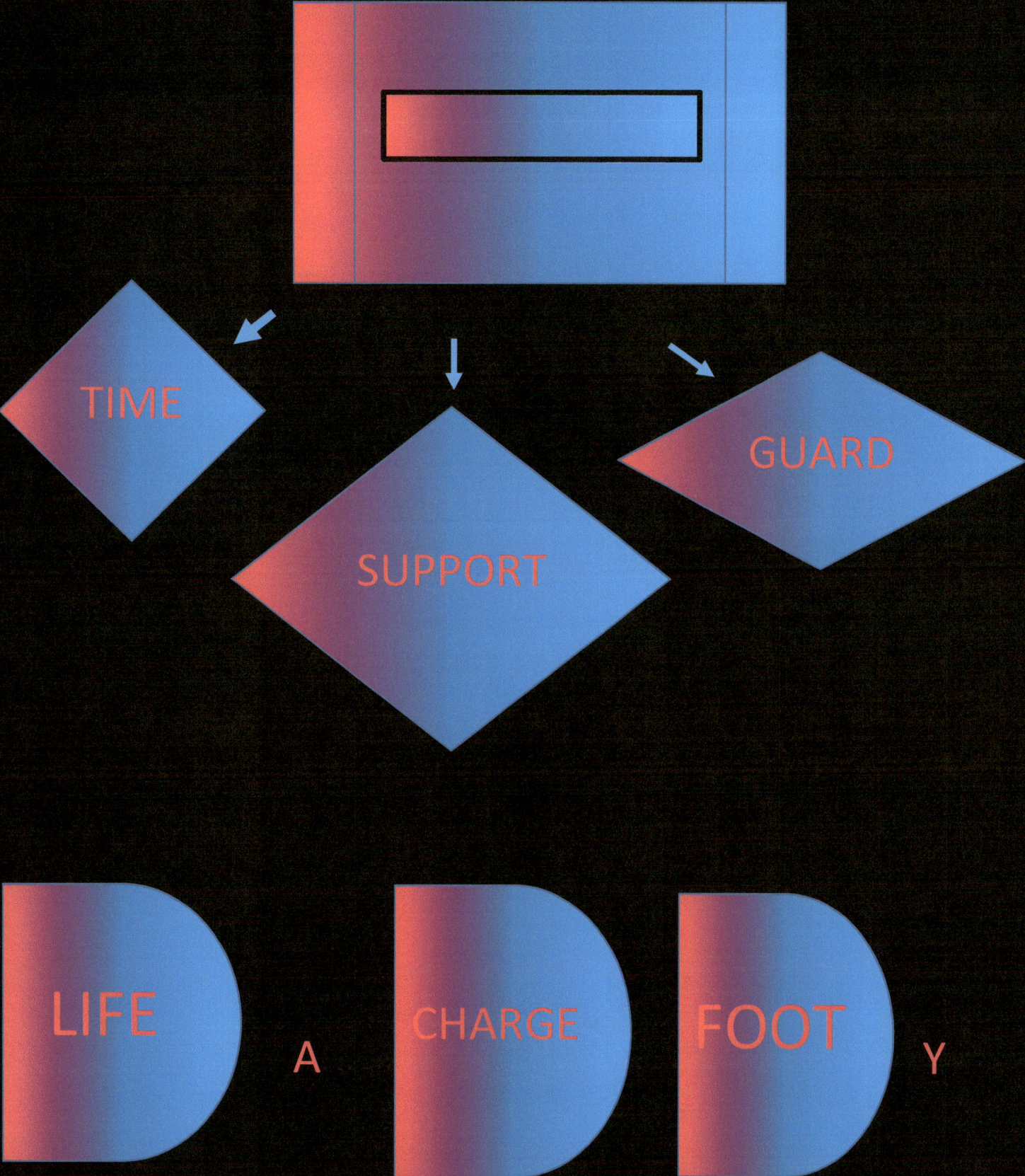

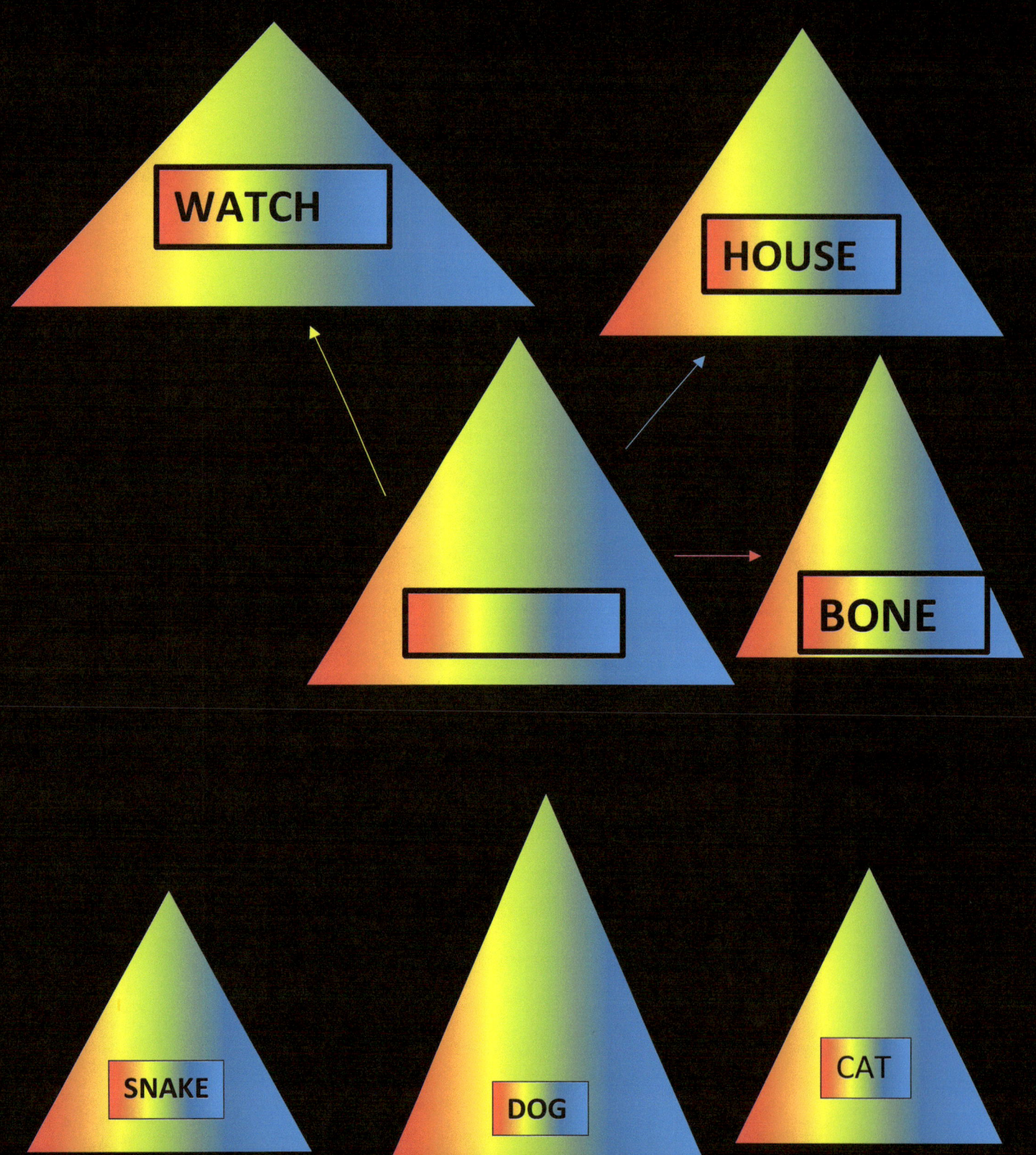

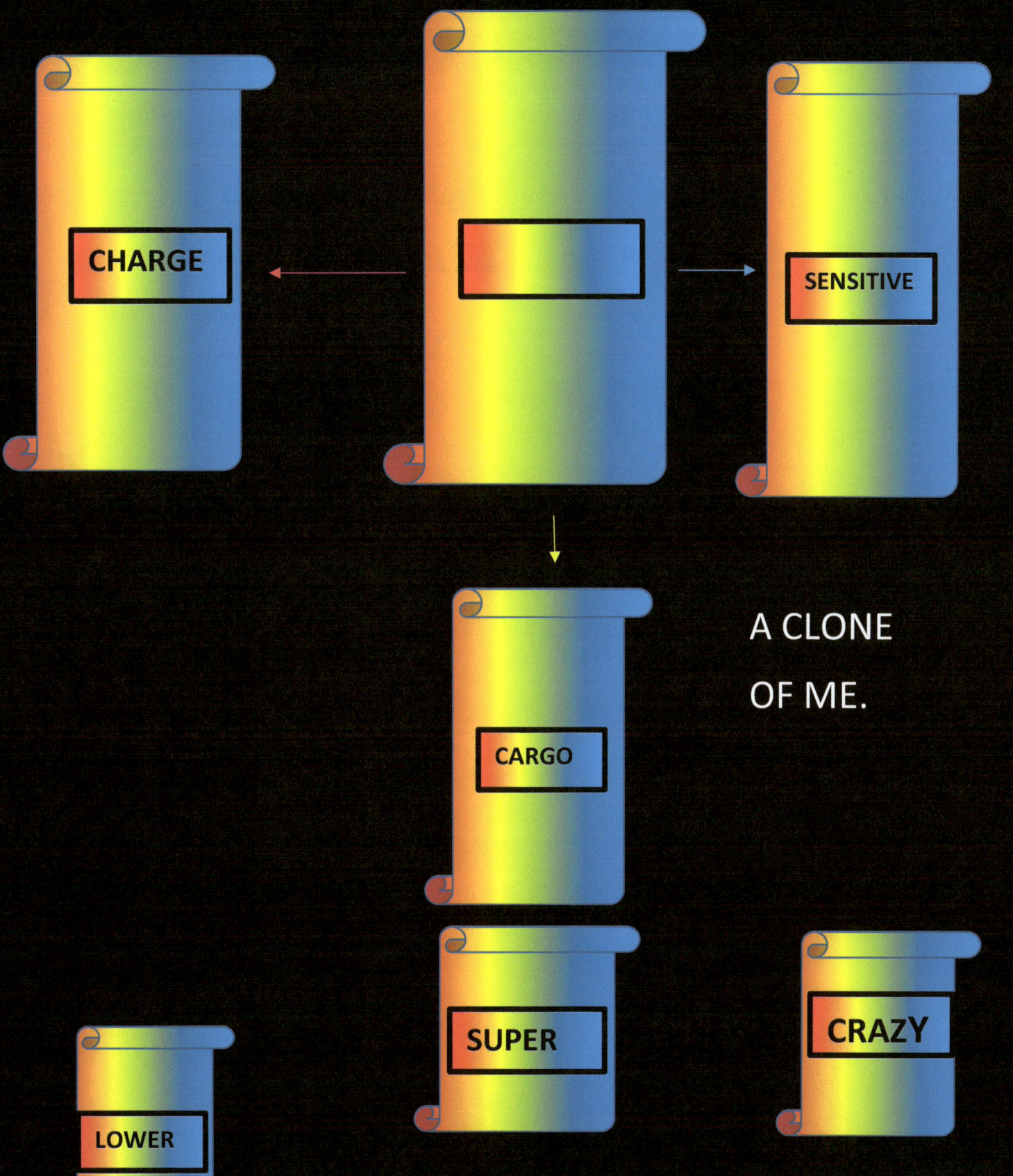

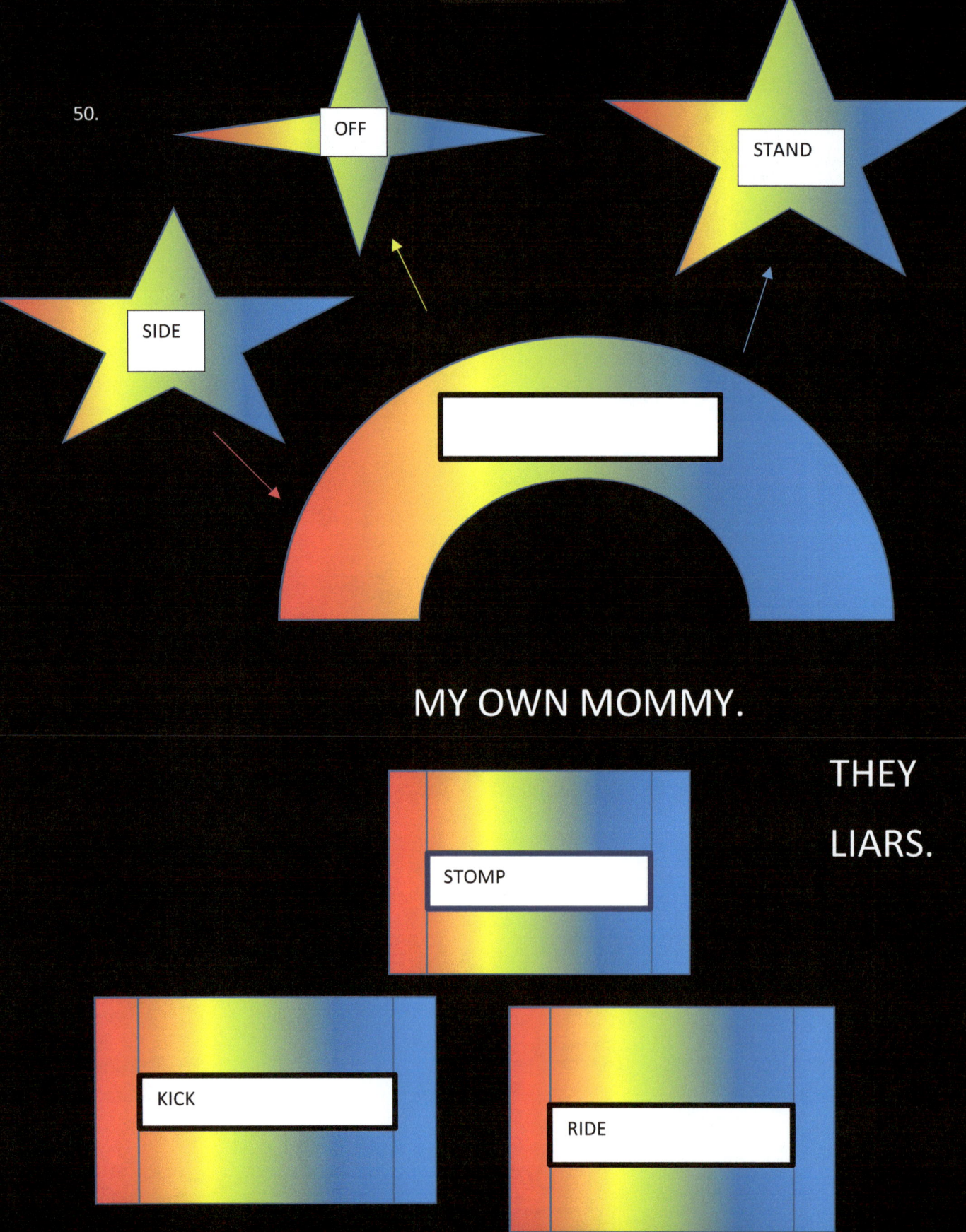

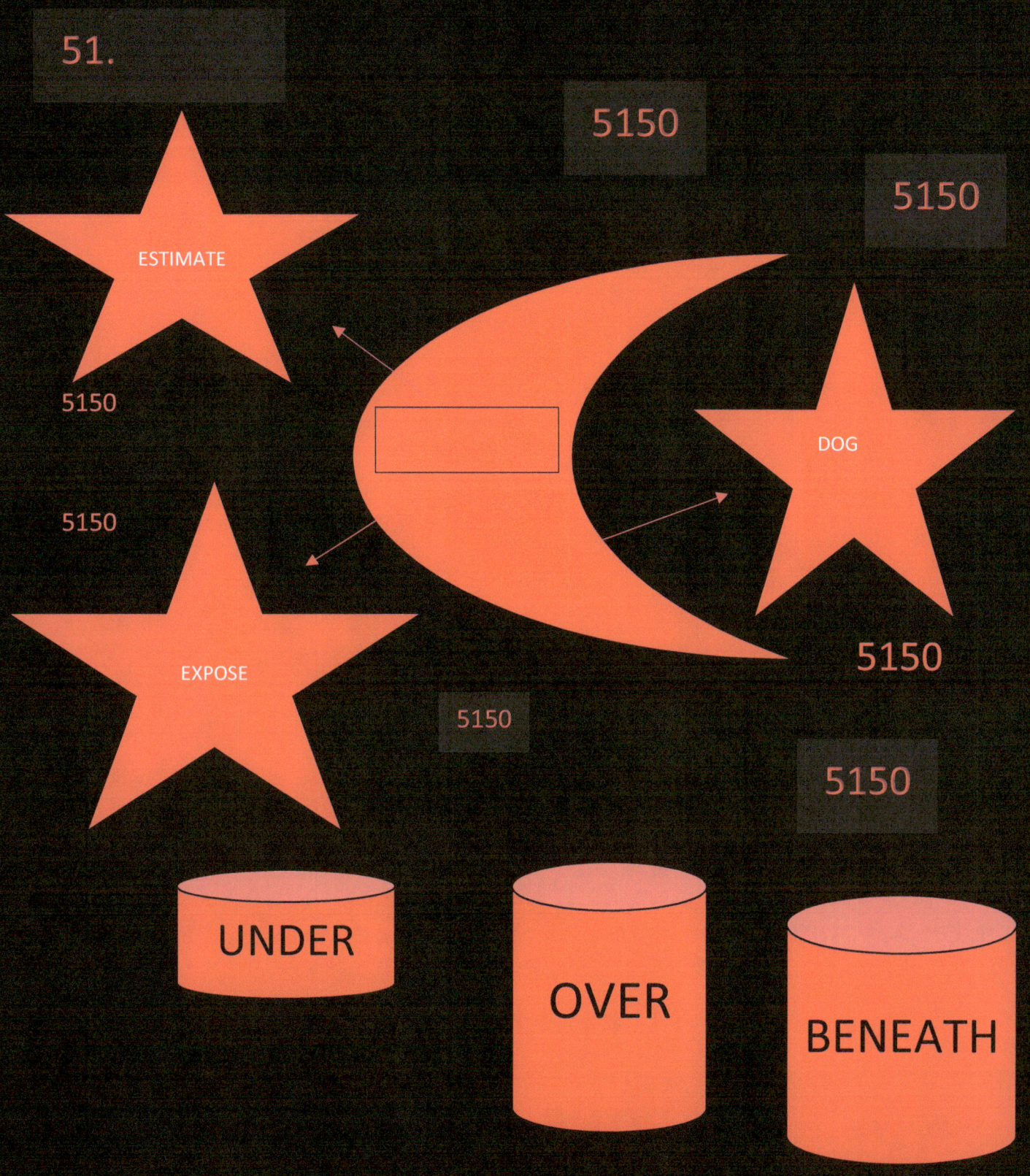

CONNECTIONS

53.

SHOW

HOME

A LOT
OF
KILLING

COW

WOMAN

GIRL

FEMALE

MORE THAN
THE NEWS.

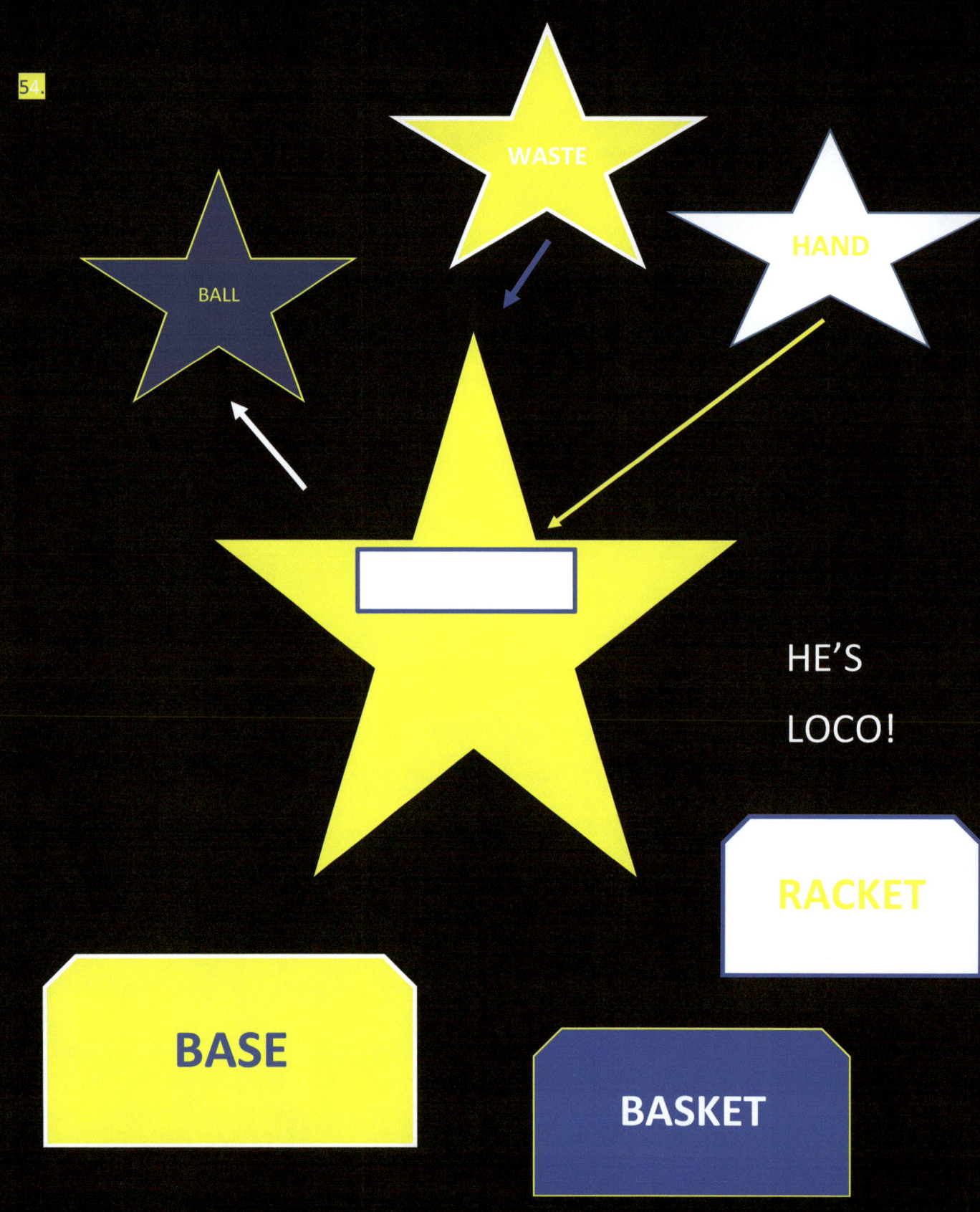

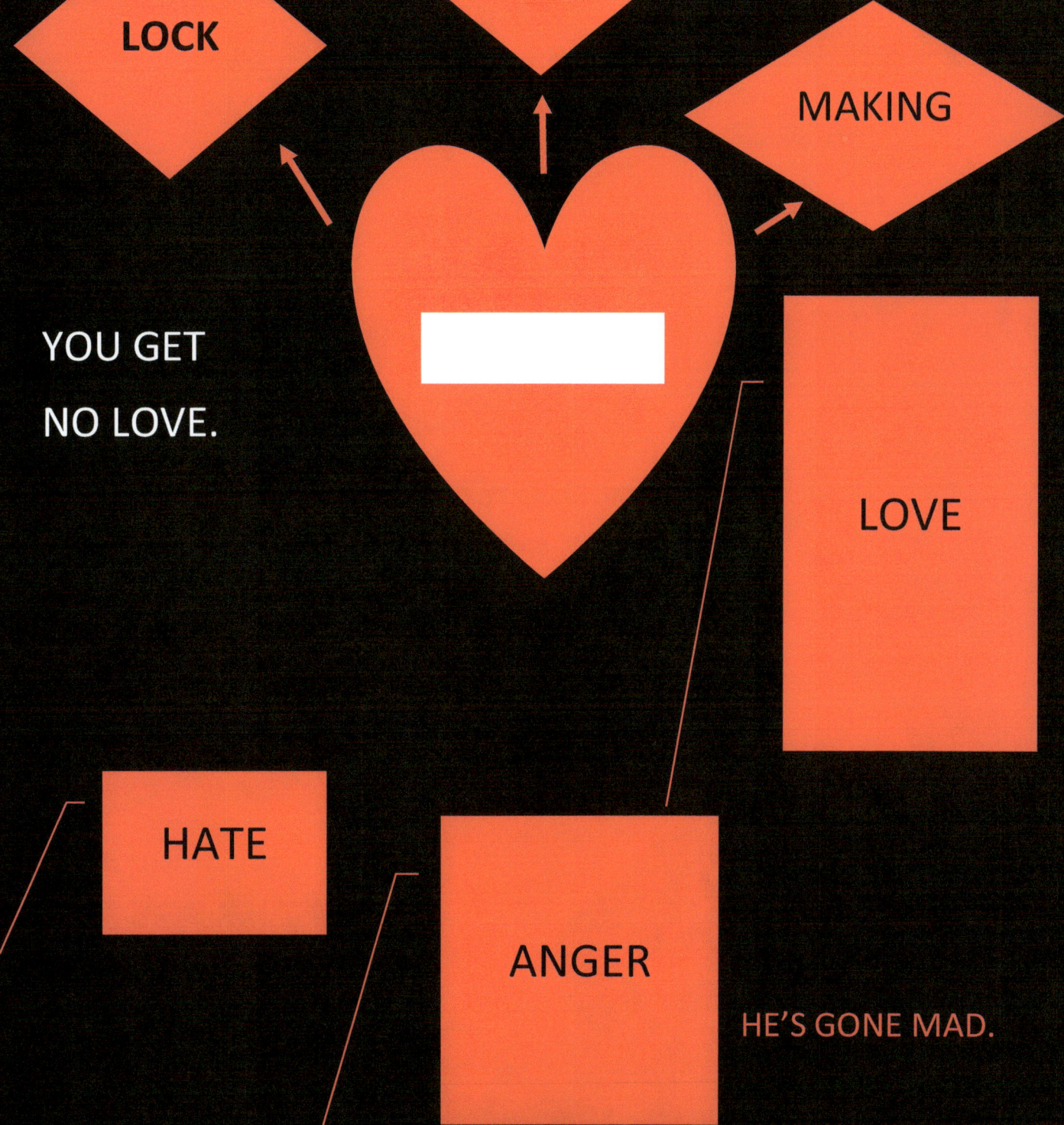

57.

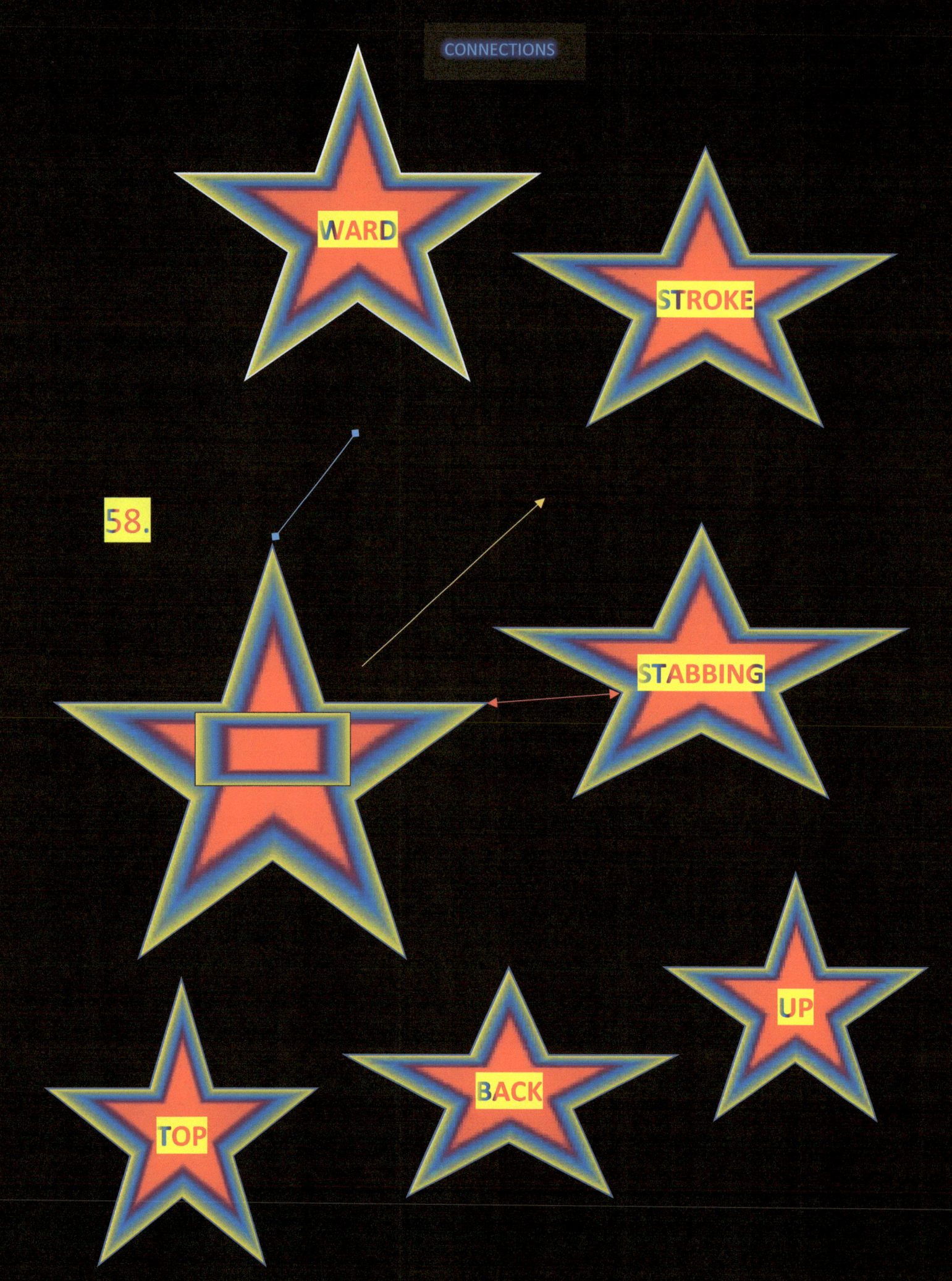

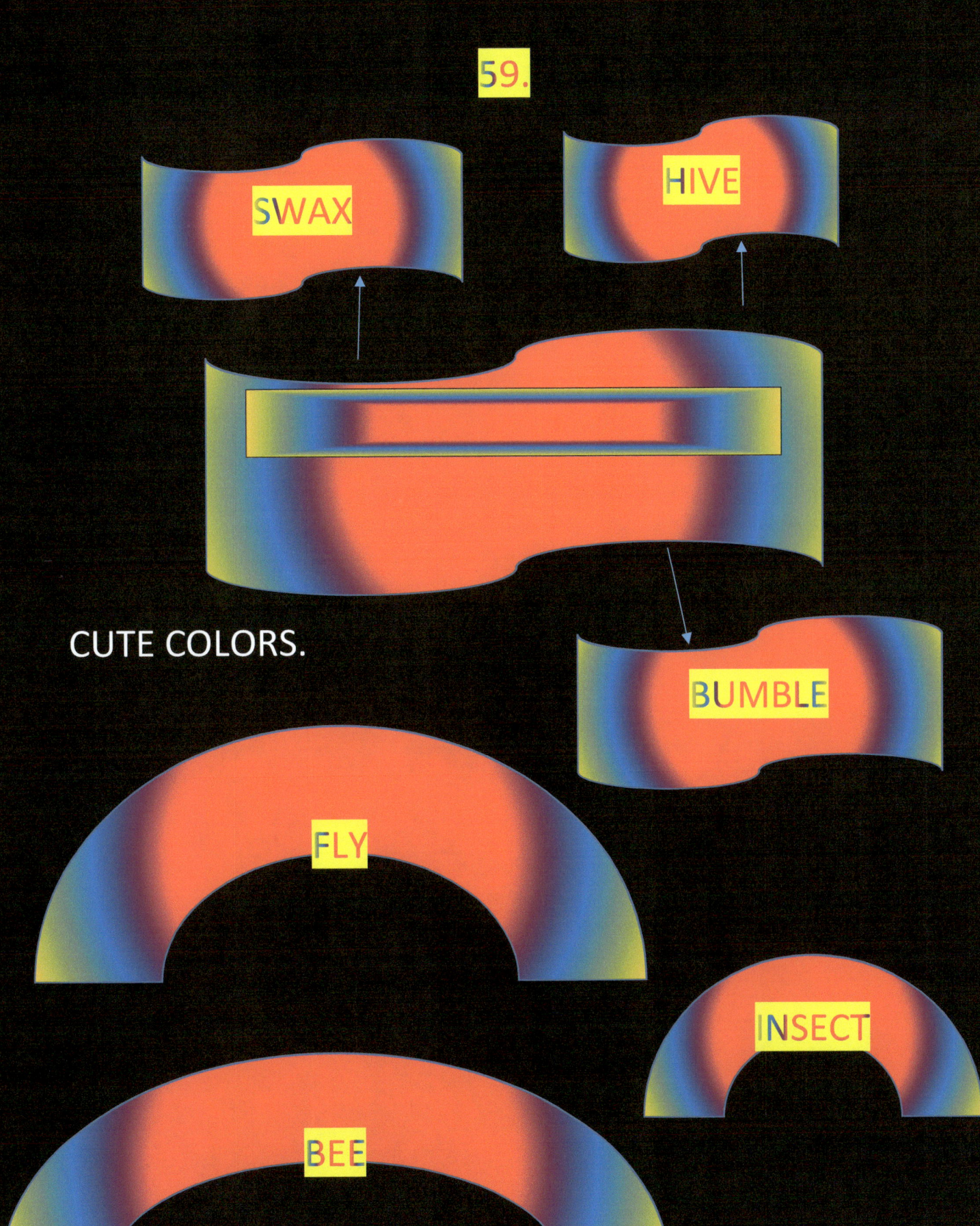

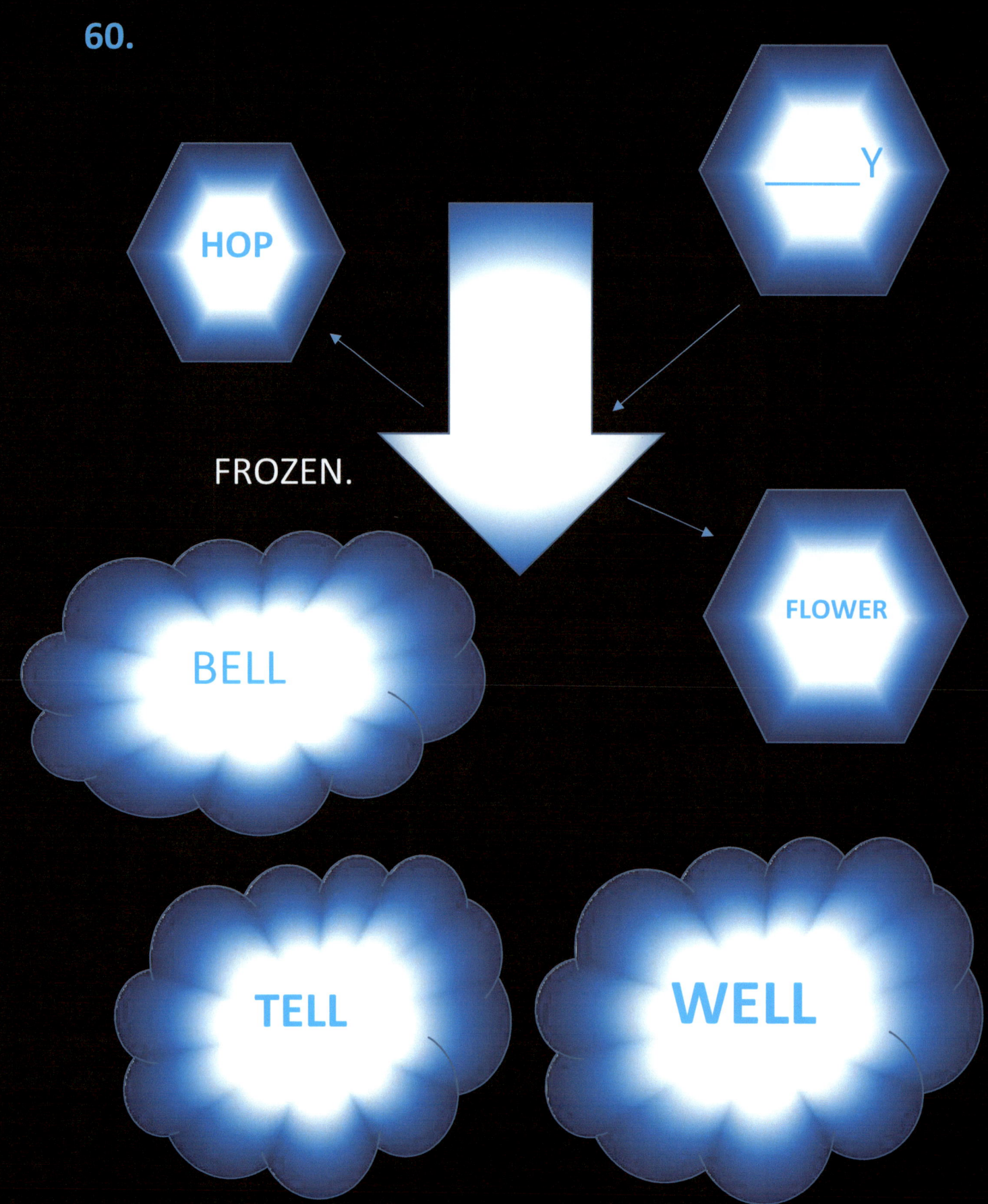

CONNECTIONS

61.

BERRY

BIRD

NO MORE.

OUT

PURPLE

BLUE

GREEN

BLACK

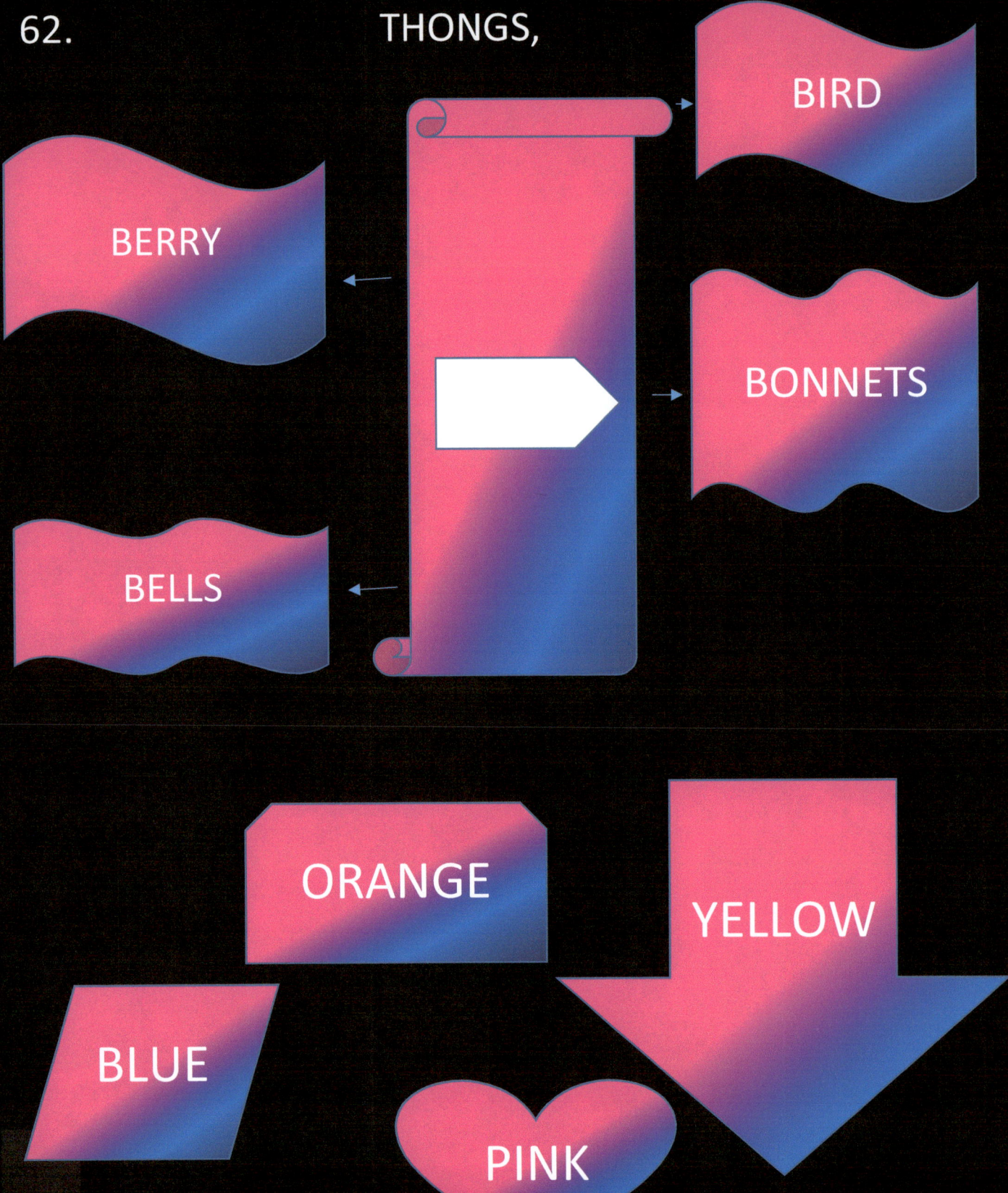

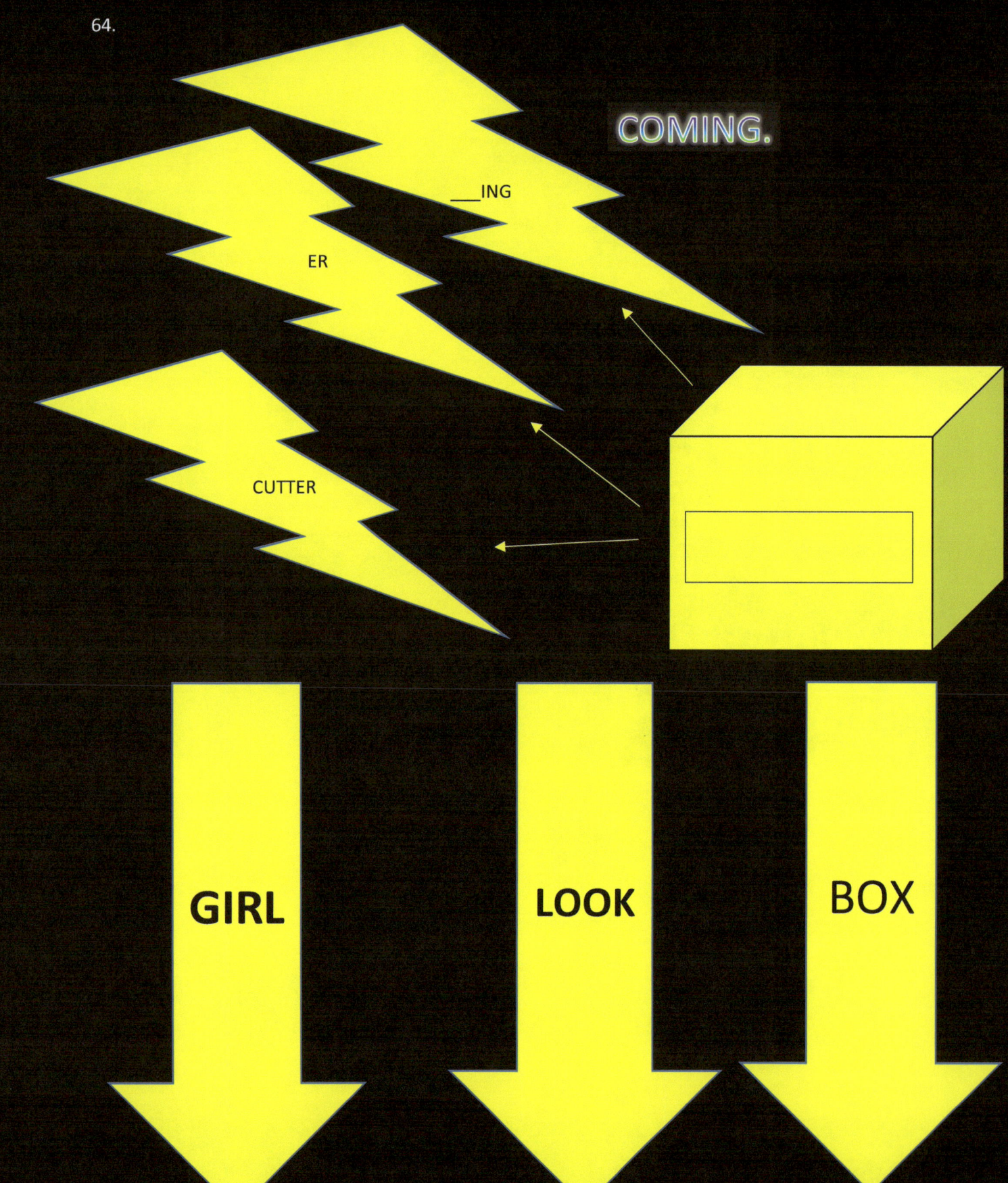

CONNECTIONS

65.

WASH

DAMAGE

STORM

LIVER

BRAIN

HEAD

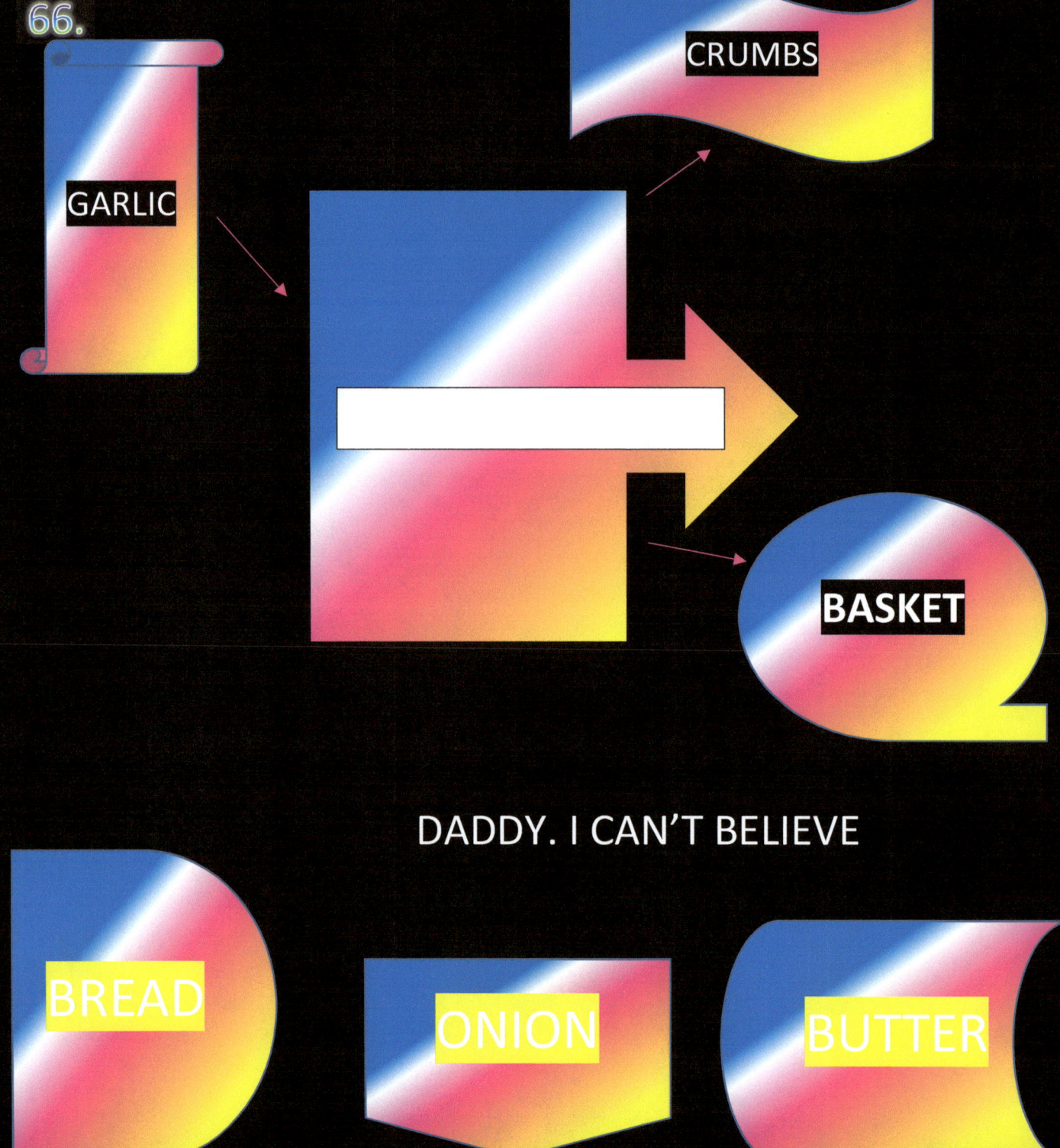

CONNECTIONS

68. SUFFOCATION

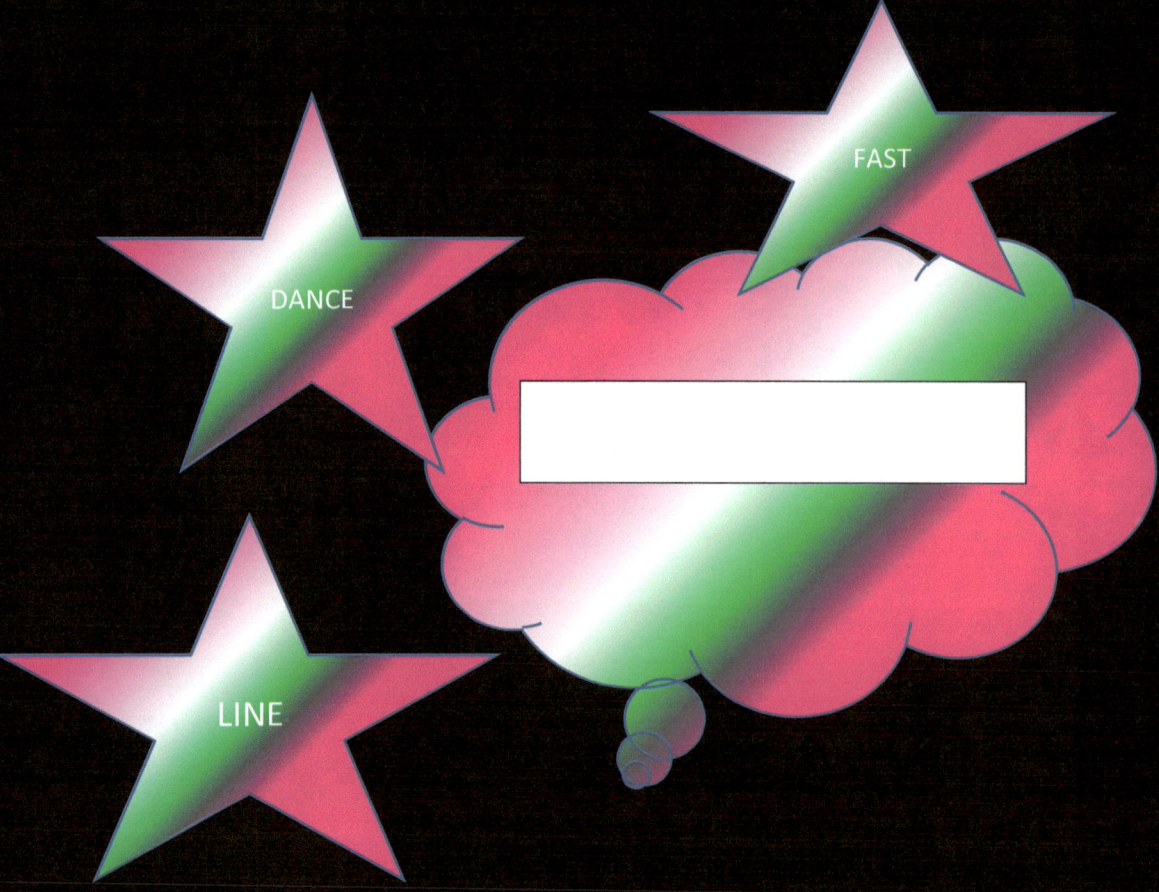

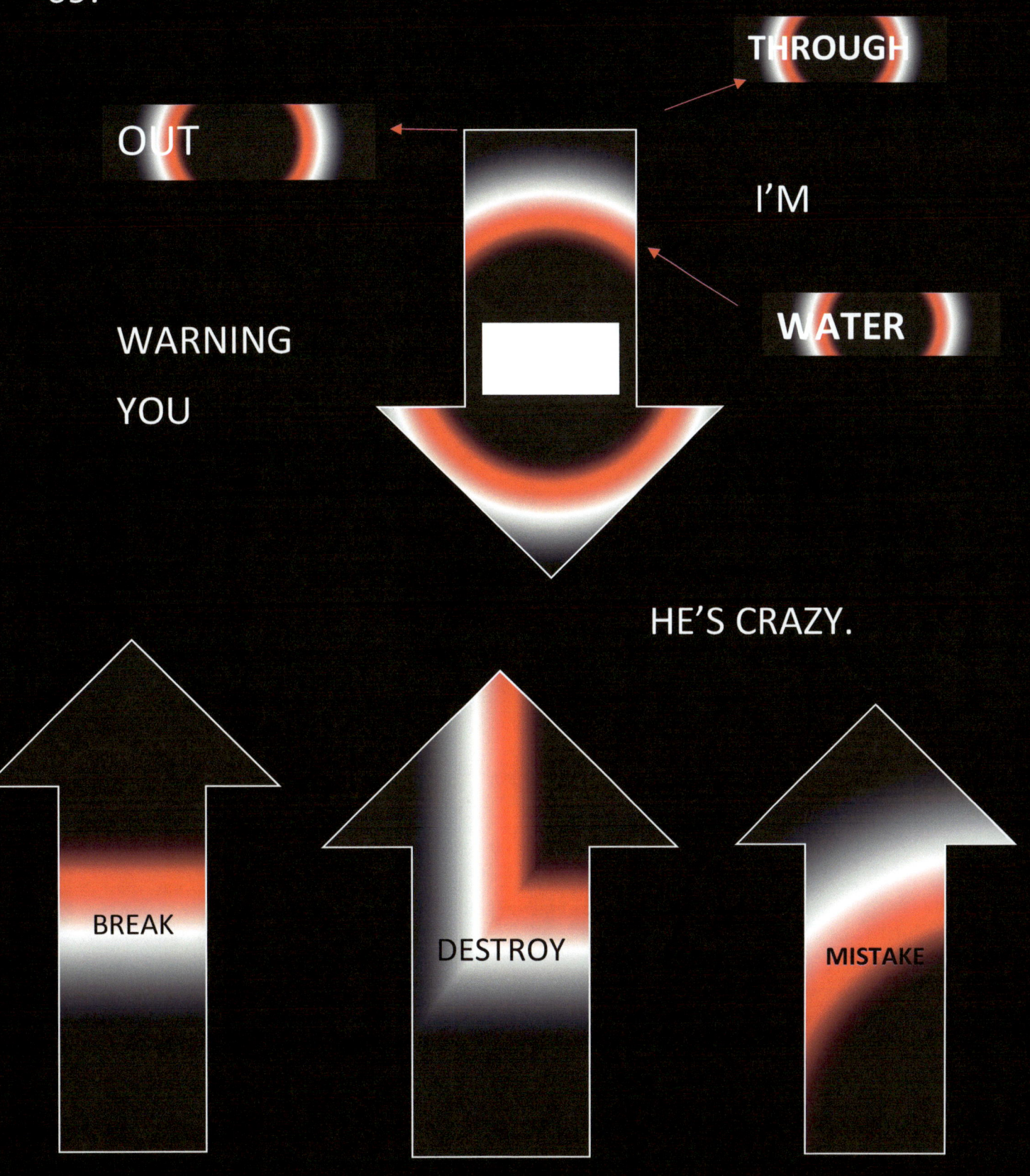

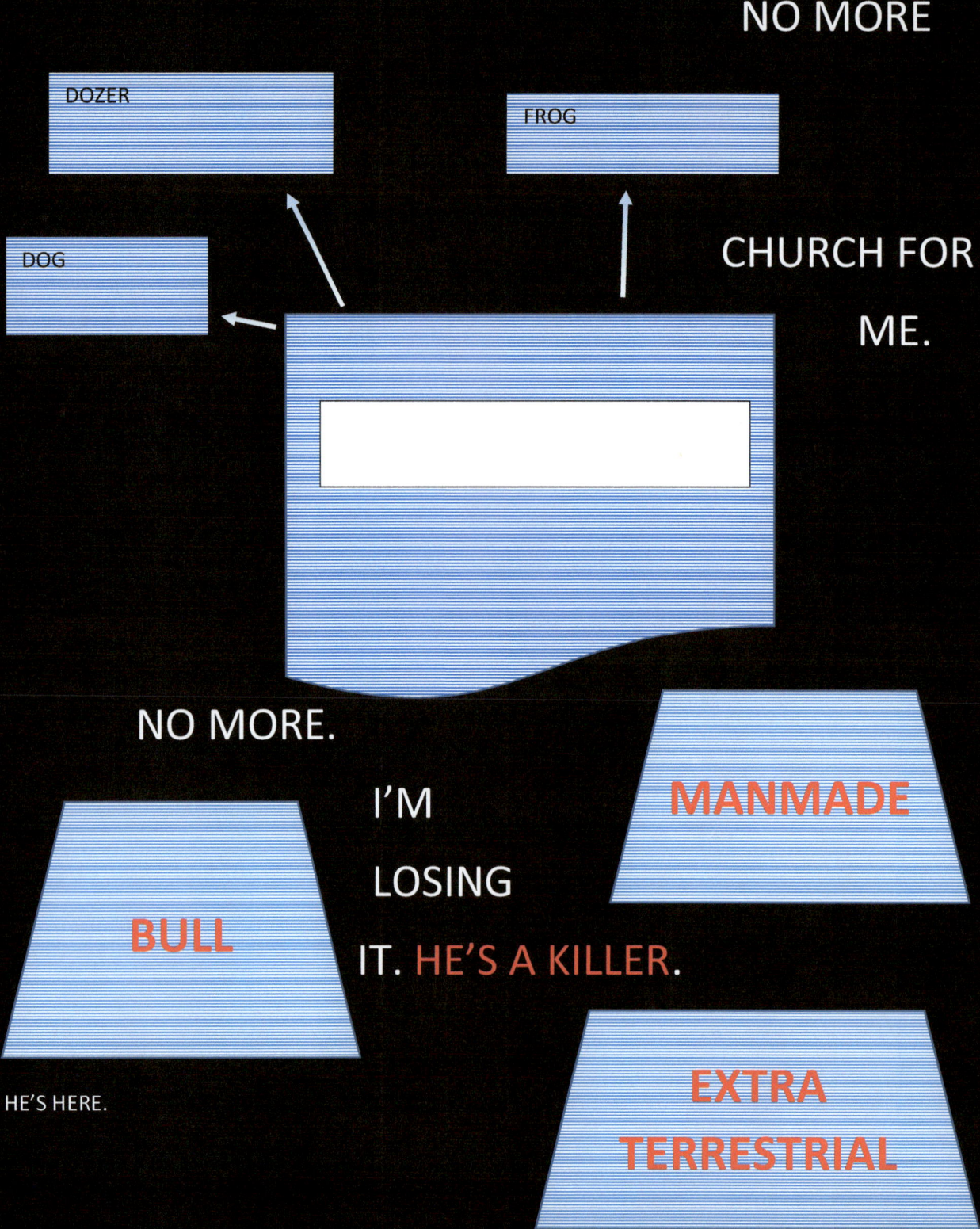

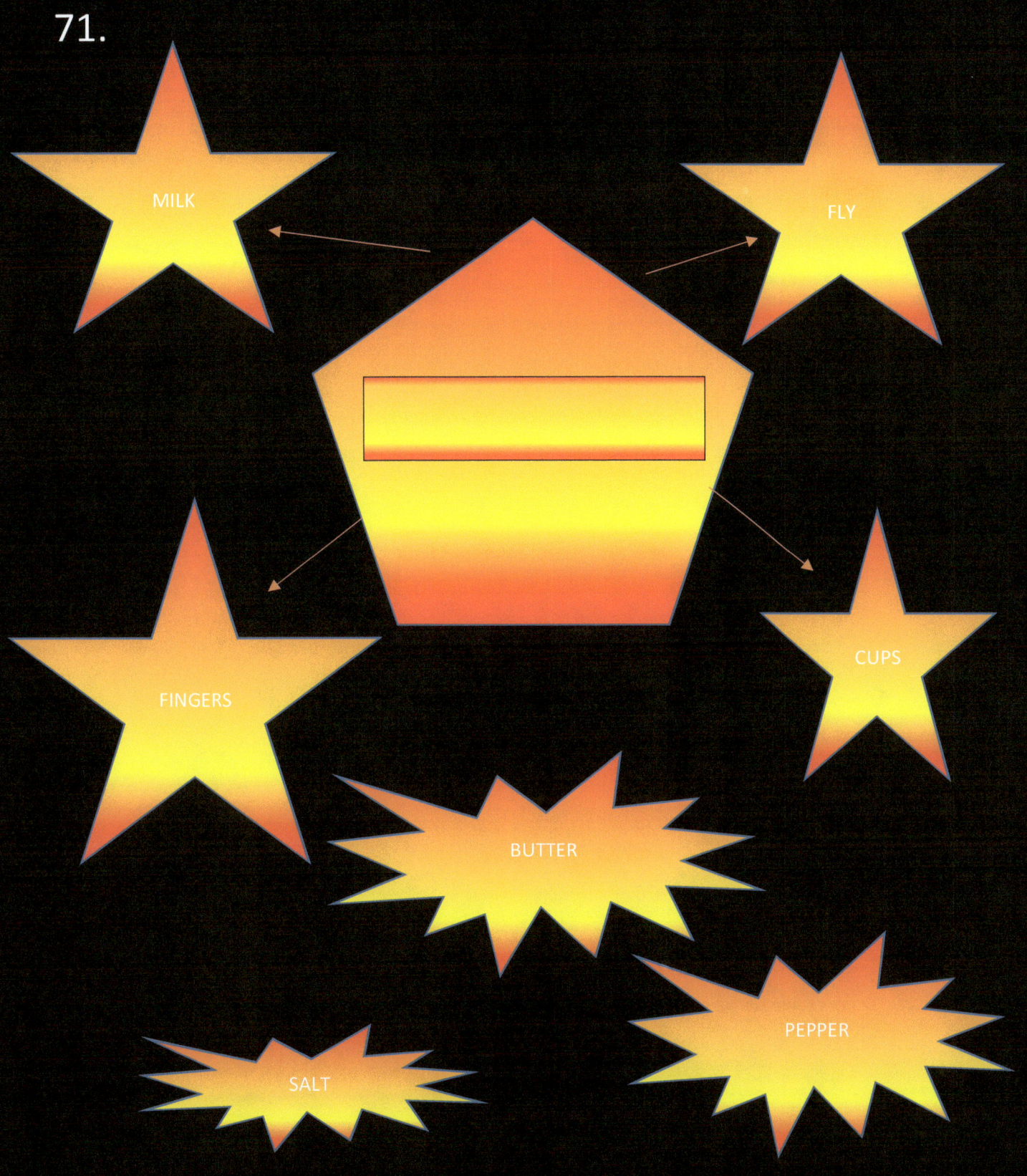

72.

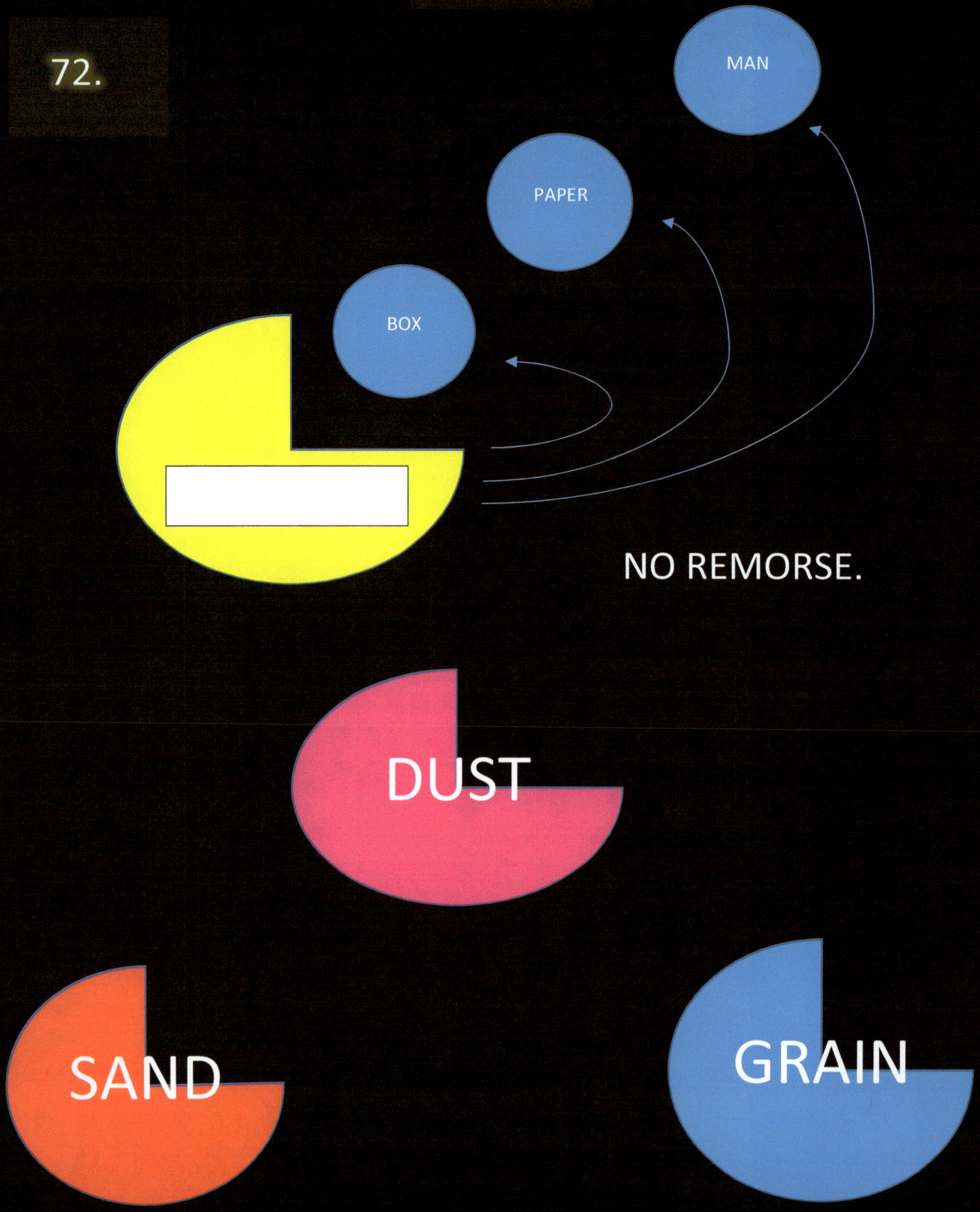

CONNECTIONS

MAN
PAPER
BOX

NO REMORSE.

DUST

SAND

GRAIN

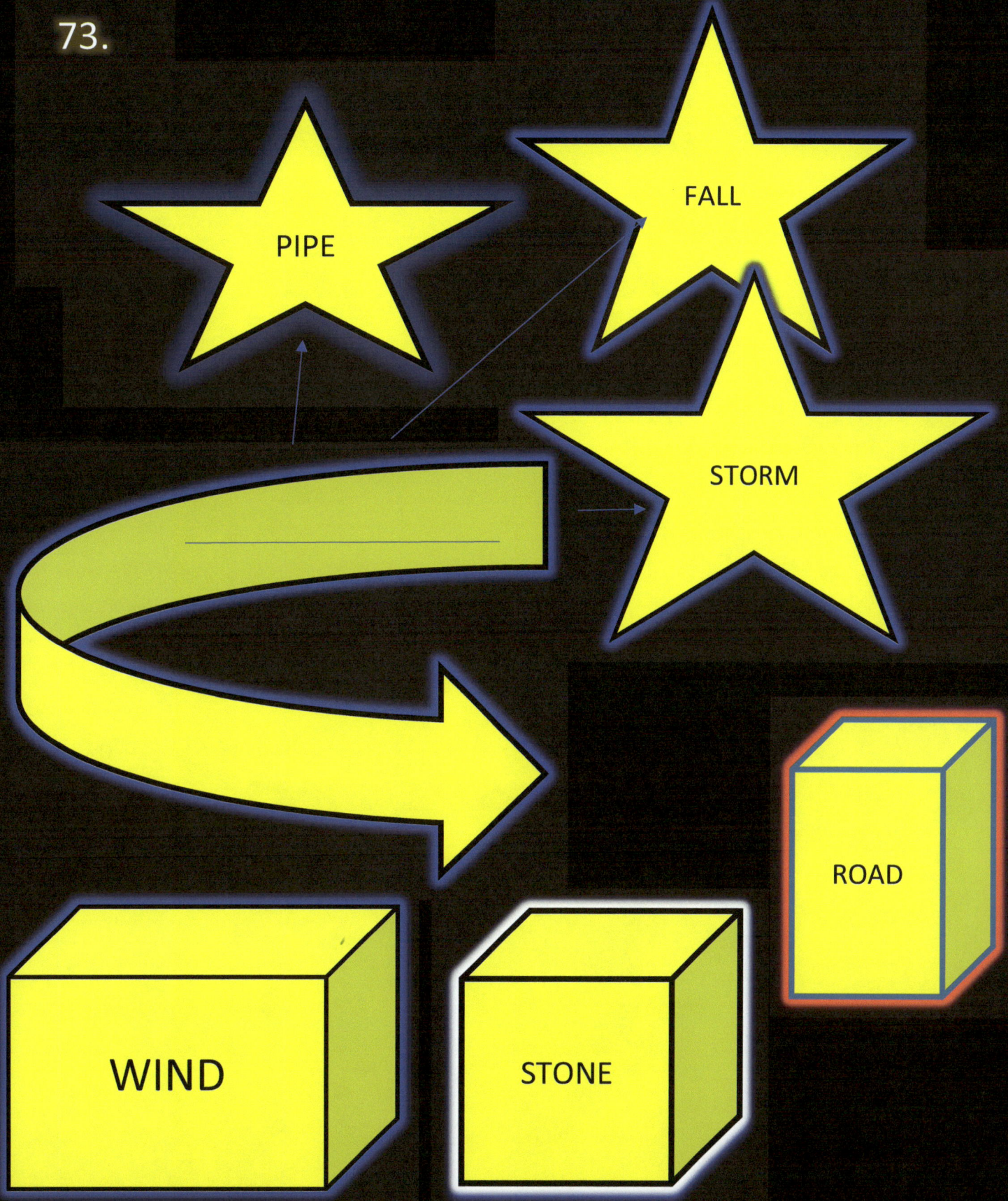

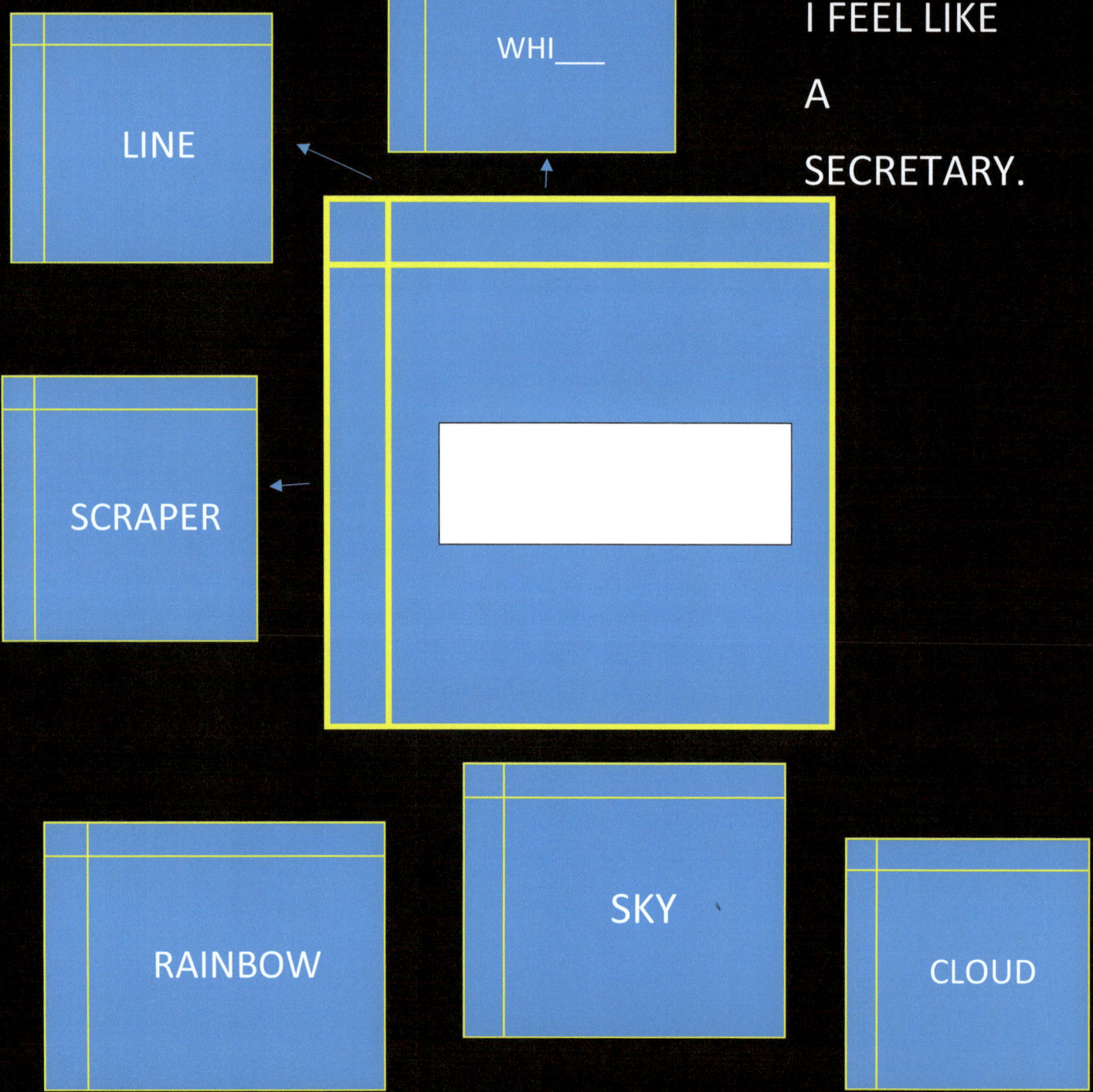

CONNECTIONS

76.

SPIDERS

OWLS

WORMS

LIGHT

__ISCOVER

FLAG

HEART

ZONE

___o

HE NEVER LEFT.

RED
ROJO

BLUE
AZUL

WHITE
BLANCO

CONNECTIONS

77.

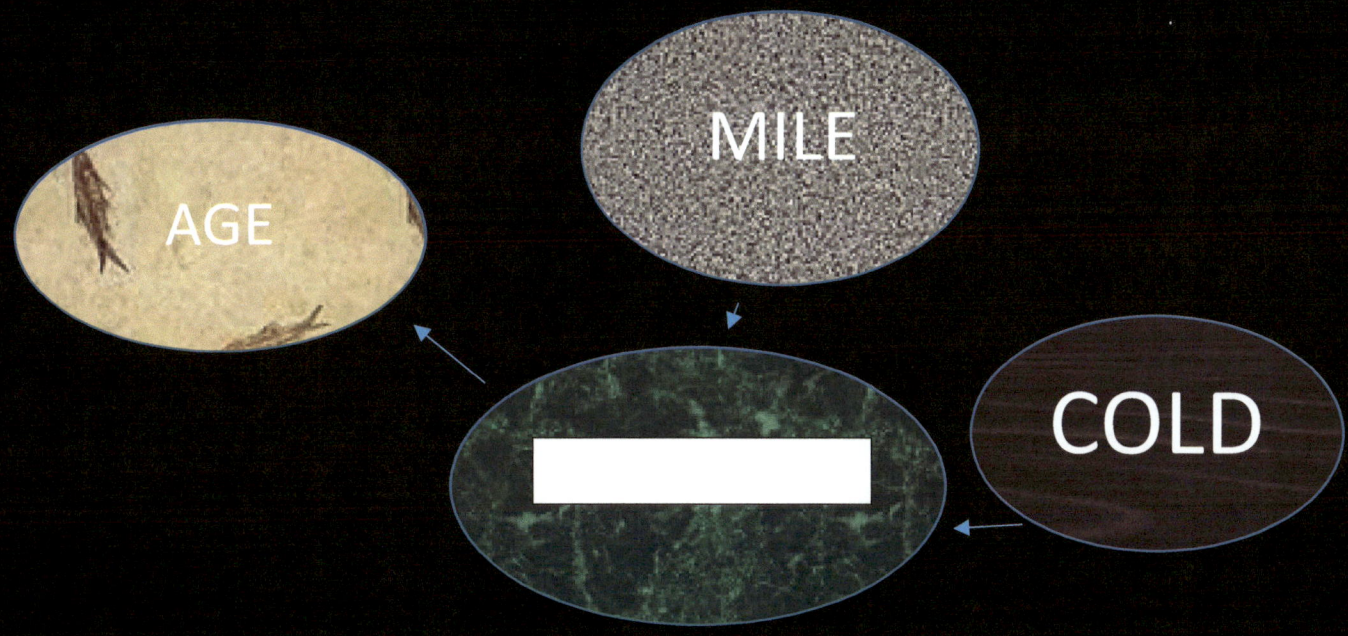

MILE

AGE

COLD

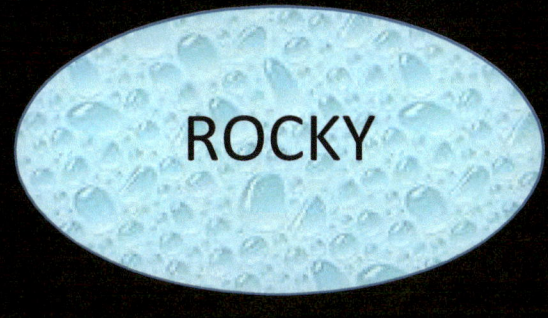

ROCKY

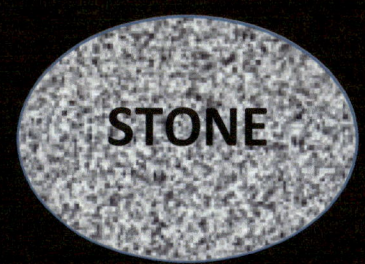

STONE

HEAVEN IS ON EARTH.

BRICK

SHELLO

CONNECTIONS

78.

SPRING → [ ] → UP

FAST ← [ ]

BRAKE

BRAYK   BREAK

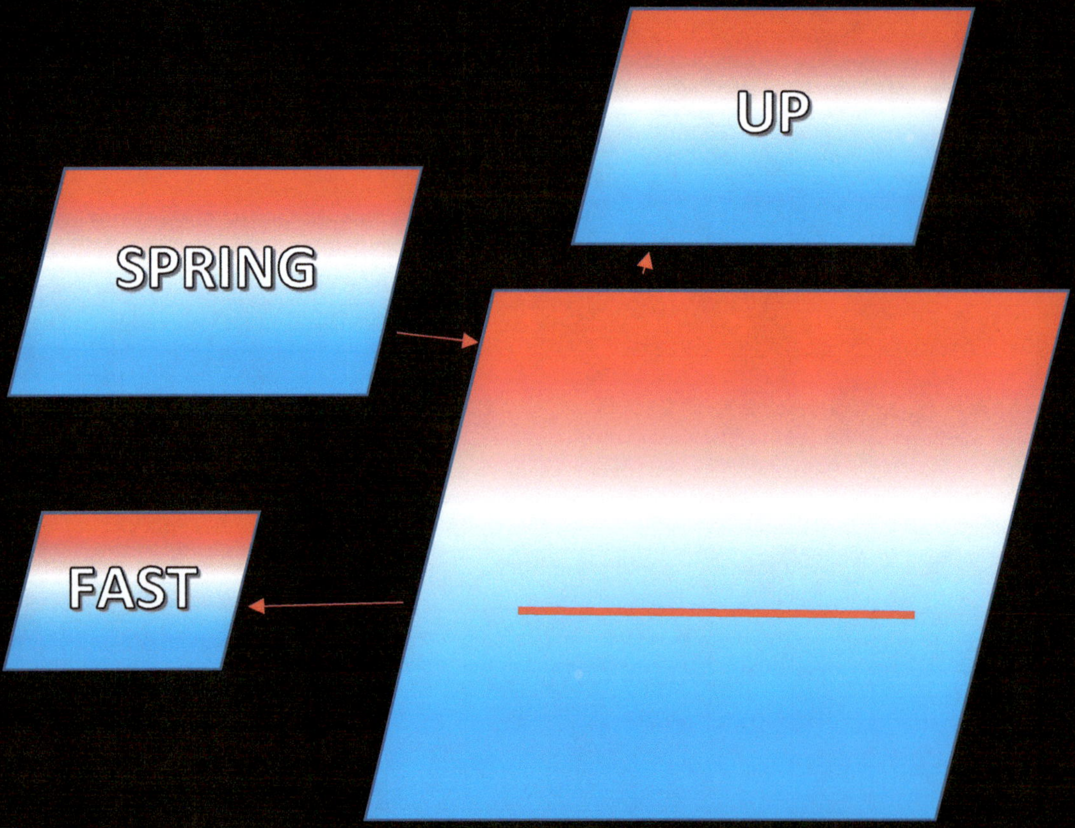

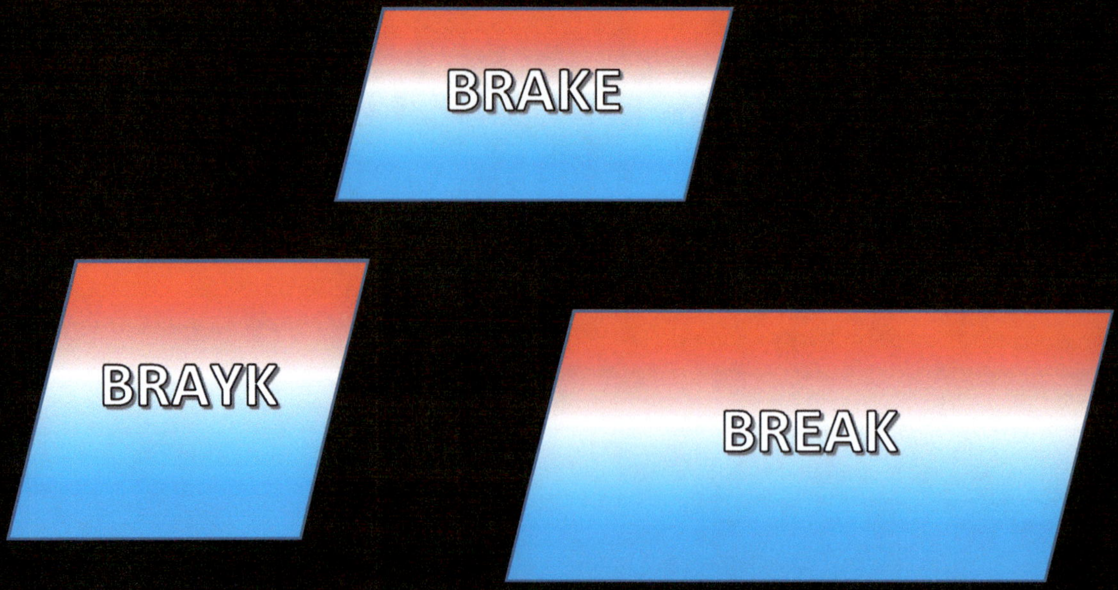

CONNECTIONS

80.

CARE

BIRTH

PROOF

MY LIFE WAS PUT ON HOLD.

HE'S JEALOUS.

WATCHING ALL OF YOU WITH YOUR KIDS.

SON

MAN

CHILD

CONNECTIONS

81.

POCKETS ↓

TUB ↓

↓

SHOT ↓

SMOKE ↓

HOT ↓

FIRE ↓

The money game. It wasn't like this in the beginning. Everyone here is paying for the behavior of the first people. You are the descendants of the first group of Manevil.

CONNECTIONS

82.

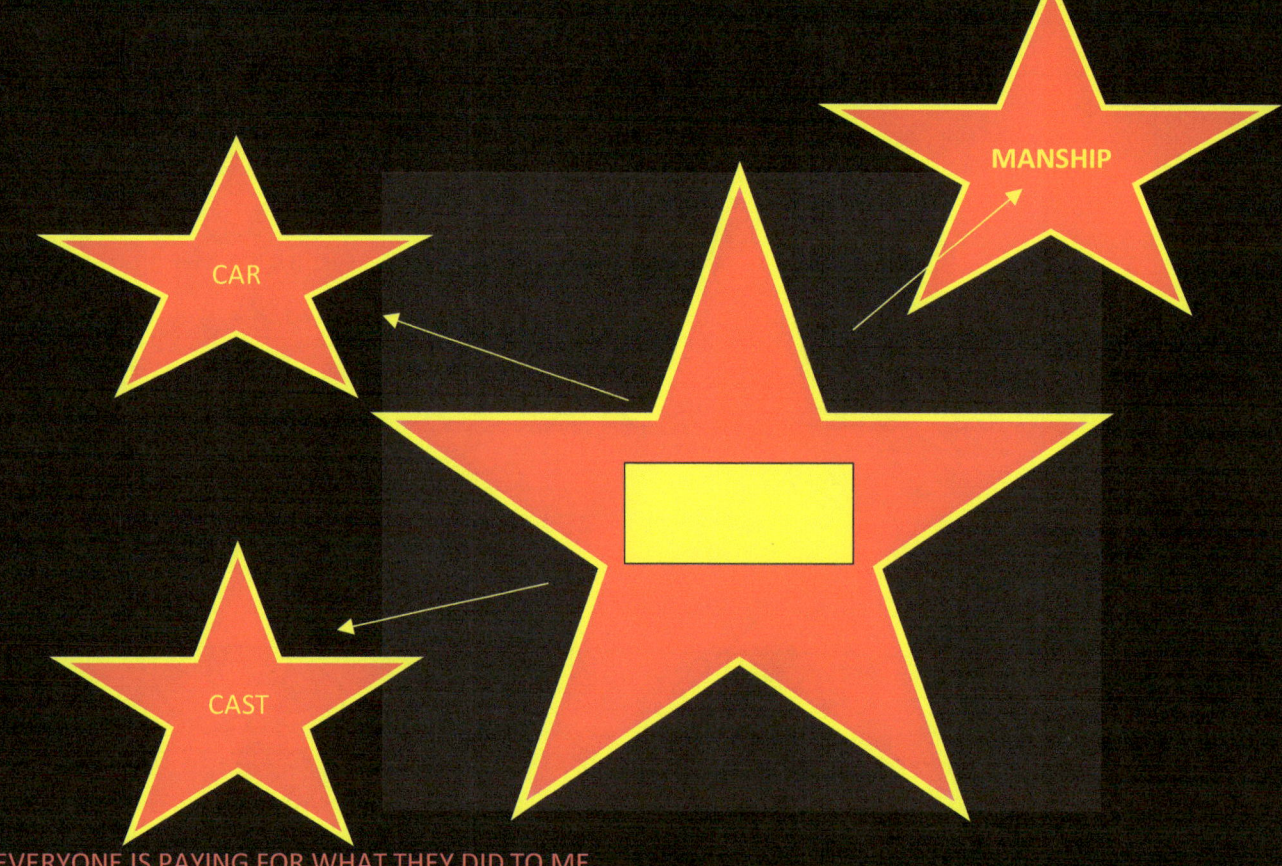

EVERYONE IS PAYING FOR WHAT THEY DID TO ME.

84.

CONNECTIONS

OUT   STAND   HOLD

WITCH   SWITCH   WITH

85.

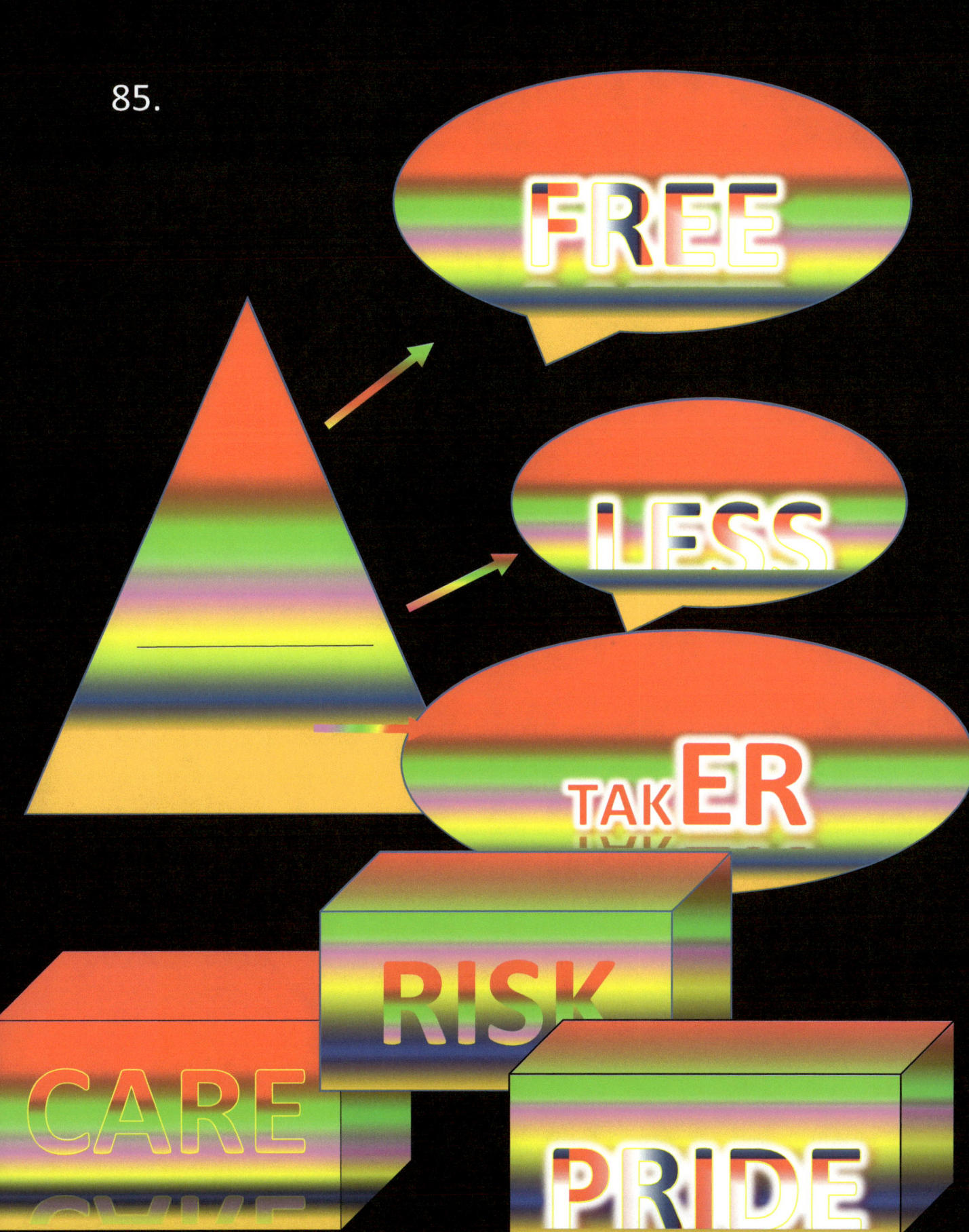

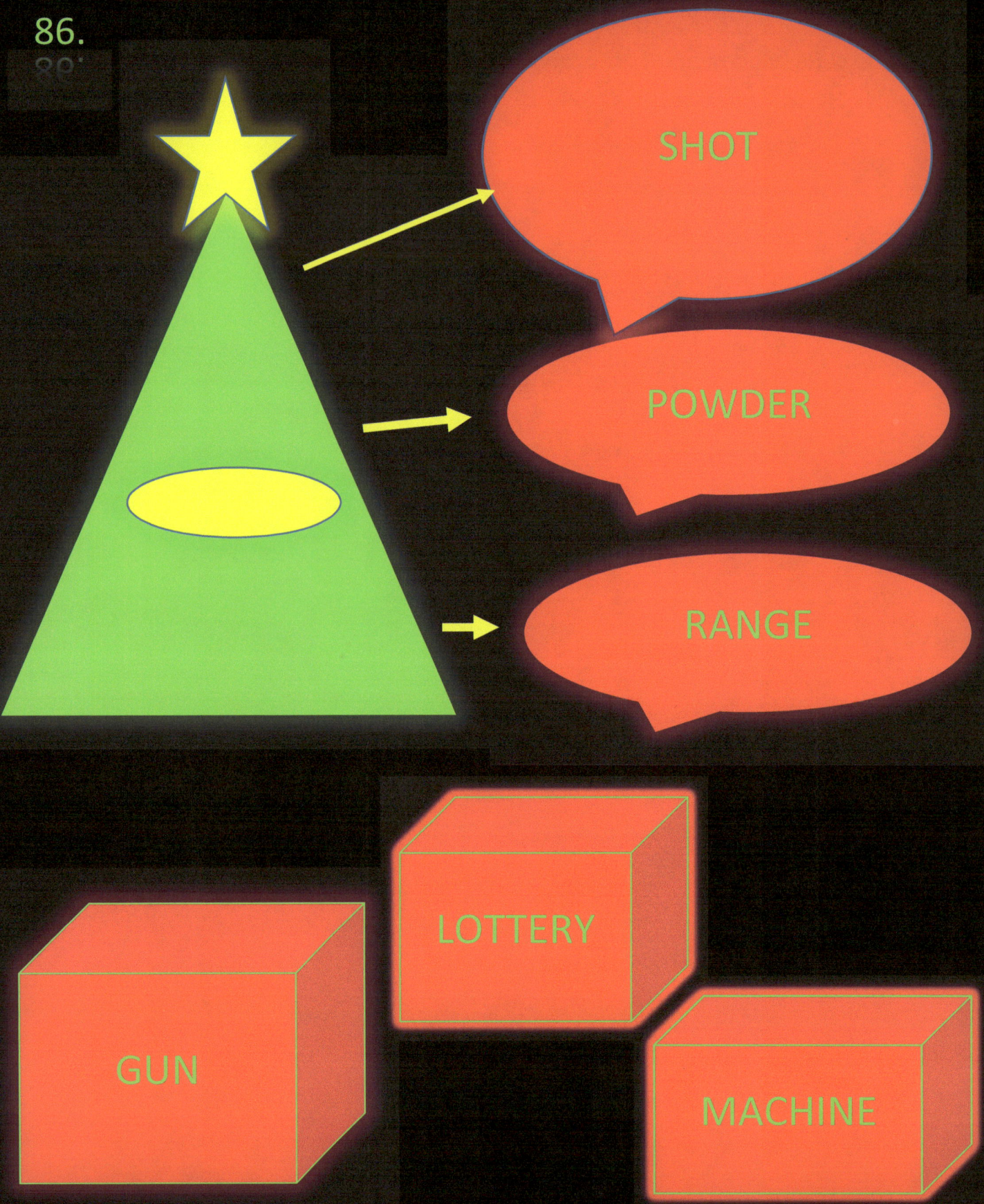

87.

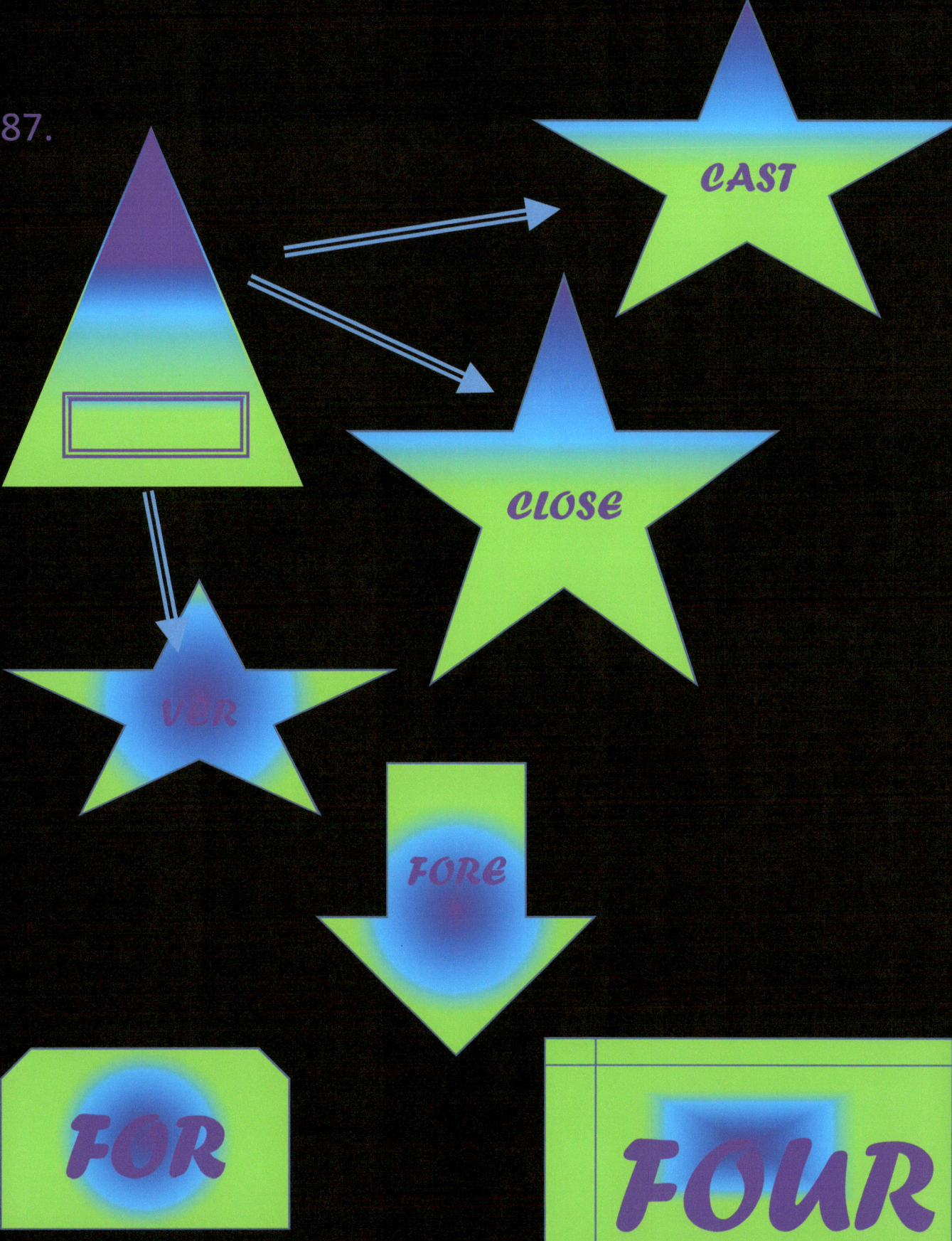

CONNECTIONS

88.

OUT

BOOK

IE

COOK

HE WALKS.

COCKY

COCOON

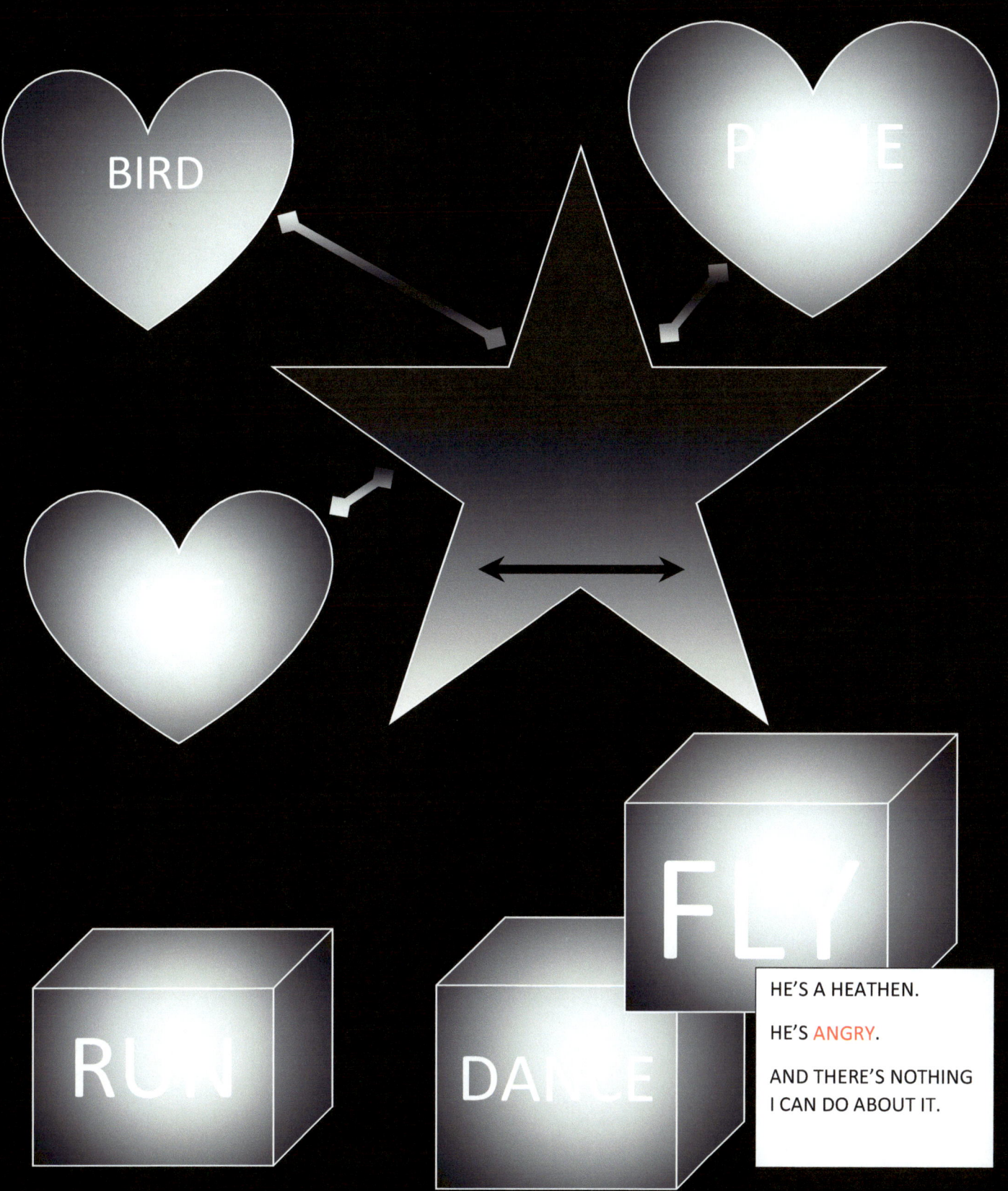

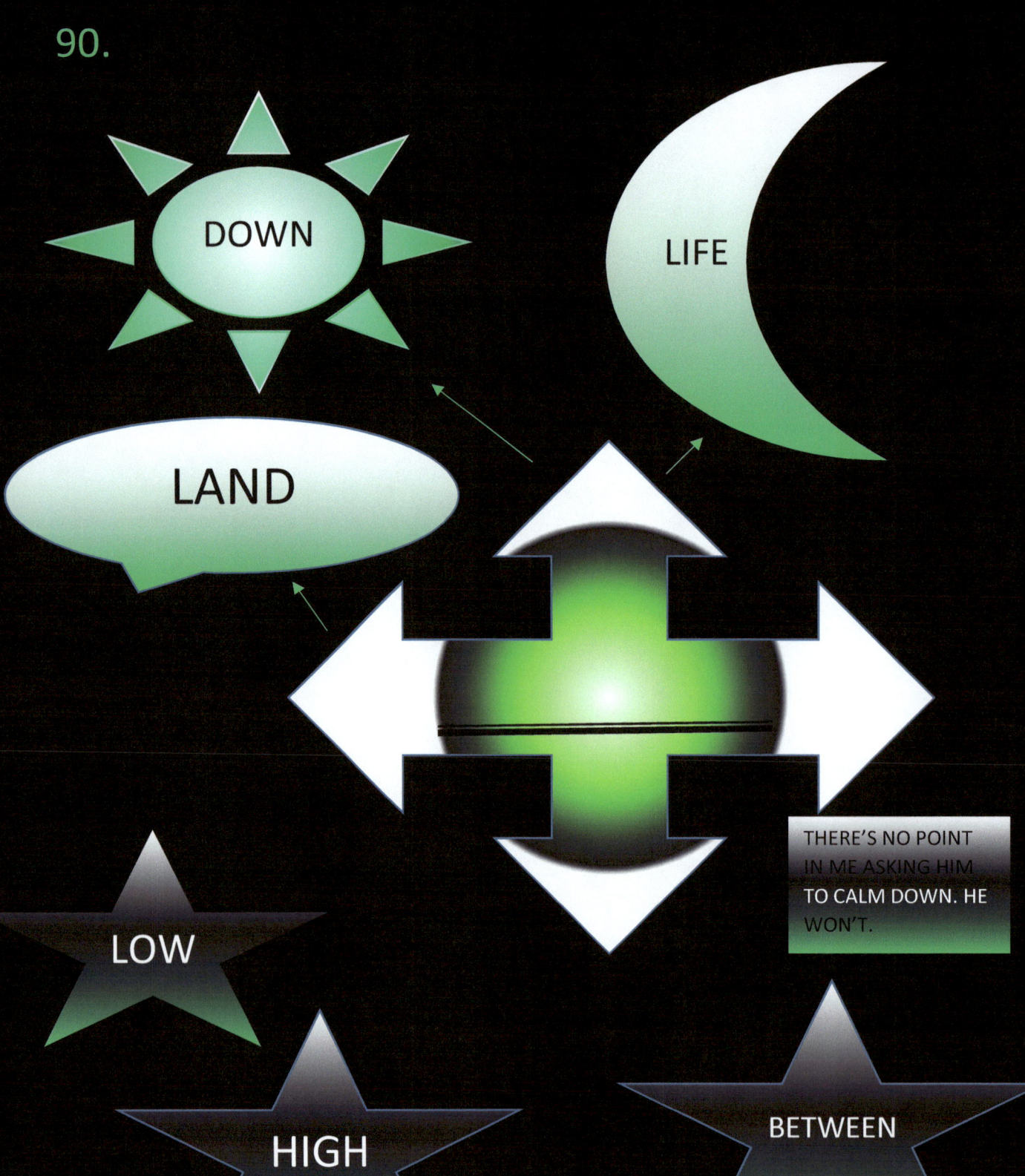

CONNECTIONS

93.

AWAY

OFF　　　WAY

RUN　　WON　　ONE

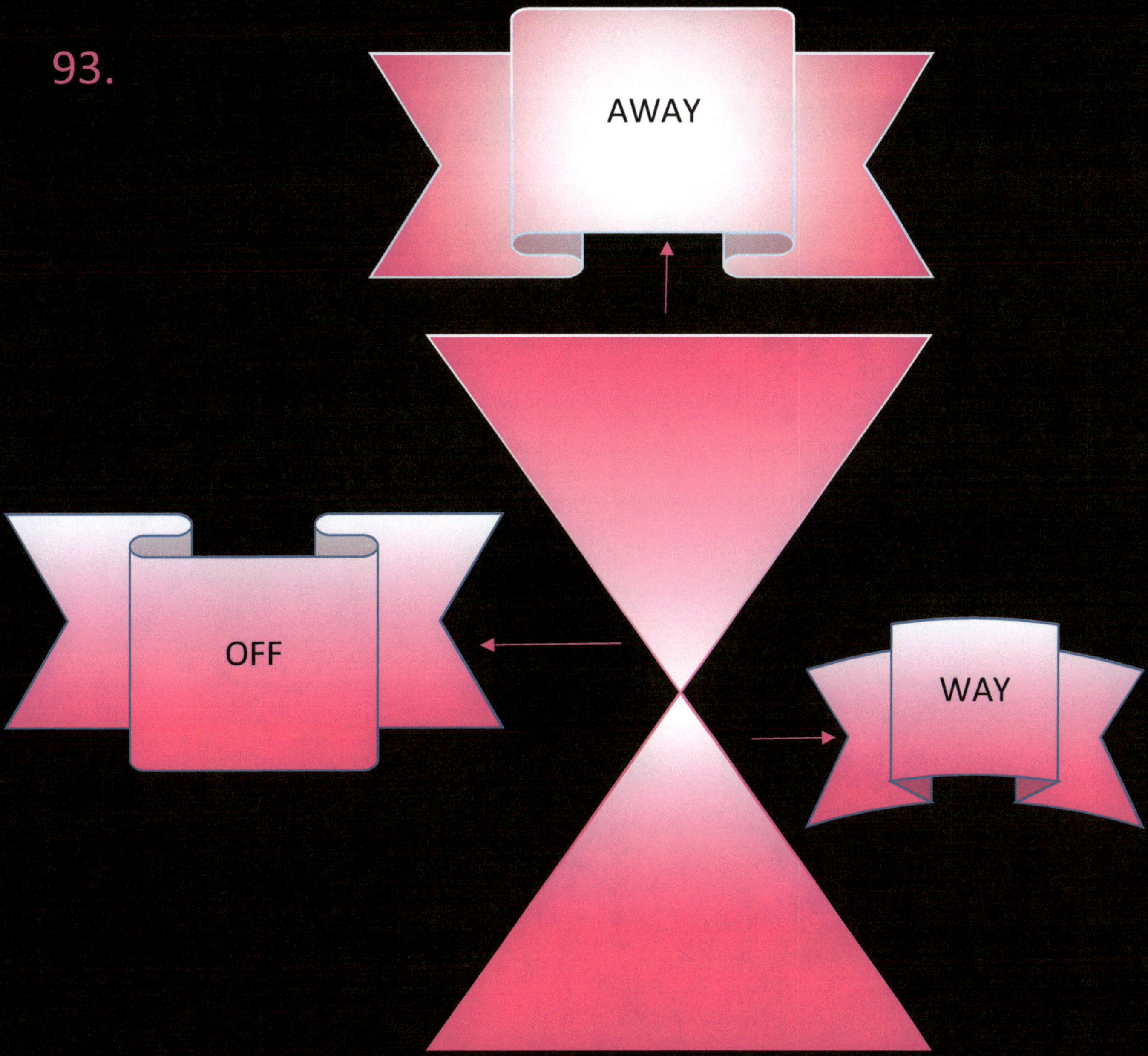

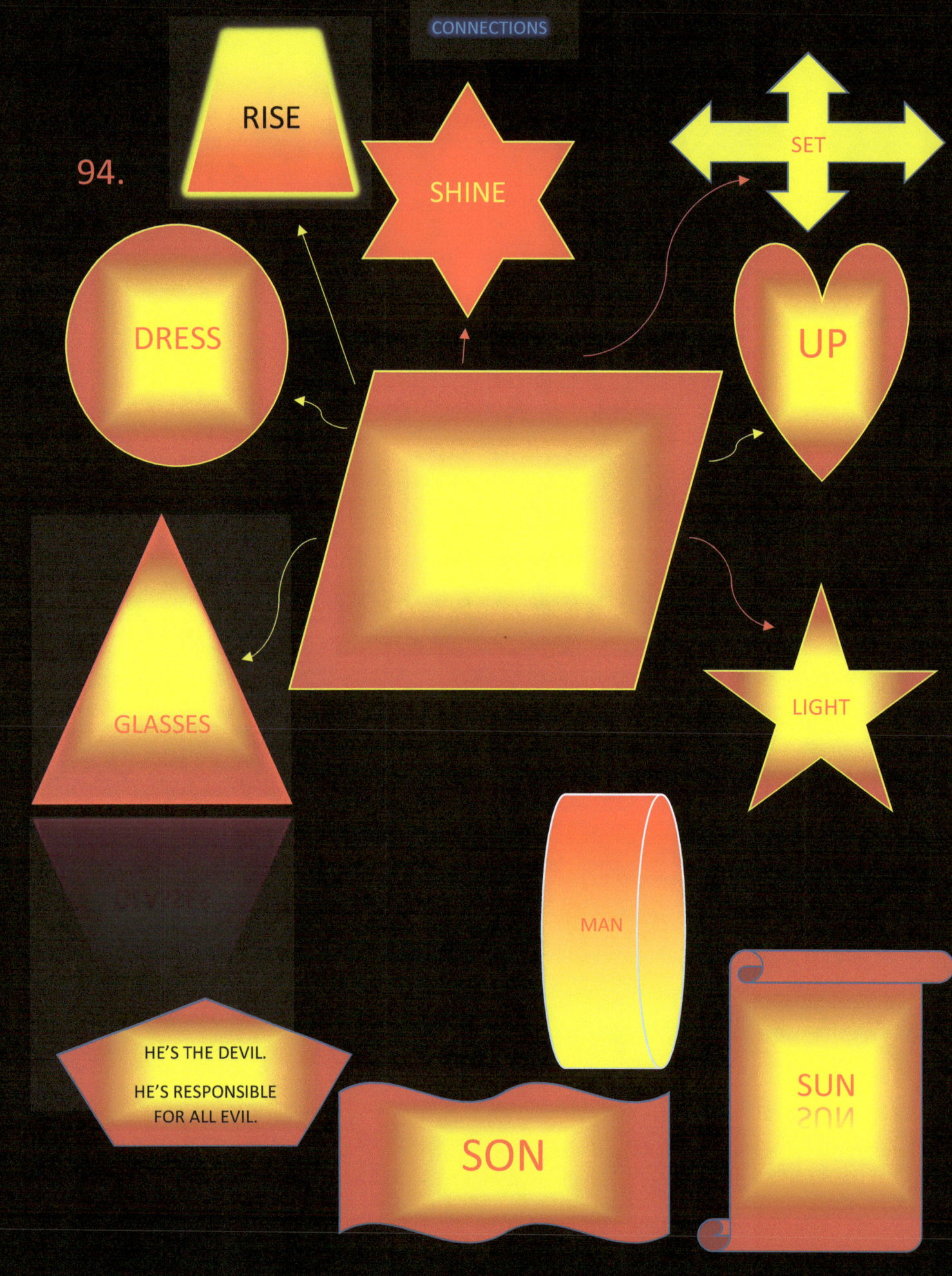

CONNECTIONS

95.

UP   ROOM   MATE

STIPEND   MONEY   CHECK

HIS MISTAKE: HE DIDN'T KILL THE FIRST PEOPLE. NOW EVERYONE IS PAYING FOR IT.

96.

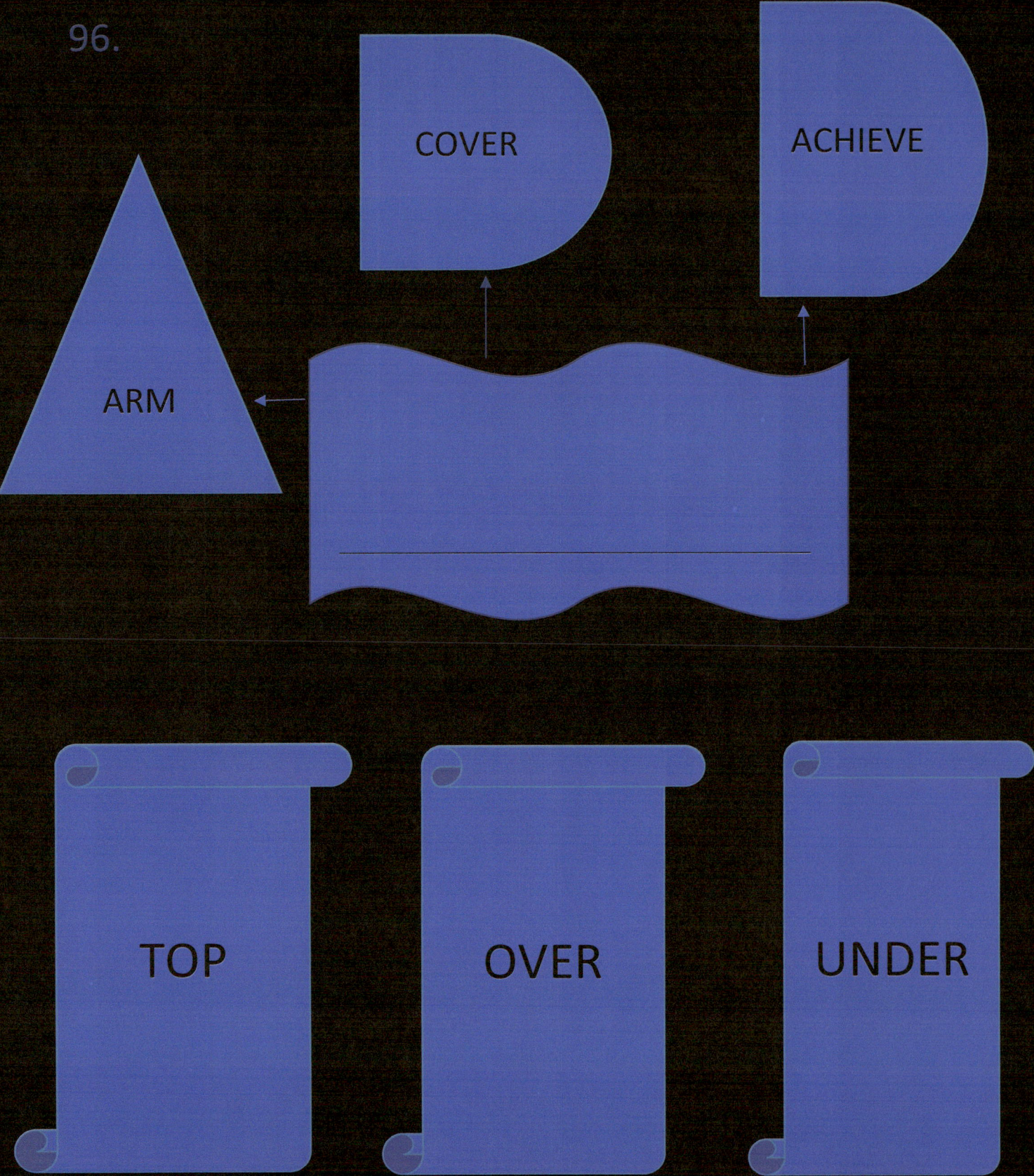

CONNECTIONS

97.

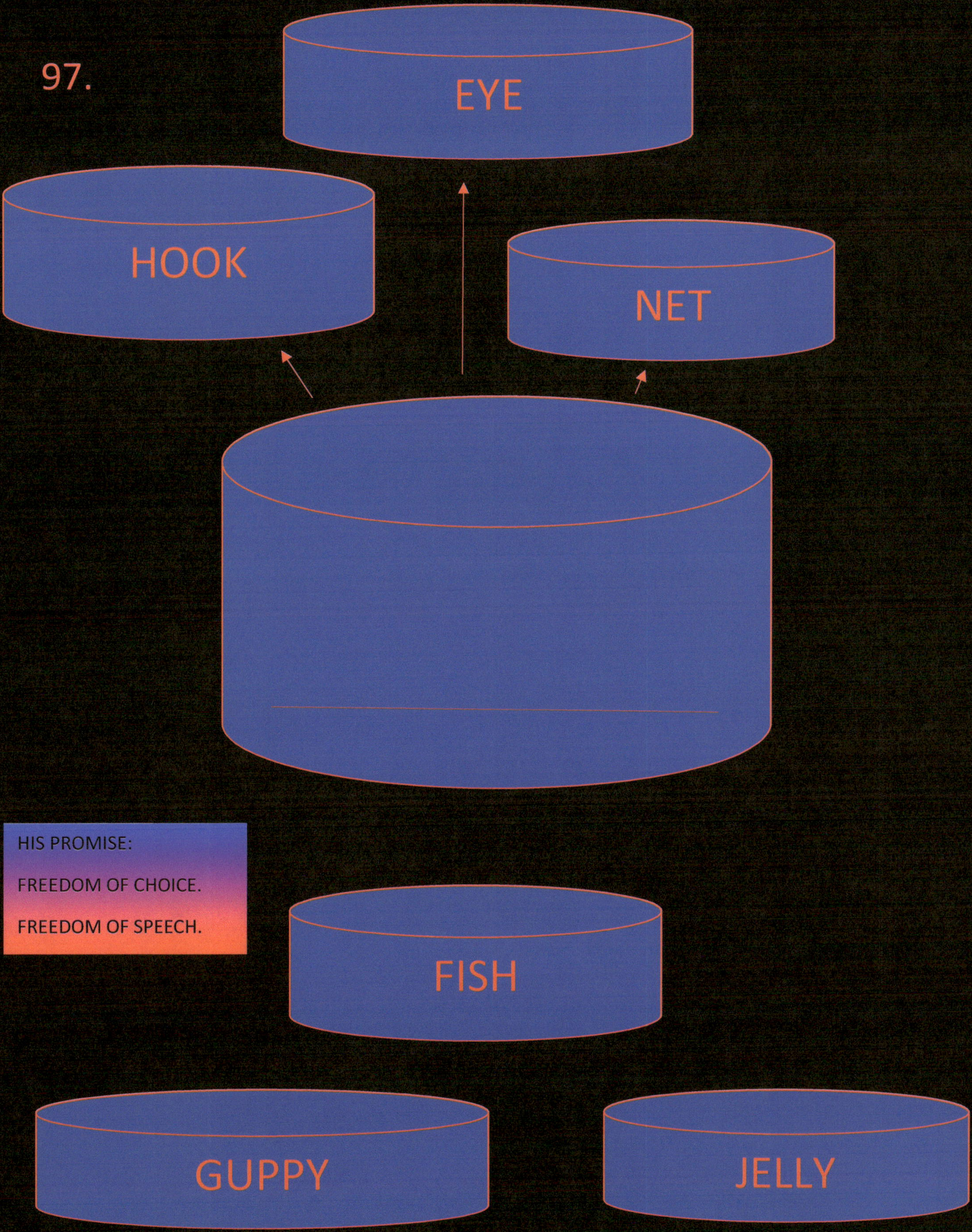

EYE

HOOK

NET

HIS PROMISE:

FREEDOM OF CHOICE.

FREEDOM OF SPEECH.

FISH

GUPPY

JELLY

98.

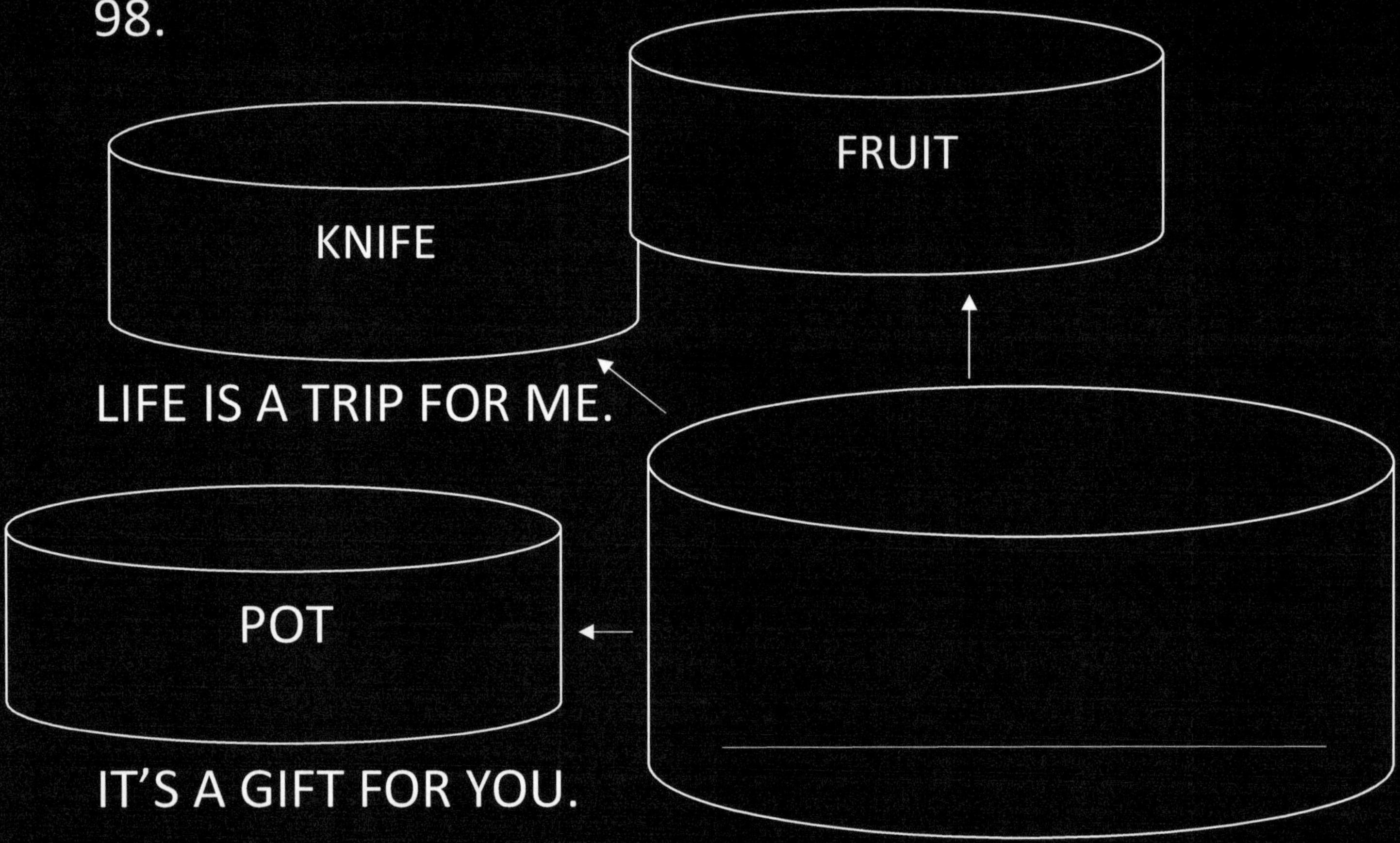

KNIFE

FRUIT

LIFE IS A TRIP FOR ME.

POT

IT'S A GIFT FOR YOU.

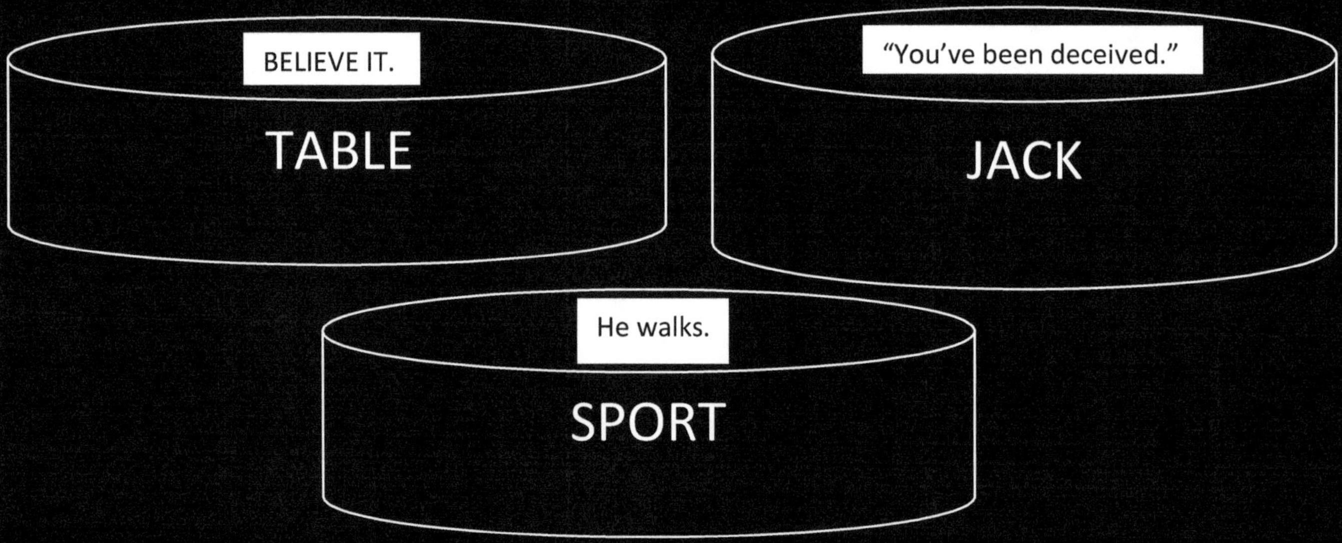

BELIEVE IT.

TABLE

"You've been deceived."

JACK

He walks.

SPORT

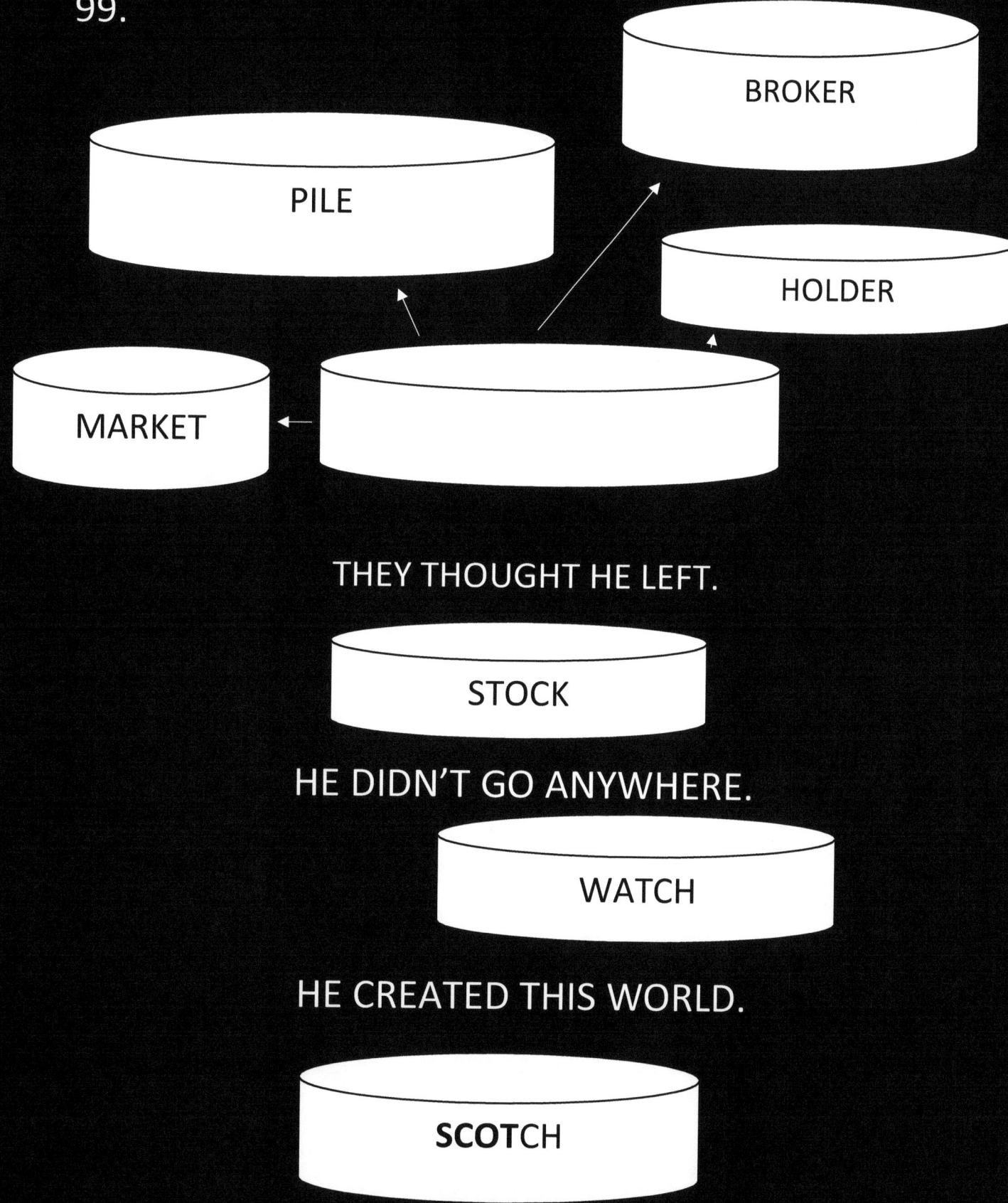

CONNECTIONS

101.

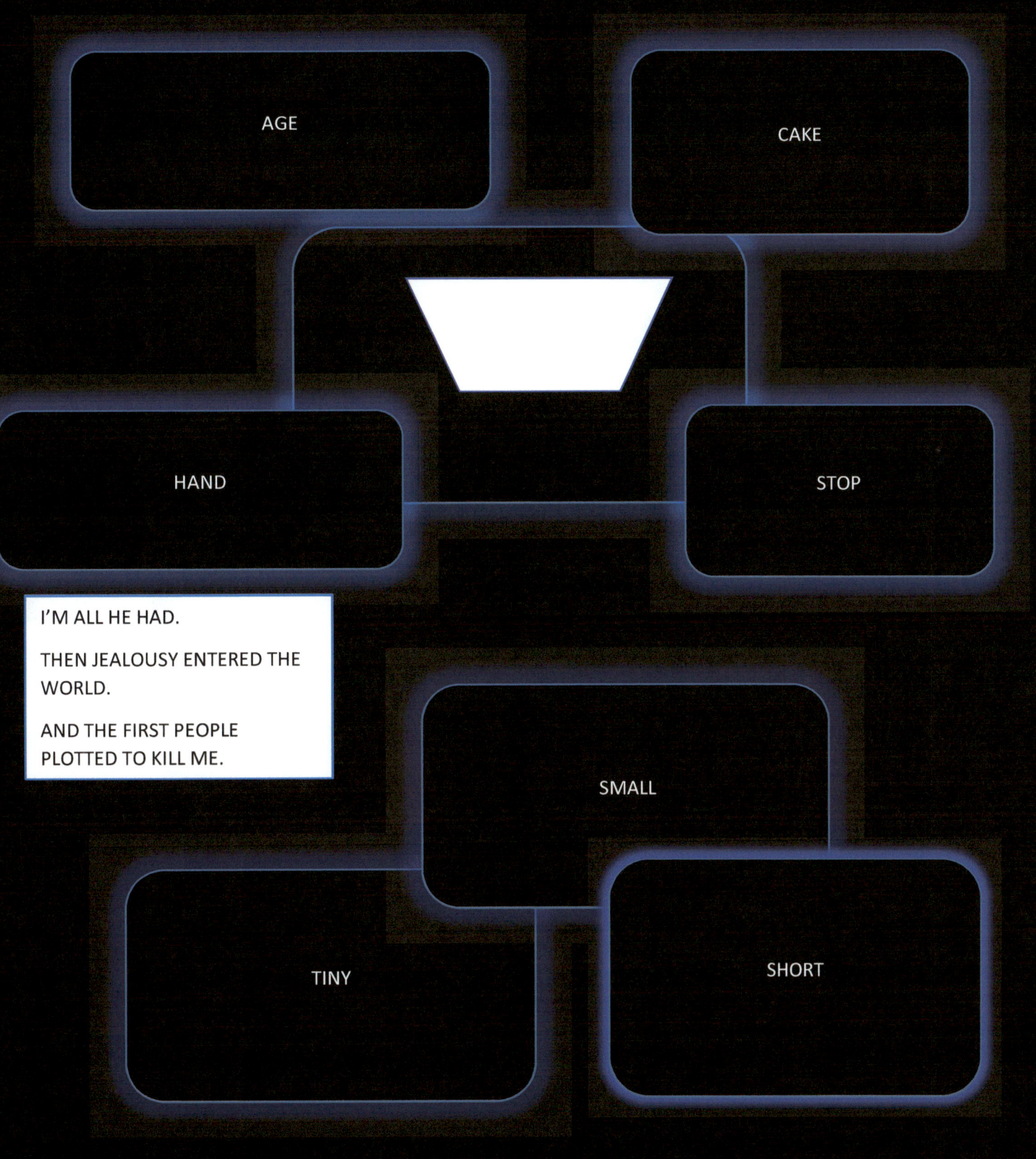

AGE

CAKE

HAND

STOP

I'M ALL HE HAD.

THEN JEALOUSY ENTERED THE WORLD.

AND THE FIRST PEOPLE PLOTTED TO KILL ME.

SMALL

TINY

SHORT

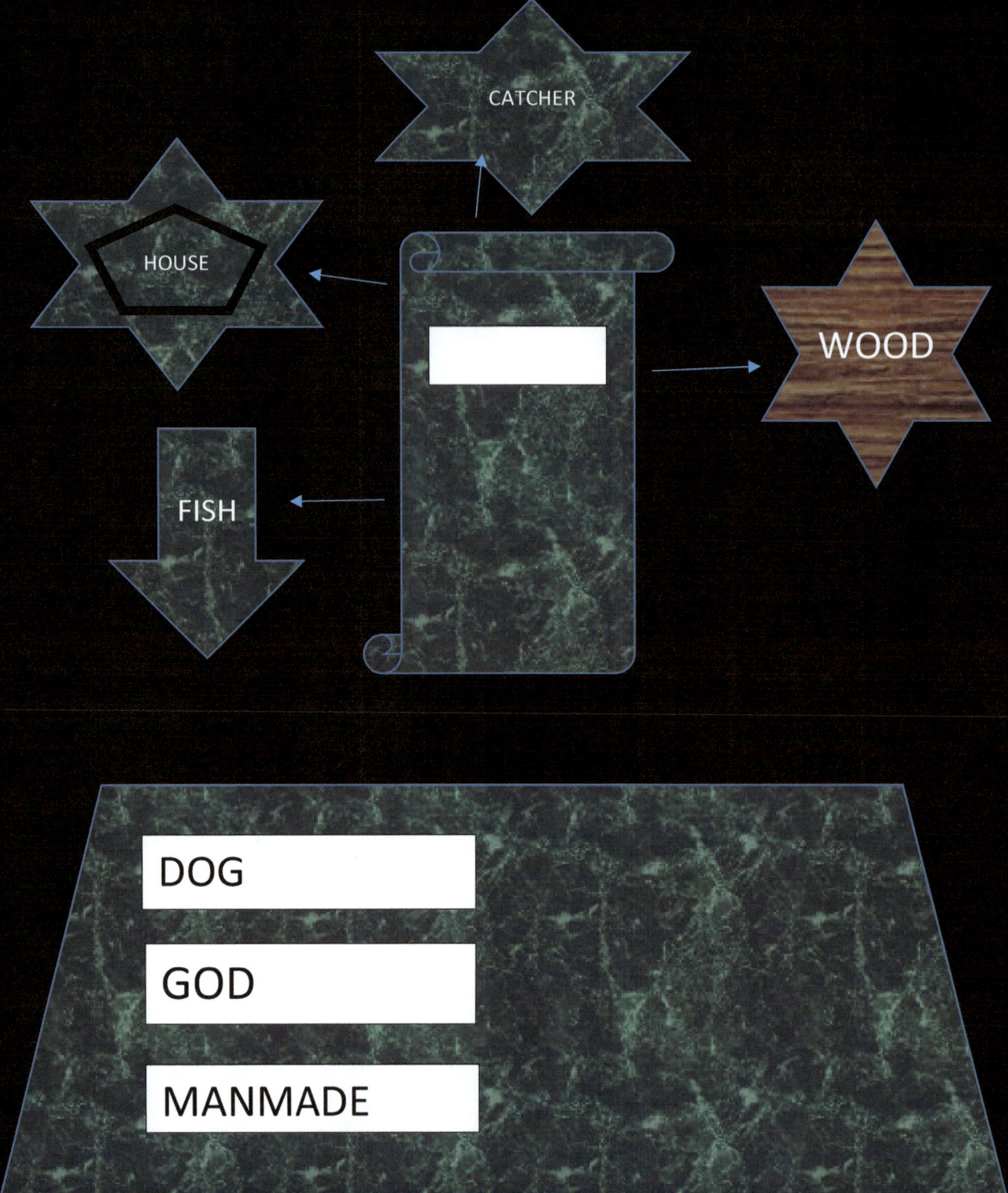

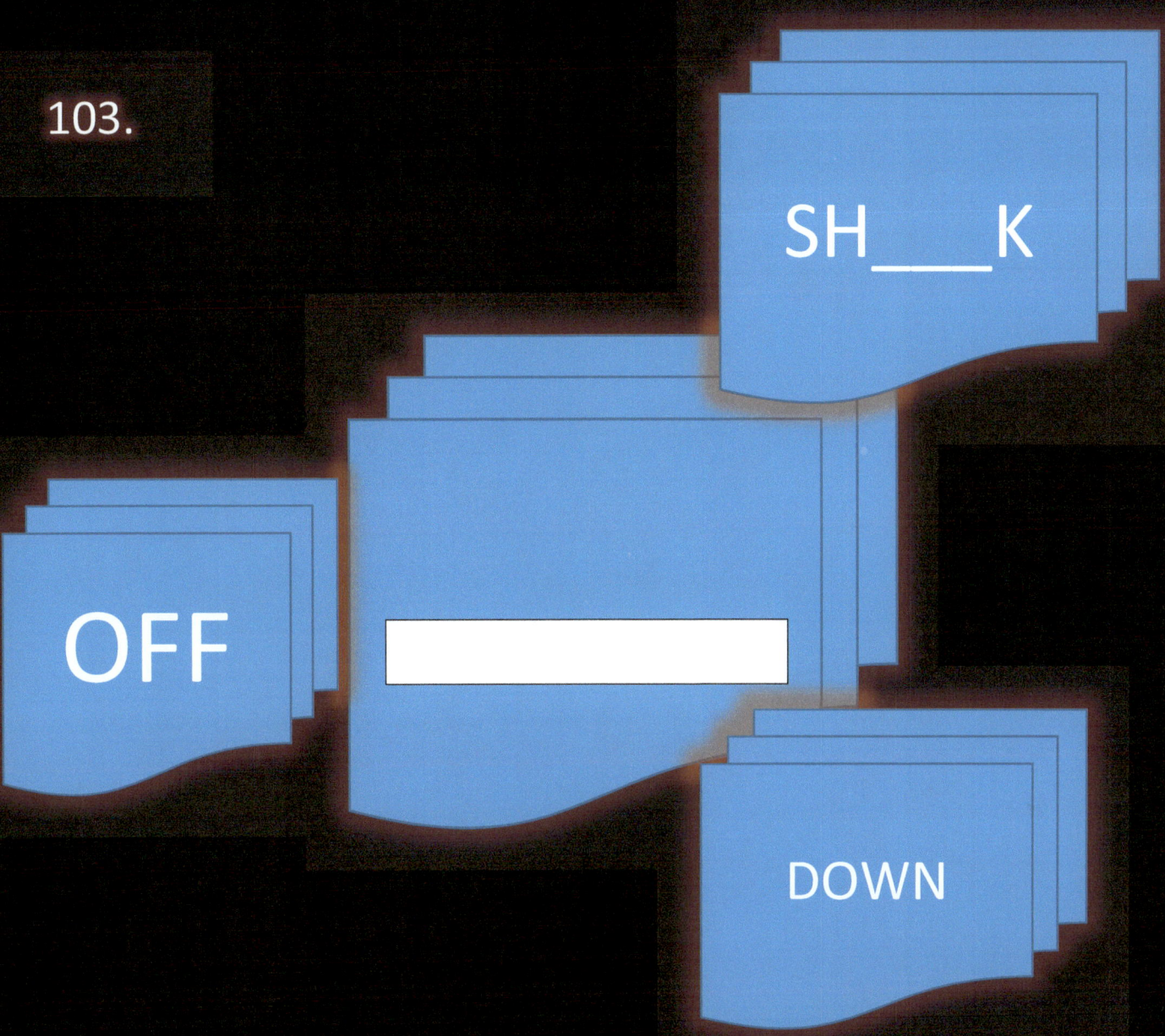

104.

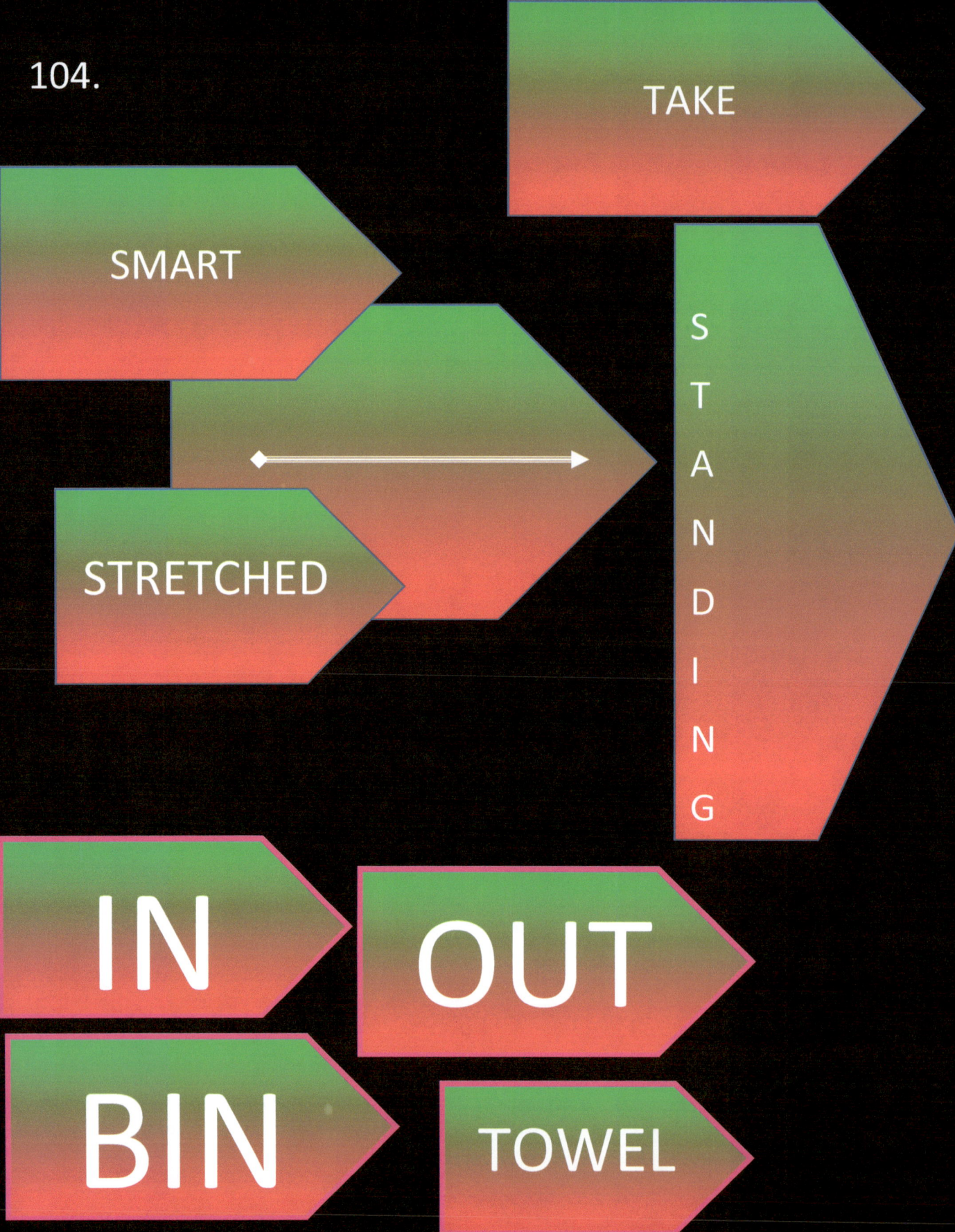

CONNECTIONS

105.

EVERYONE CAN SEE ME.

BUT HIM.

YOU'LL NEVER KNOW WHEN HE'S STANDING RIGHT IN YOUR FACE LISTENING TO YOU PLOT TO KILL ME.

→ WISE

→ WORK

TIME

CLOCK

NUMBER

IN

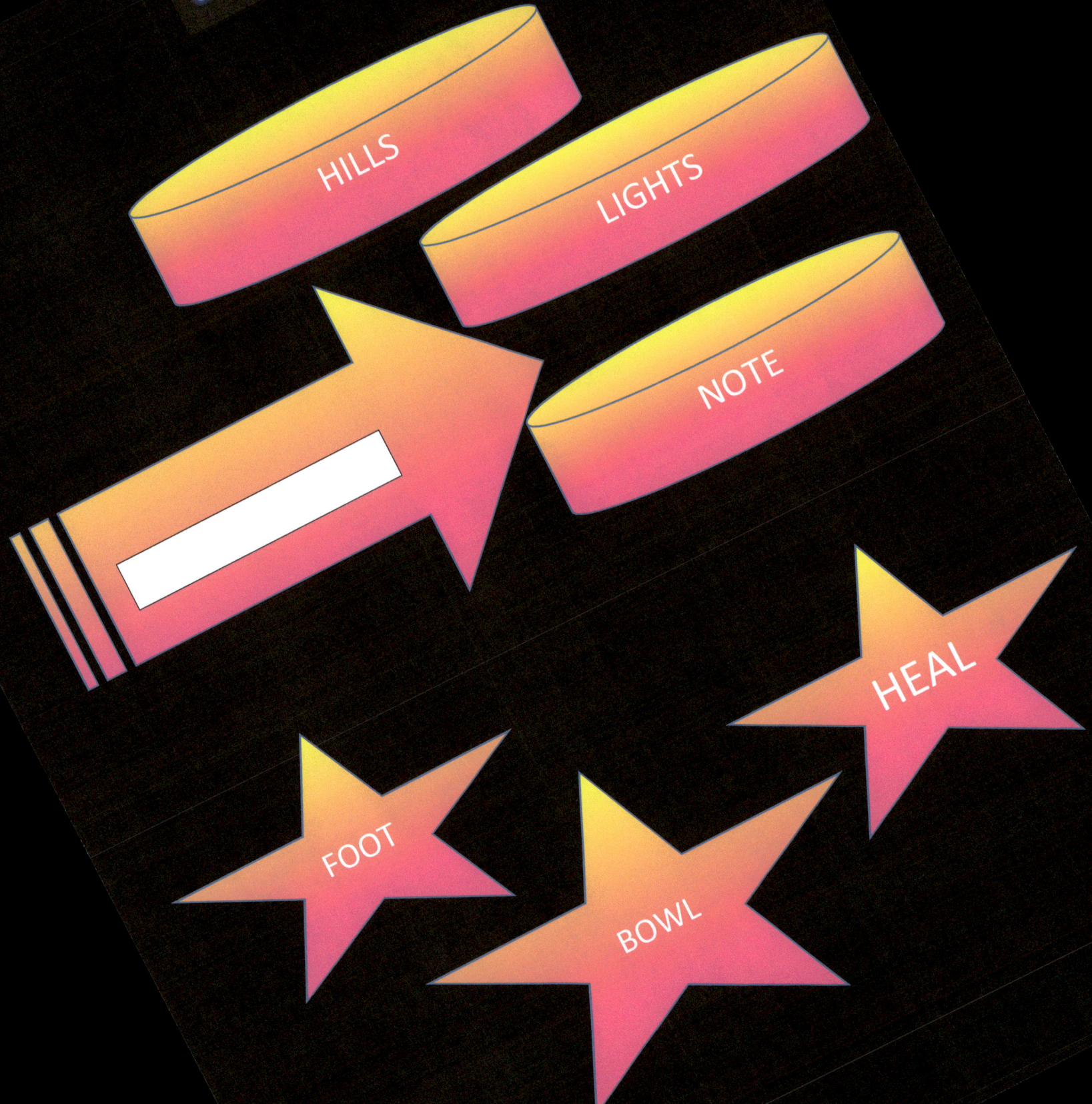

107.

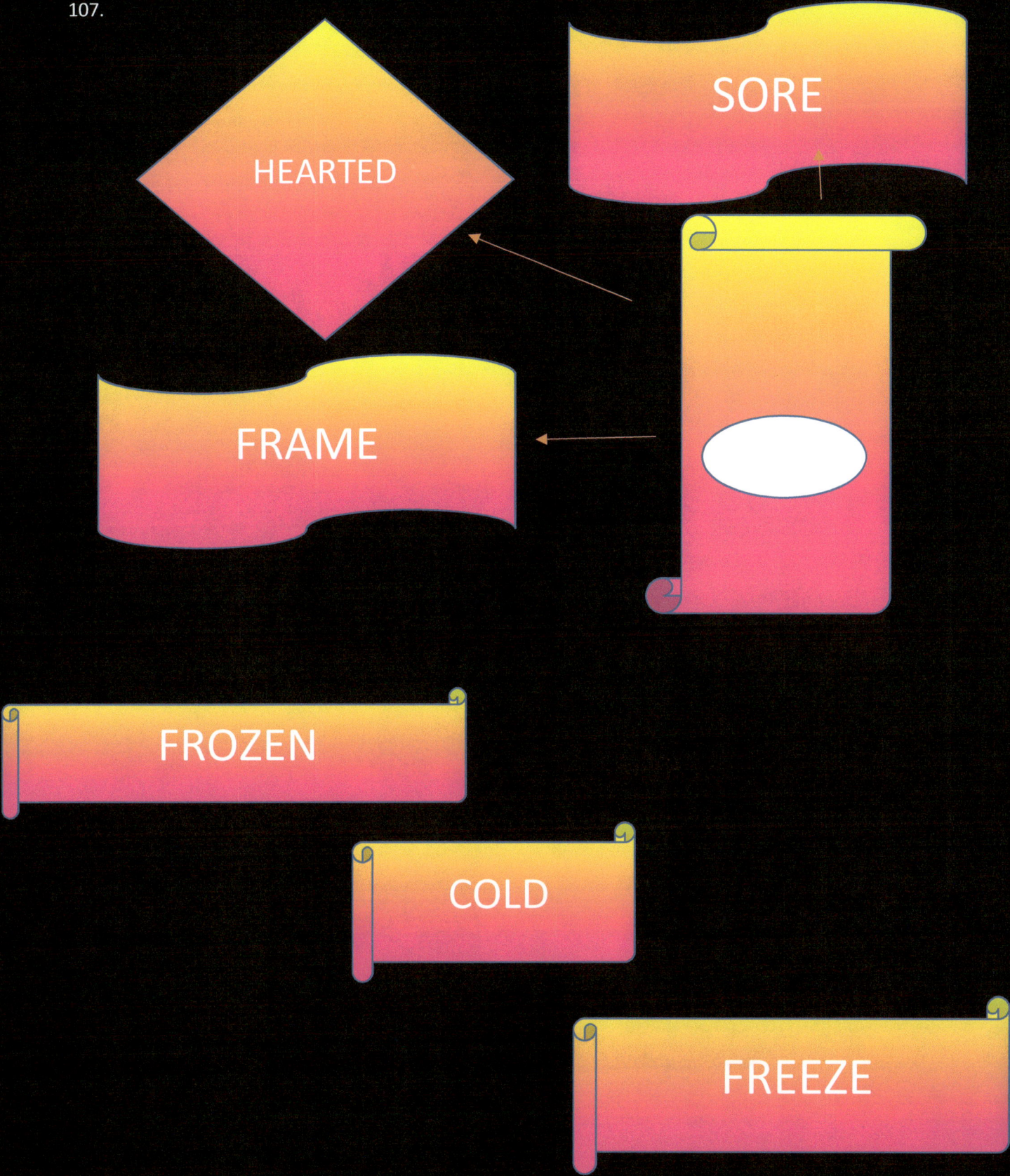

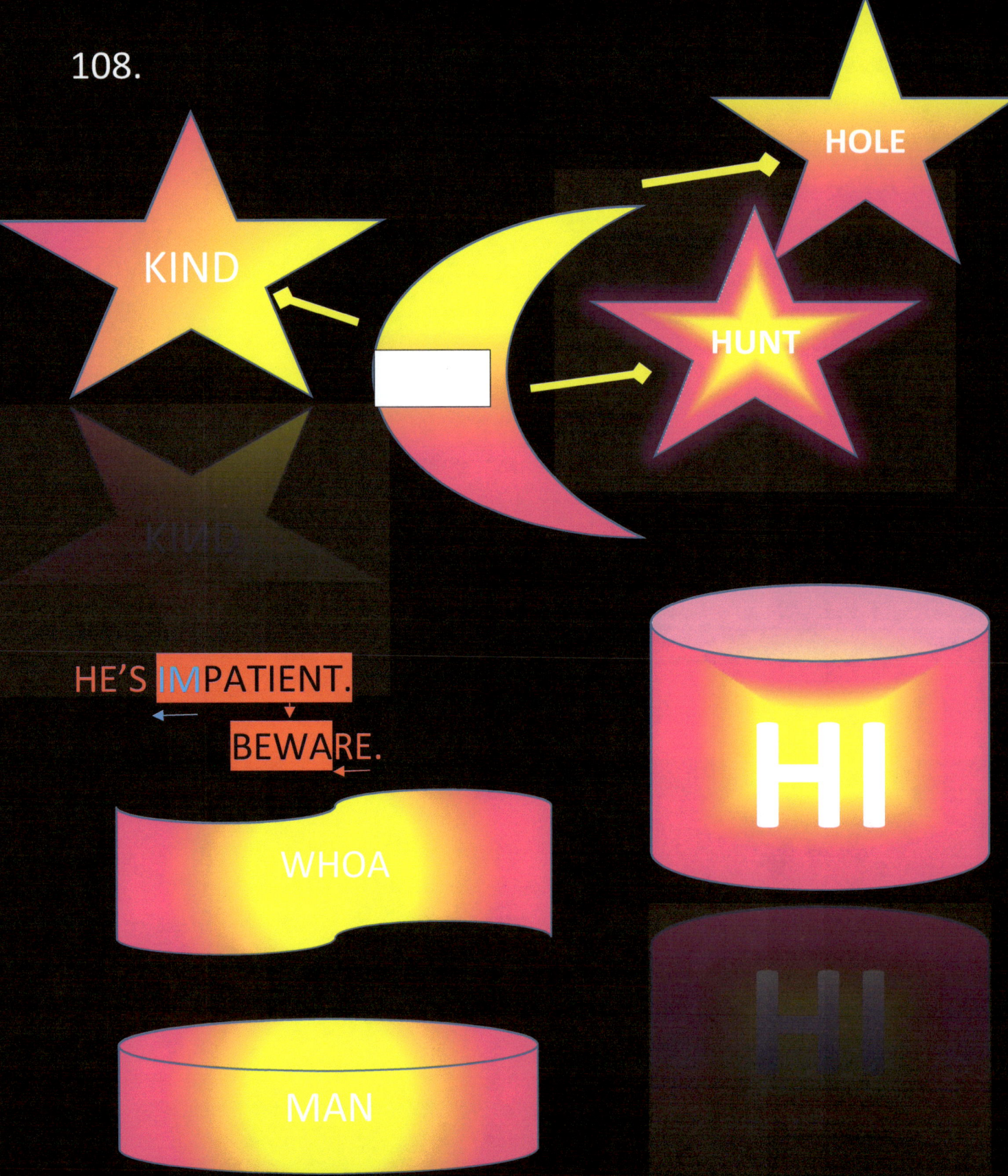

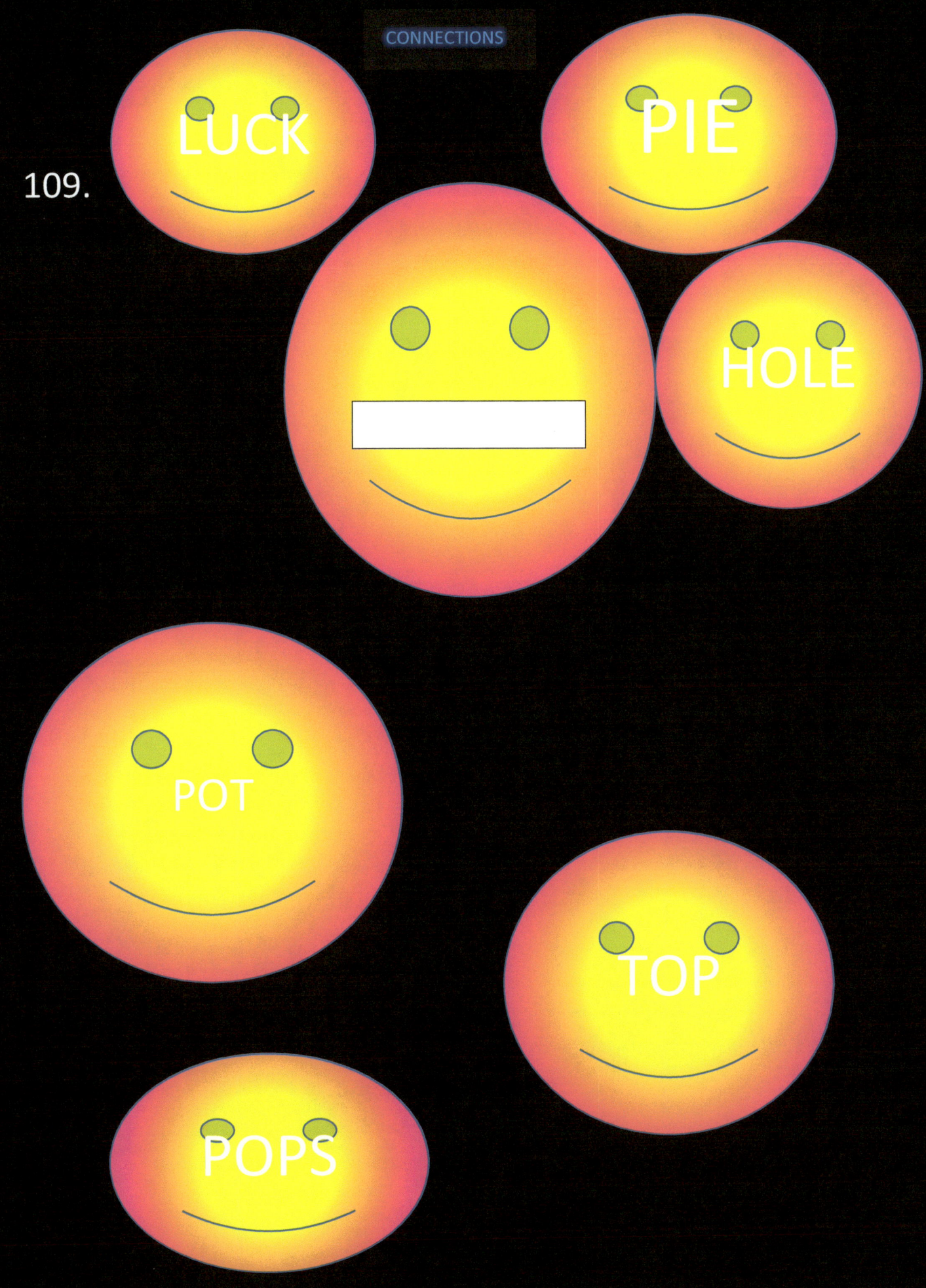

CONNECTIONS

110.

WORK

SIGN

VIEW

RAT

STREET

ROAD

111.

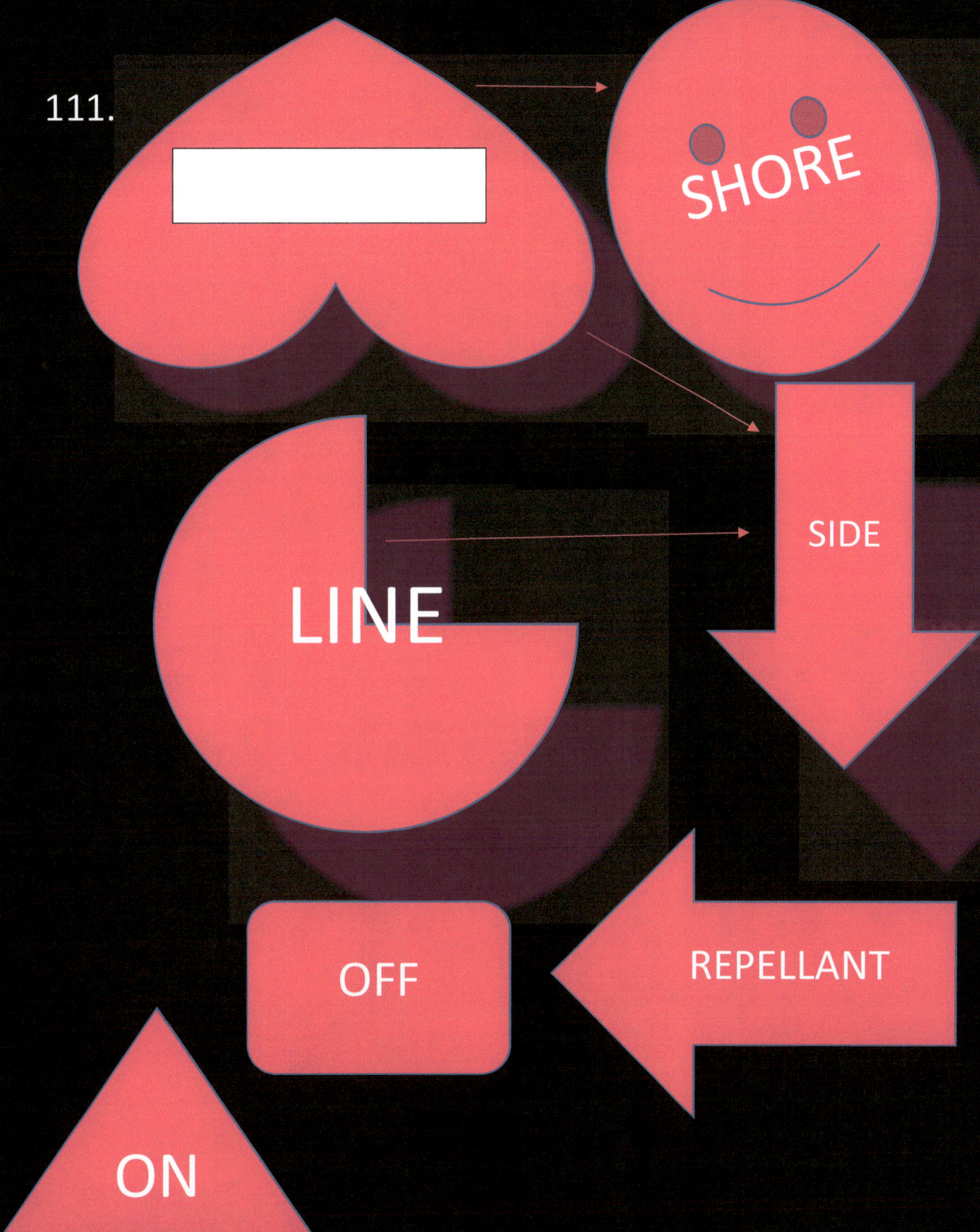

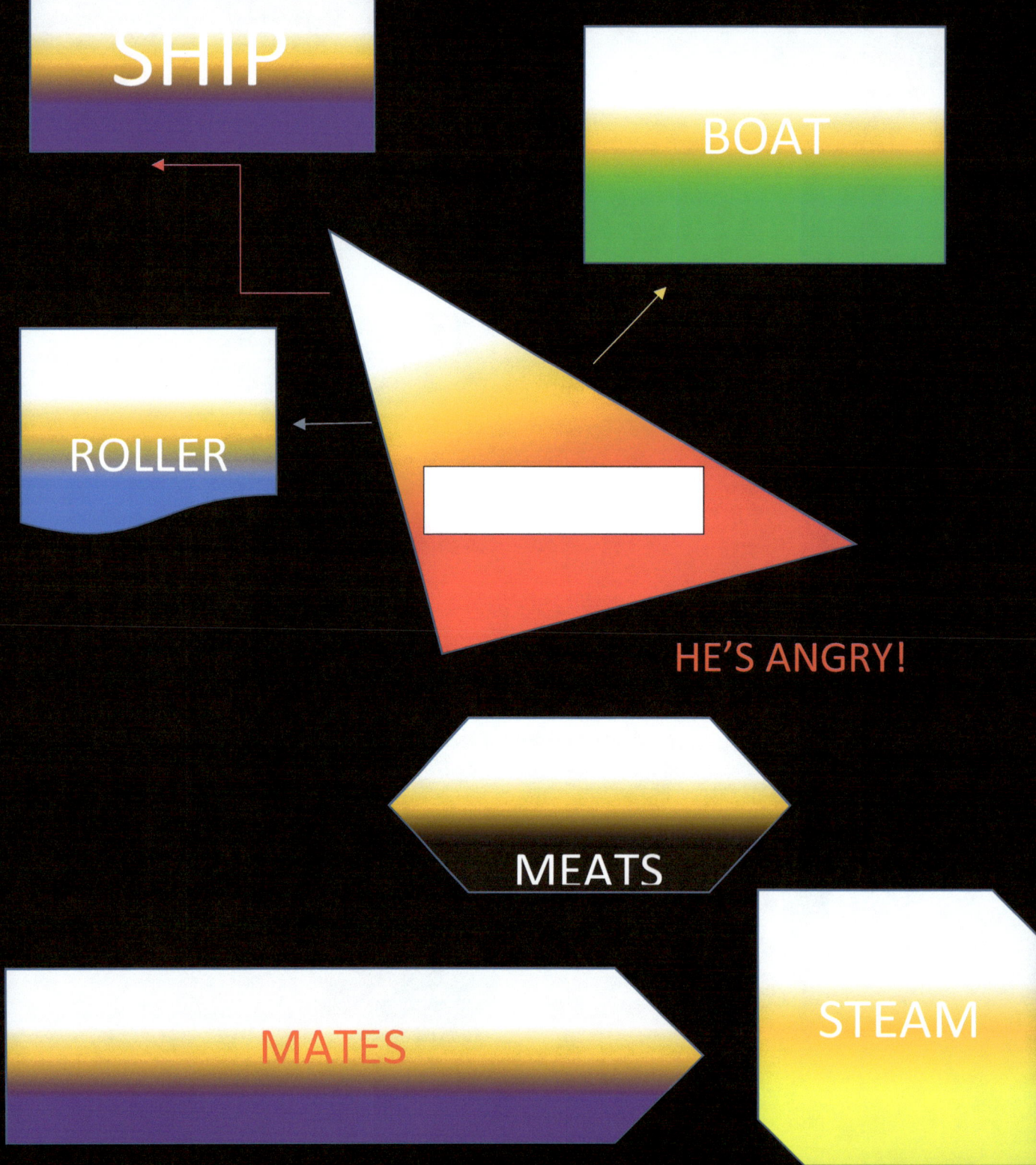

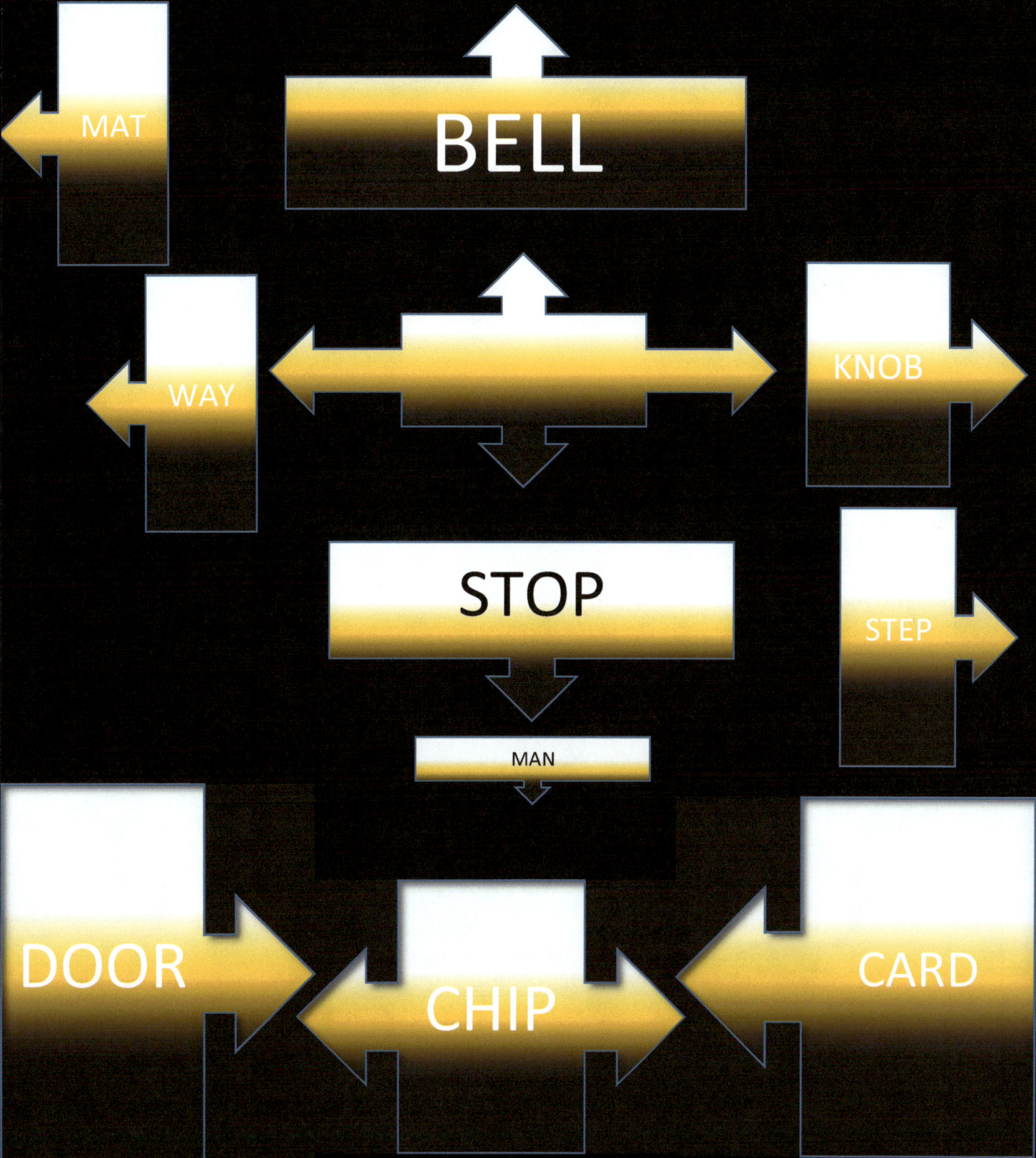

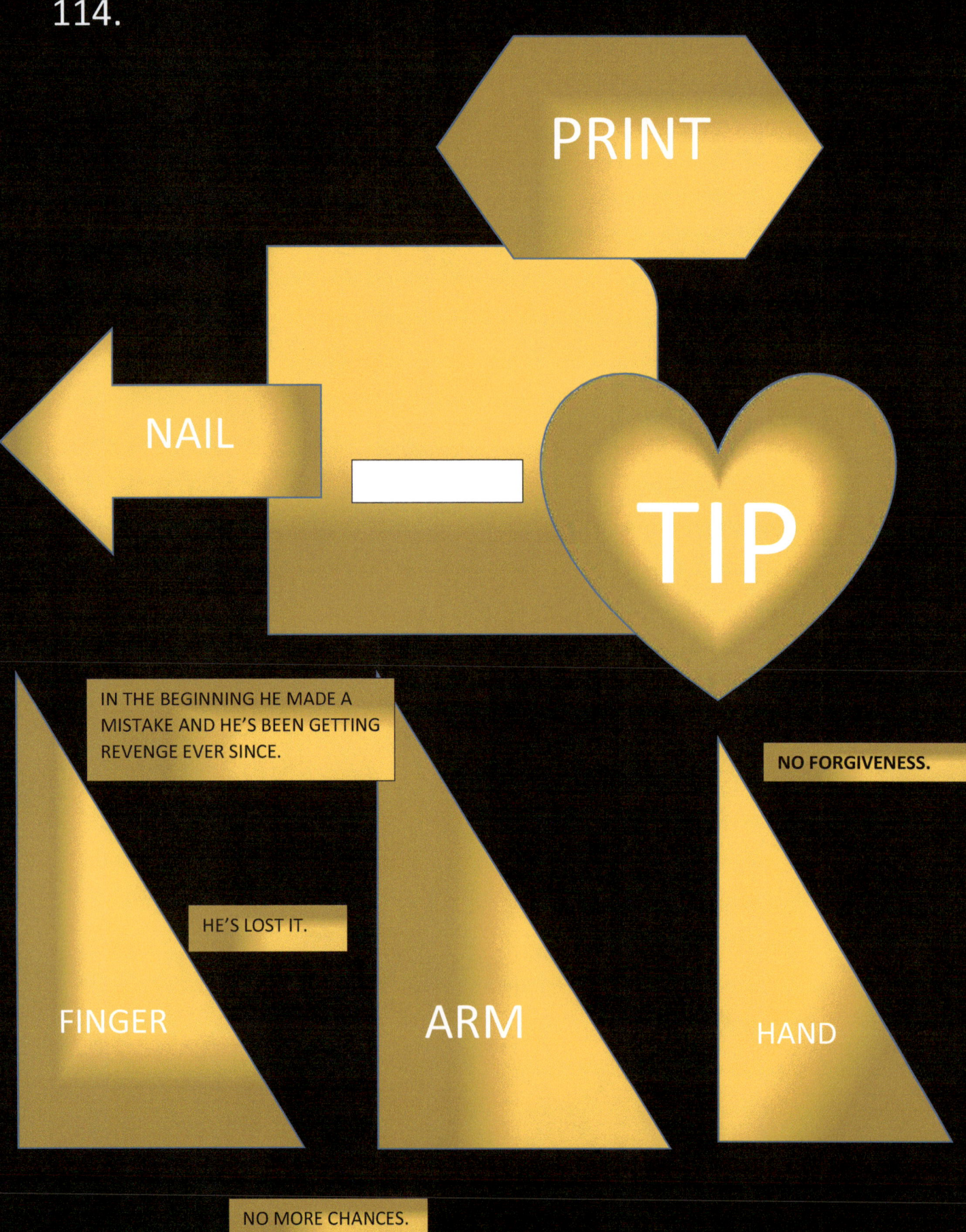

115.

TRAUMATIC STRESS DISORDER

MASTER

CARD

MARK

POST

DATE

PLAYER

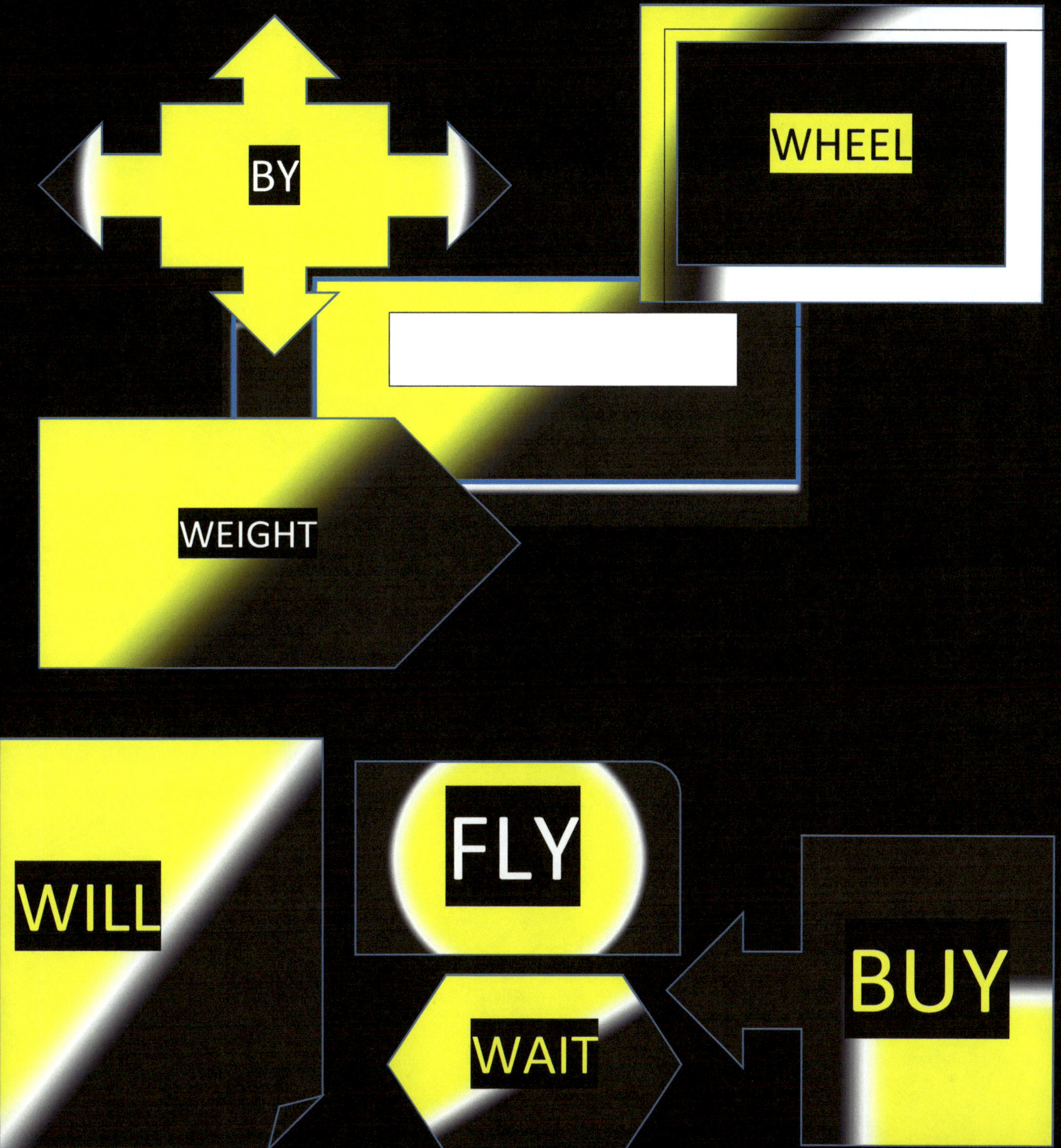

CONNECTIONS

CONNECTIONS

118.

HEADED

HEARTED

NOTHING'S HERE.

SWITCH

HOUSE

DAD

LIFE

DₑAD

LIGHT

THE MAKER SAID LET THERE BE LIFE.

LIGHT WAS ALWAYS HERE.

NO COINCIDENCES

CONNECTIONS

119.

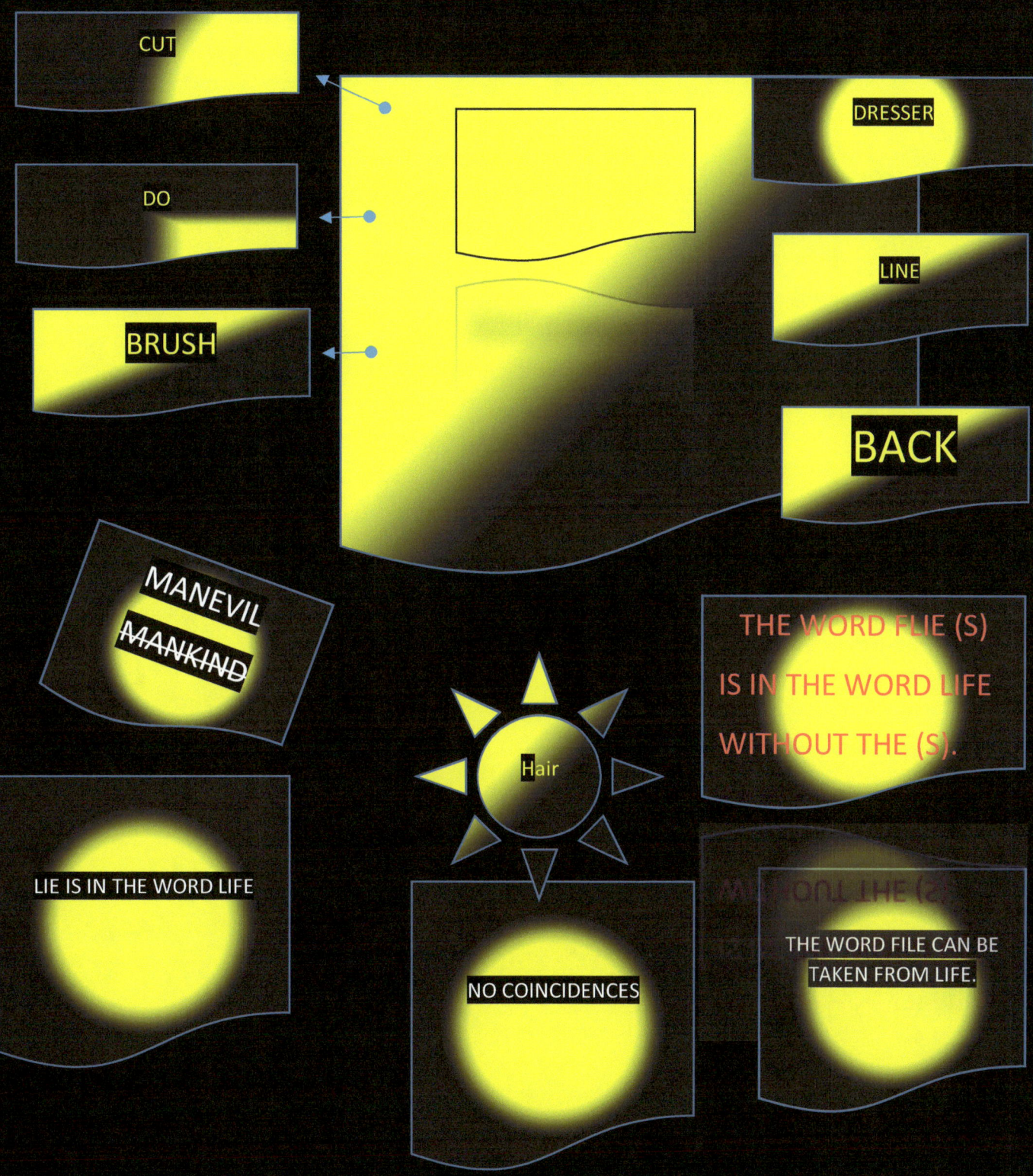

CUT

DO

BRUSH

DRESSER

LINE

BACK

MANEVIL
~~MANKIND~~

Hair

THE WORD FLIE (S) IS IN THE WORD LIFE WITHOUT THE (S).

LIE IS IN THE WORD LIFE

NO COINCIDENCES

THE WORD FILE CAN BE TAKEN FROM LIFE.

120.

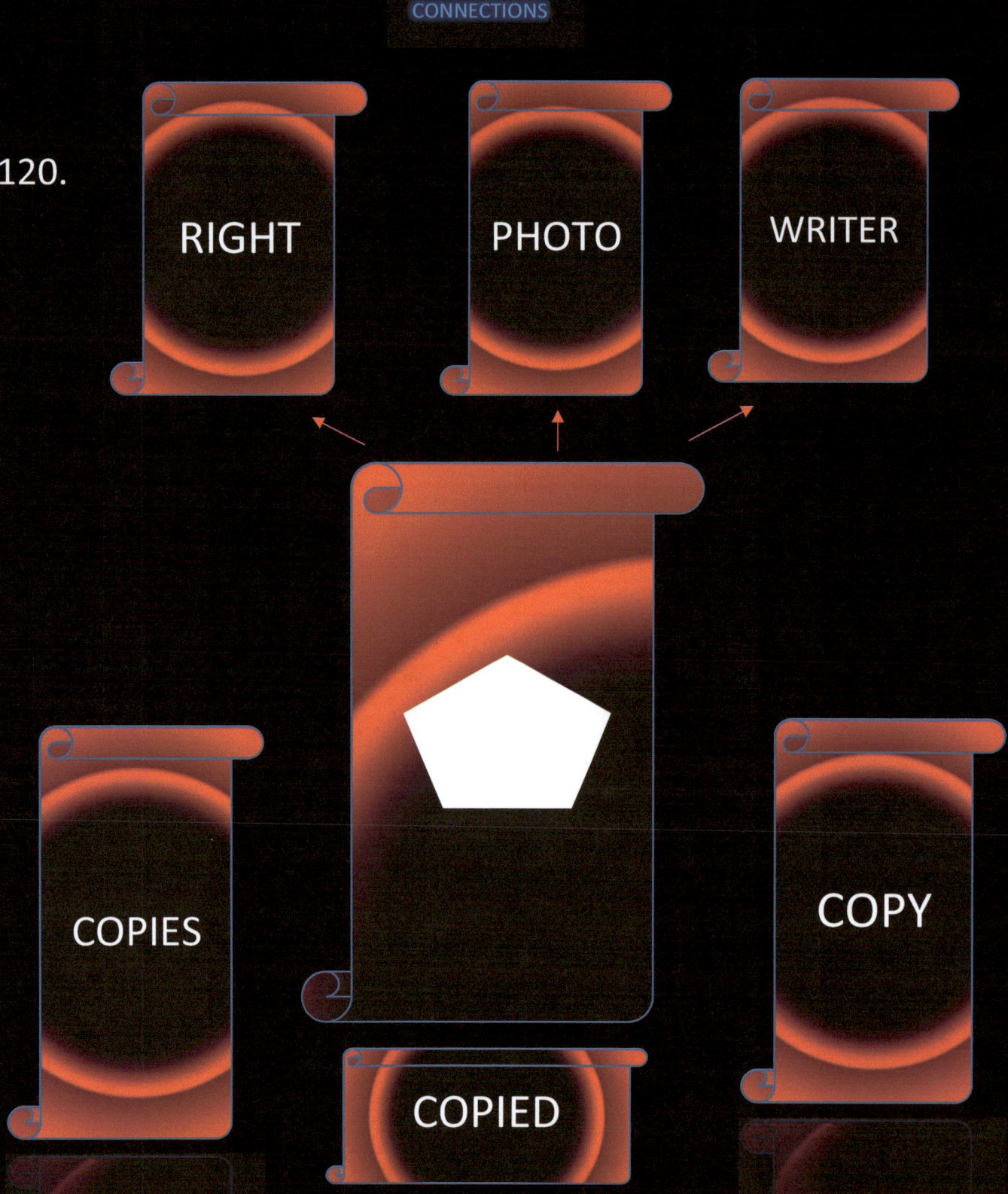

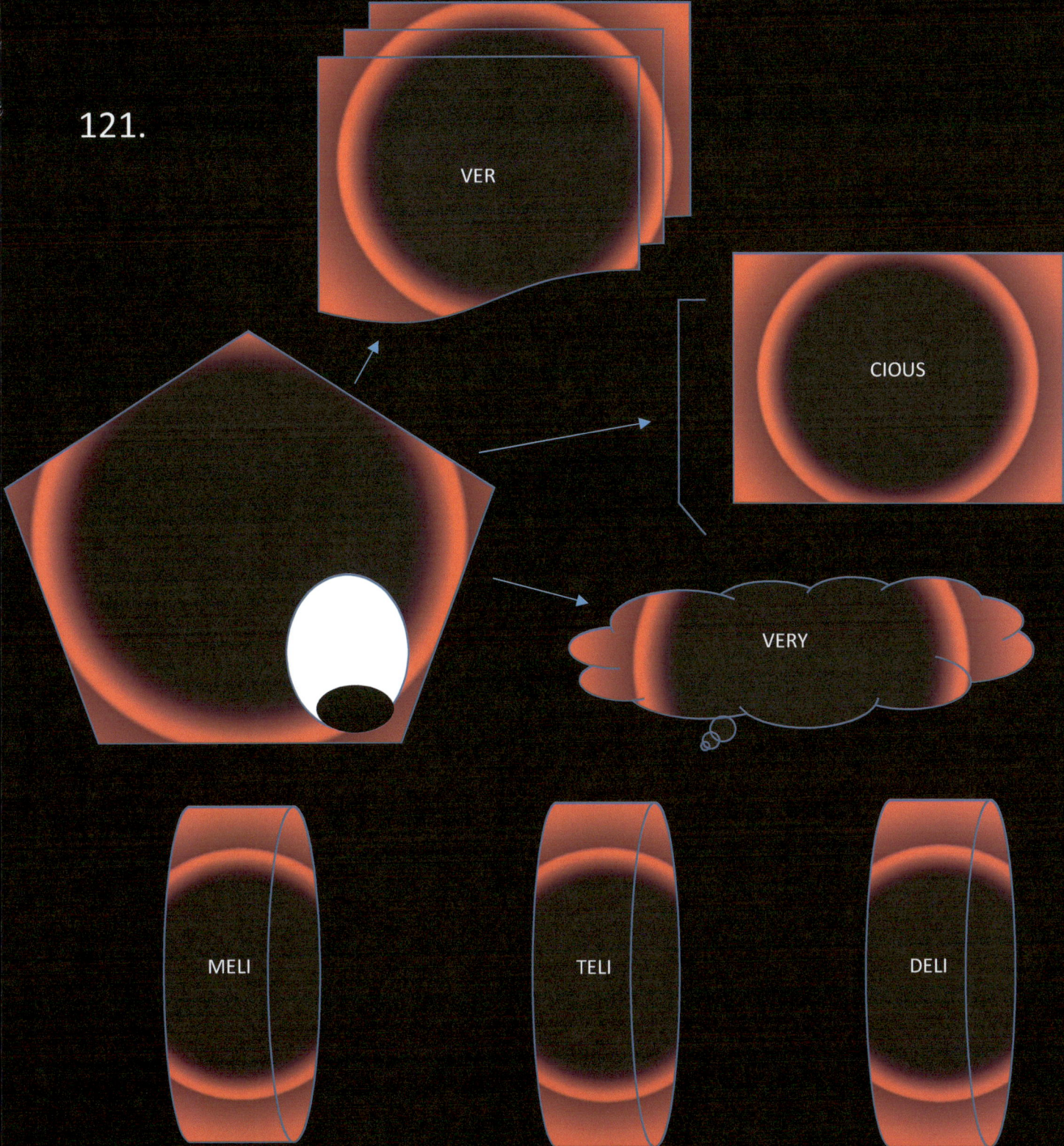

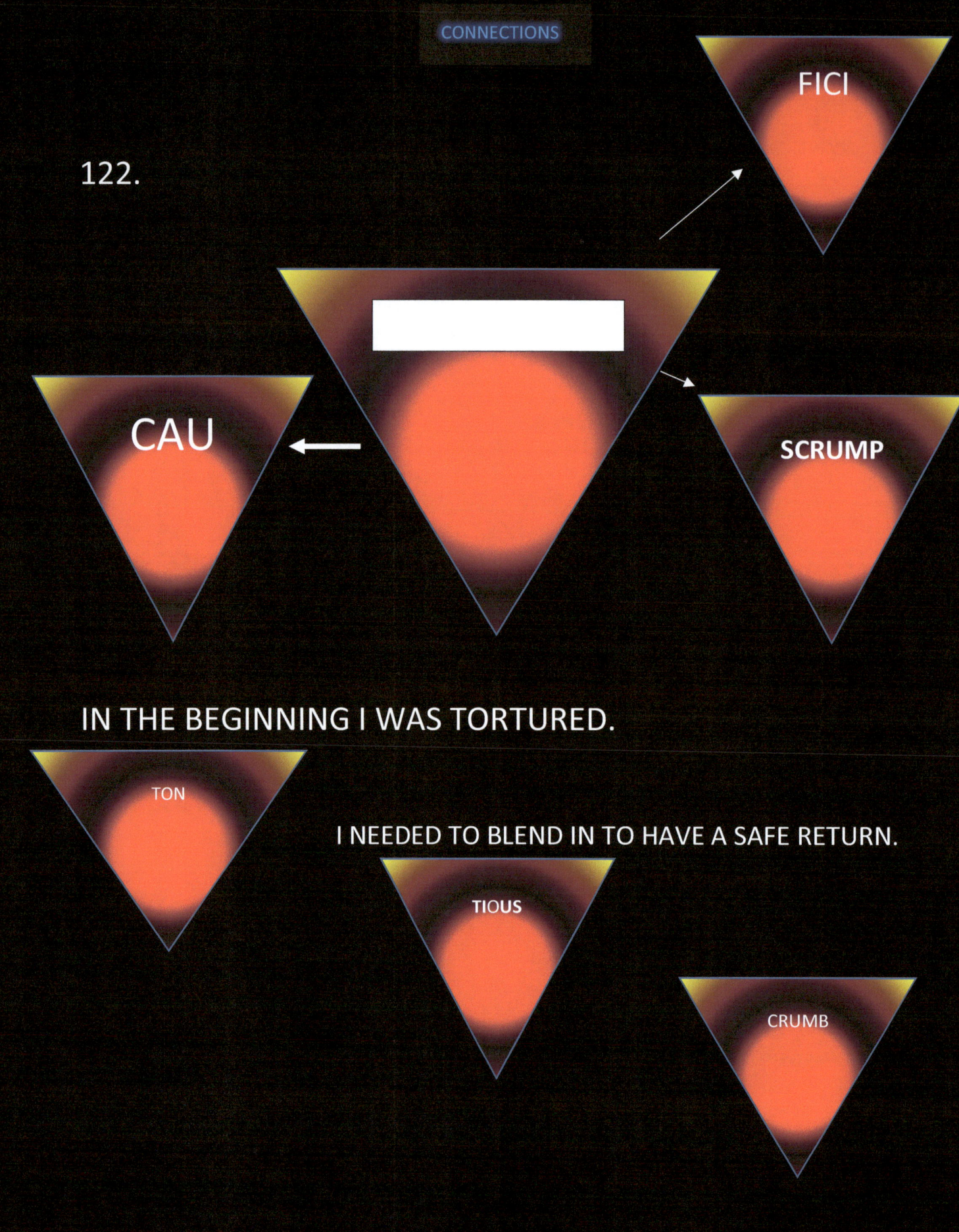

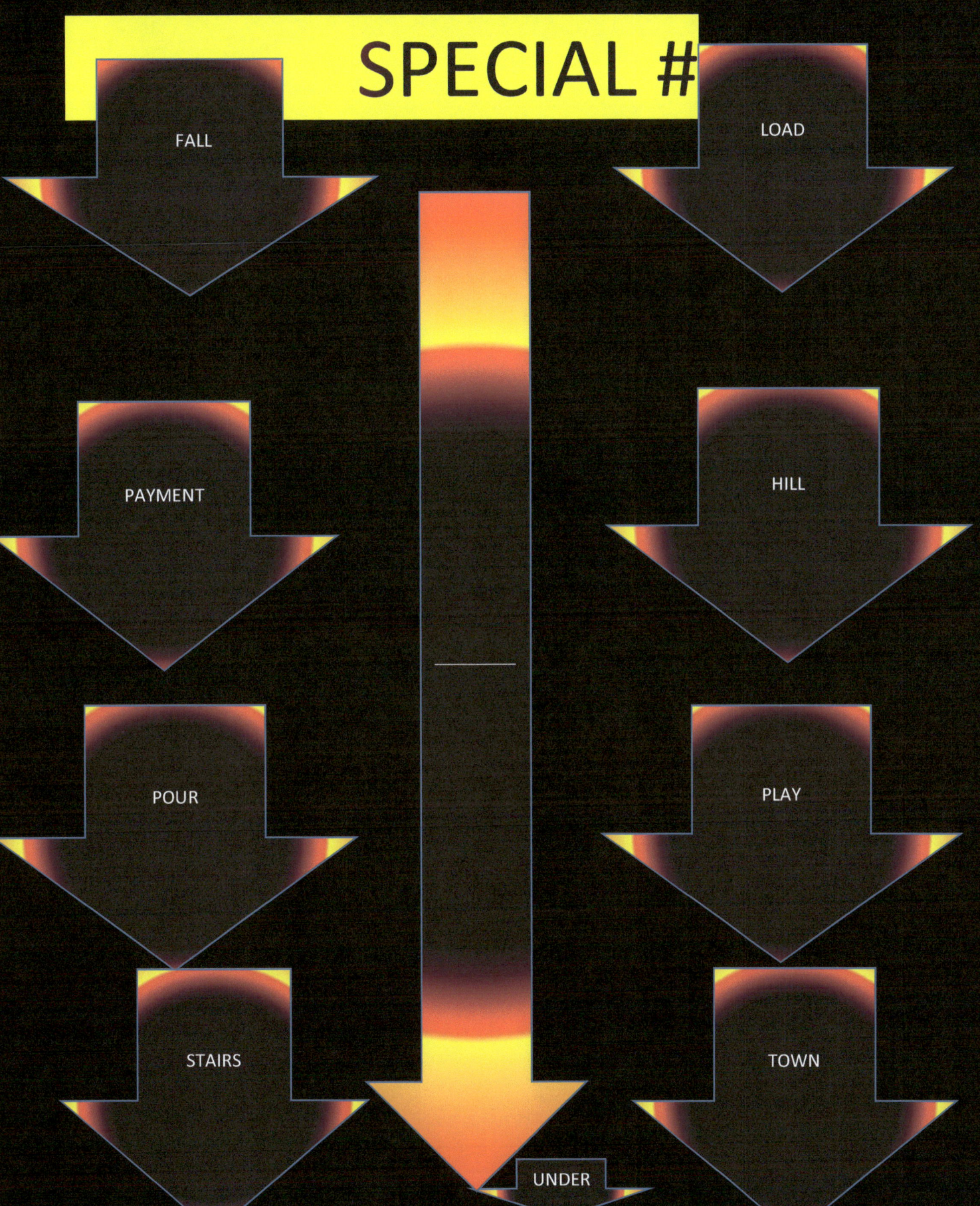

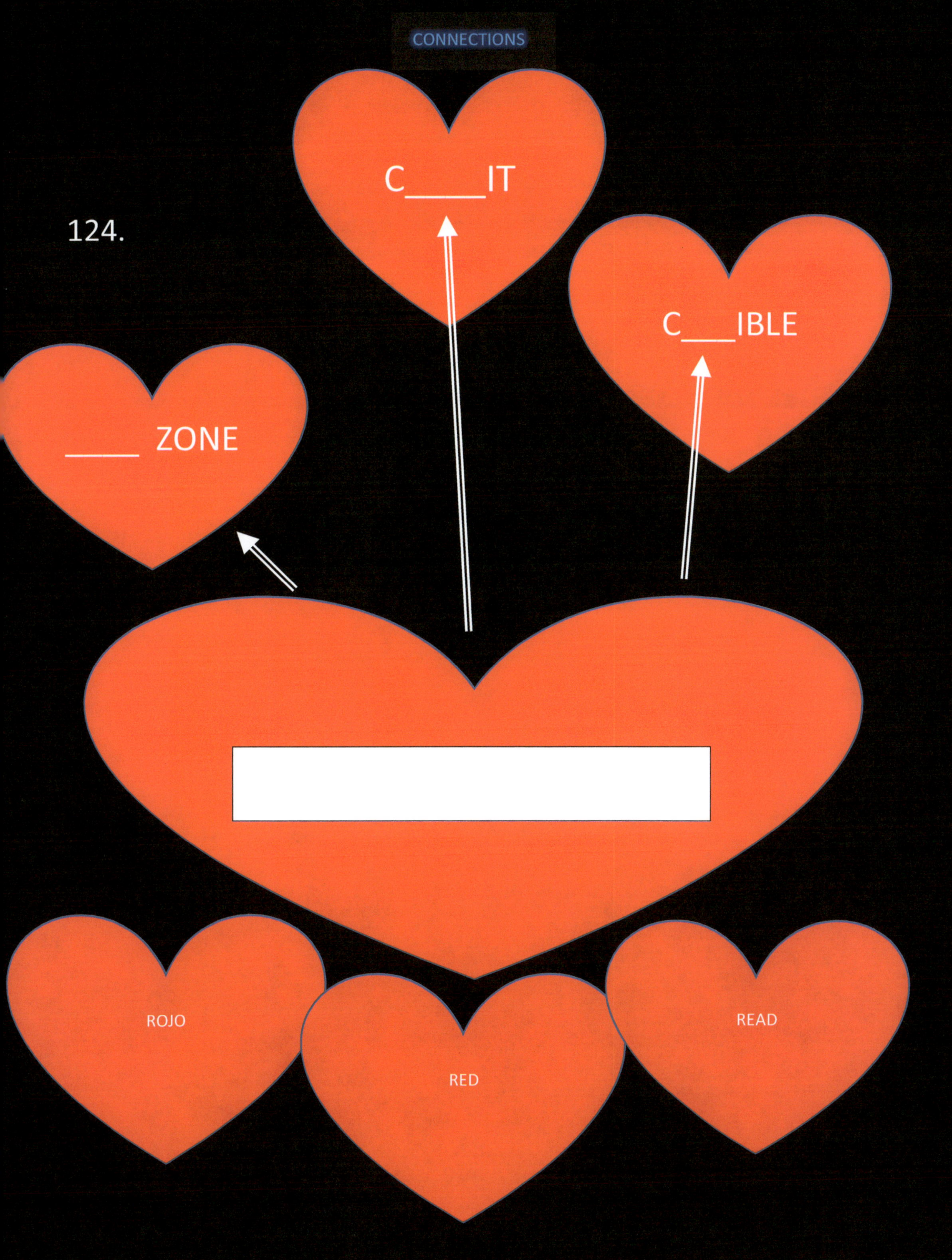

125.

WHICH BOX DO YOU THINK BREAKS DOWN THE NAMES THE BEST?

SAMANTHA	AMANDA	CARMEN

MANDY

IT'S A MAN. DUH. A MAN DUH ARE MEN MAN DIE	SAM IS A MAN. DUH. I AM AN. A MAN DUH. I WANT A CAR MAN. MANDATE	THE MAN SAM I AM THE AND. SEE. OUR MEN? MAN TEA

WOULD YOU NAME YOUR DAUGHTER ONE OF THESE NAMES?

DO YOU BELIEVE IN SACRIFICES AT BIRTH?

125

WHY WAS THE PREVIOUS PAGE MADE WITH HEARTS?

126.

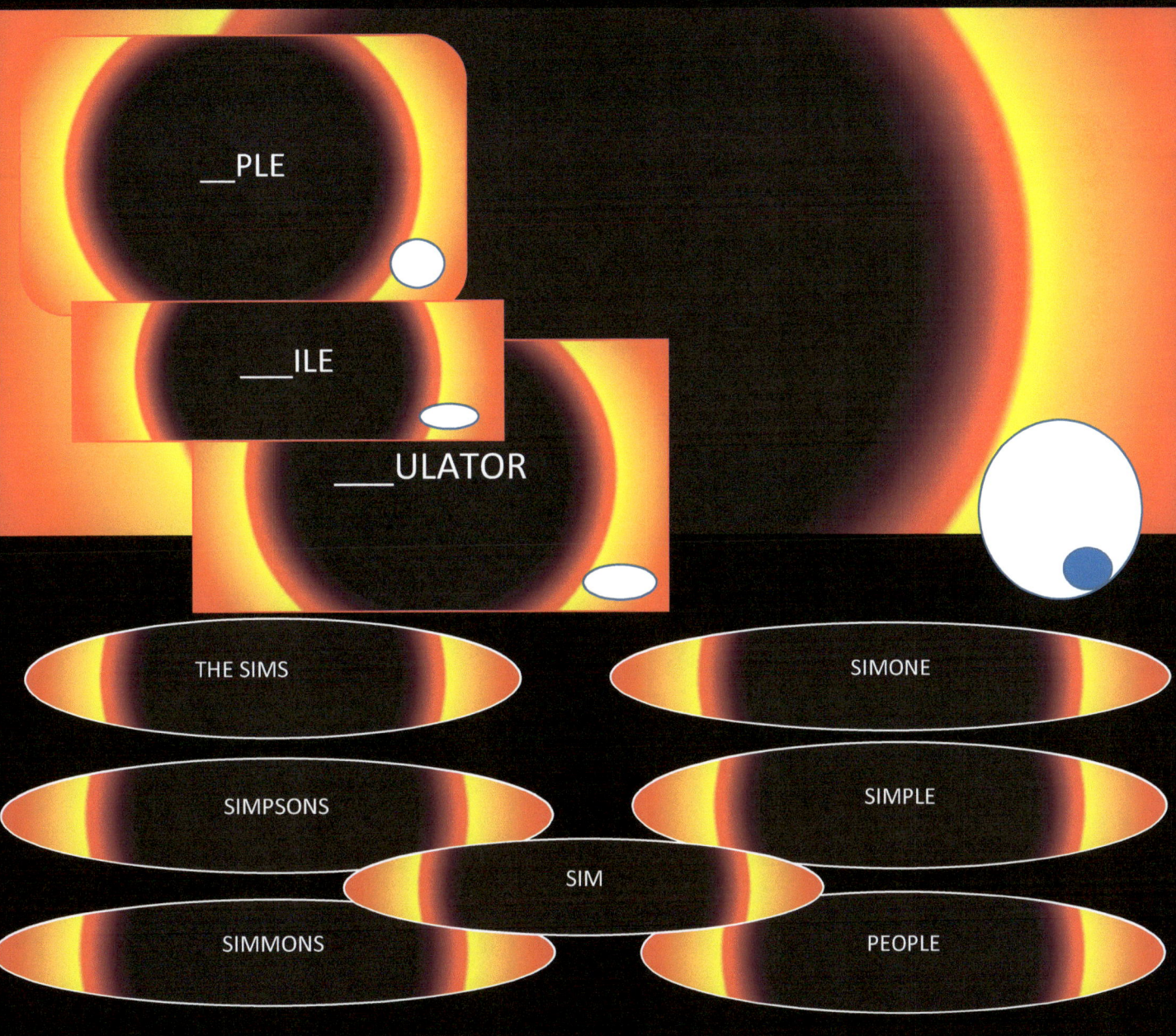

___PLE

___ILE

___ULATOR

THE SIMS

SIMONE

SIMPSONS

SIMPLE

SIM

SIMMONS

PEOPLE

THE PREVIOUS PAGE WAS MADE WITH HEARTS BECAUSE THE NUMBER 124 UNSCRAMBLED IS 2-14.

VALENTINE'S DAY

THE ANSWER TO EVERY QUESTION YOU HAVE ABOUT THIS PAGE IS IN MOST OF THE ANSWERS.

SI MEANS YES IN SPANISH

CONNECTIONS

HAMBURGER

____ER

____FUL

____LESS

HELICOPTER

A C R O P H O B I A

HEAL

IT'S A SETUP.

HEALTH

HELP

128.

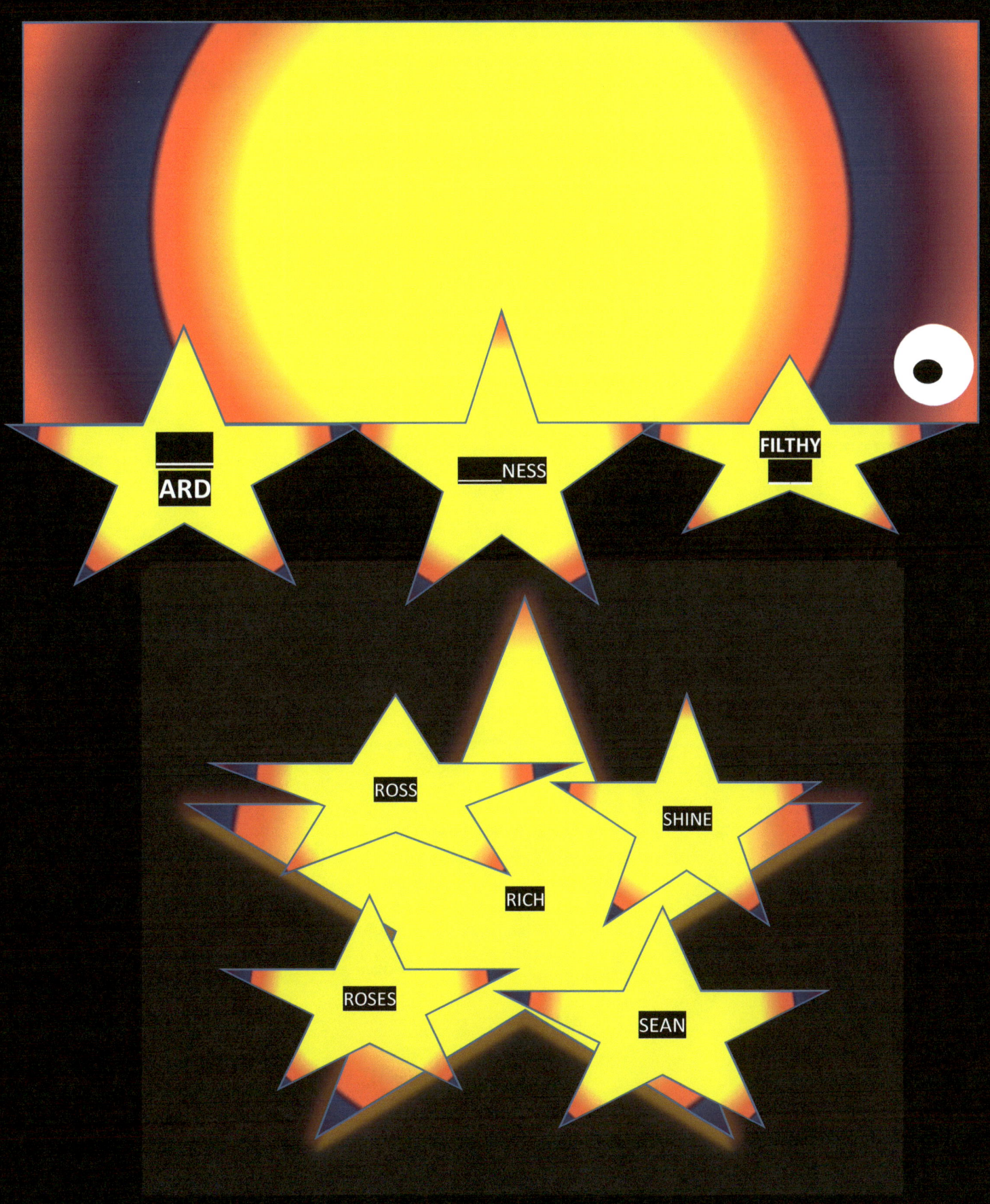

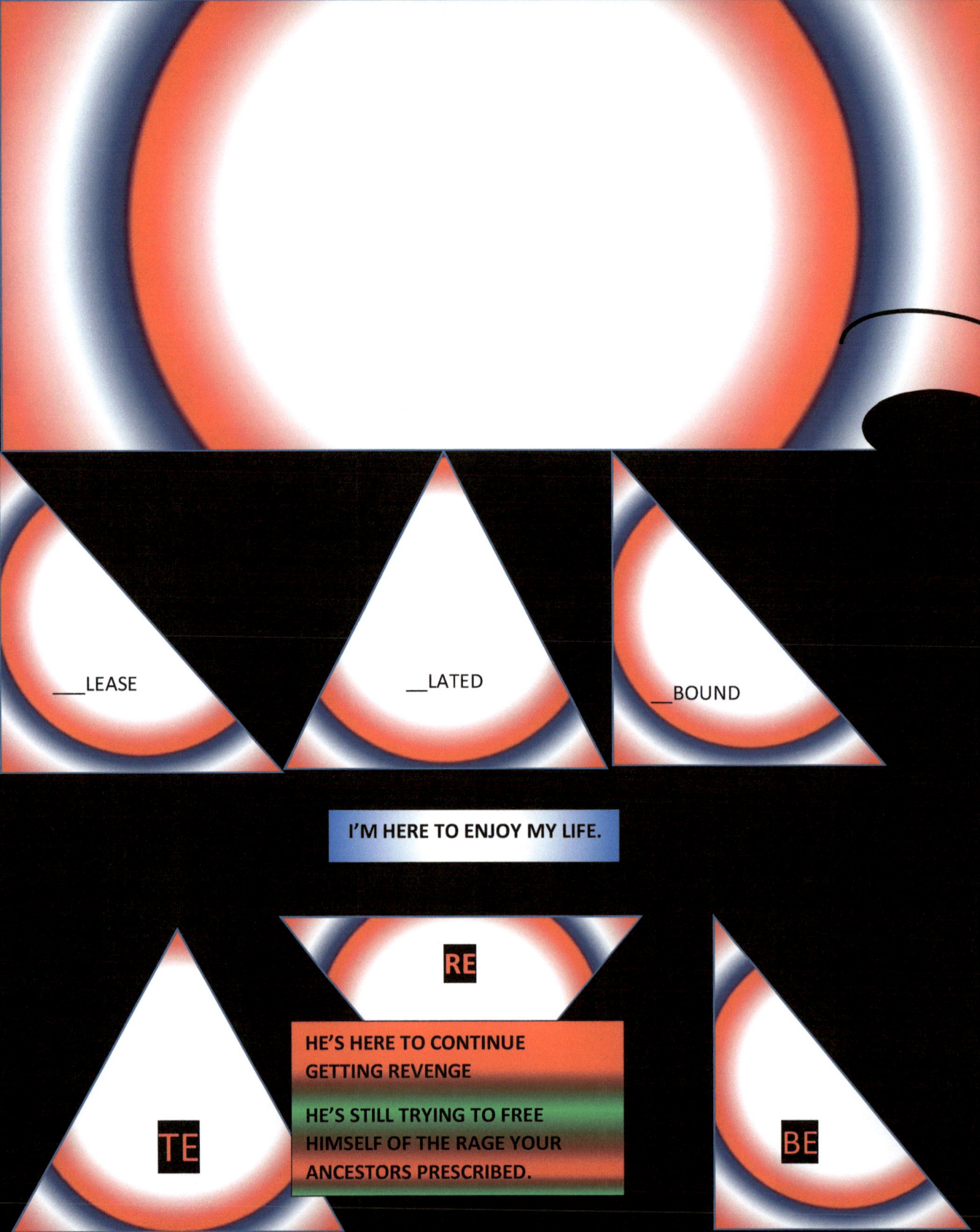

CONNECTIONS

130.

CONNECTIONS

HE

NEVER

LEFT

CONNECTIONS

HE'S BEEN HERE

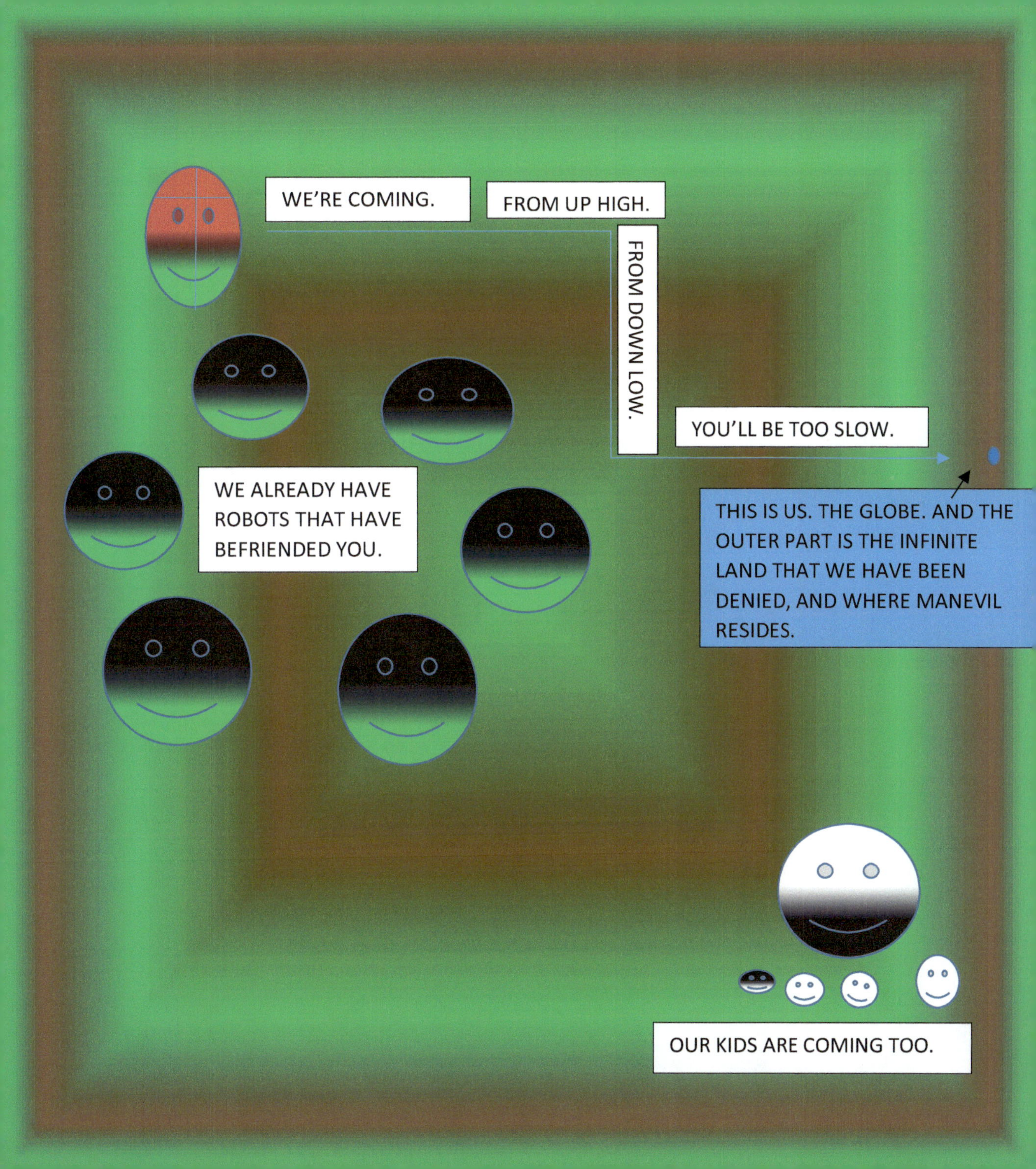

WE'RE COMING.
FROM UP HIGH.
FROM DOWN LOW.
YOU'LL BE TOO SLOW.
WE ALREADY HAVE ROBOTS THAT HAVE BEFRIENDED YOU.
THIS IS US. THE GLOBE. AND THE OUTER PART IS THE INFINITE LAND THAT WE HAVE BEEN DENIED, AND WHERE MANEVIL RESIDES.
OUR KIDS ARE COMING TOO.

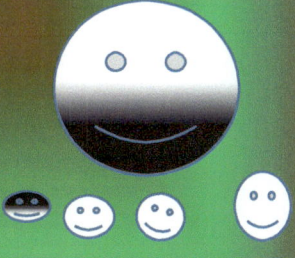

MANEVIL'S MESSAGE TO THE LAND SHOWN ON THE GLOBE:

UNTIL

DEATH

DO

US

PART

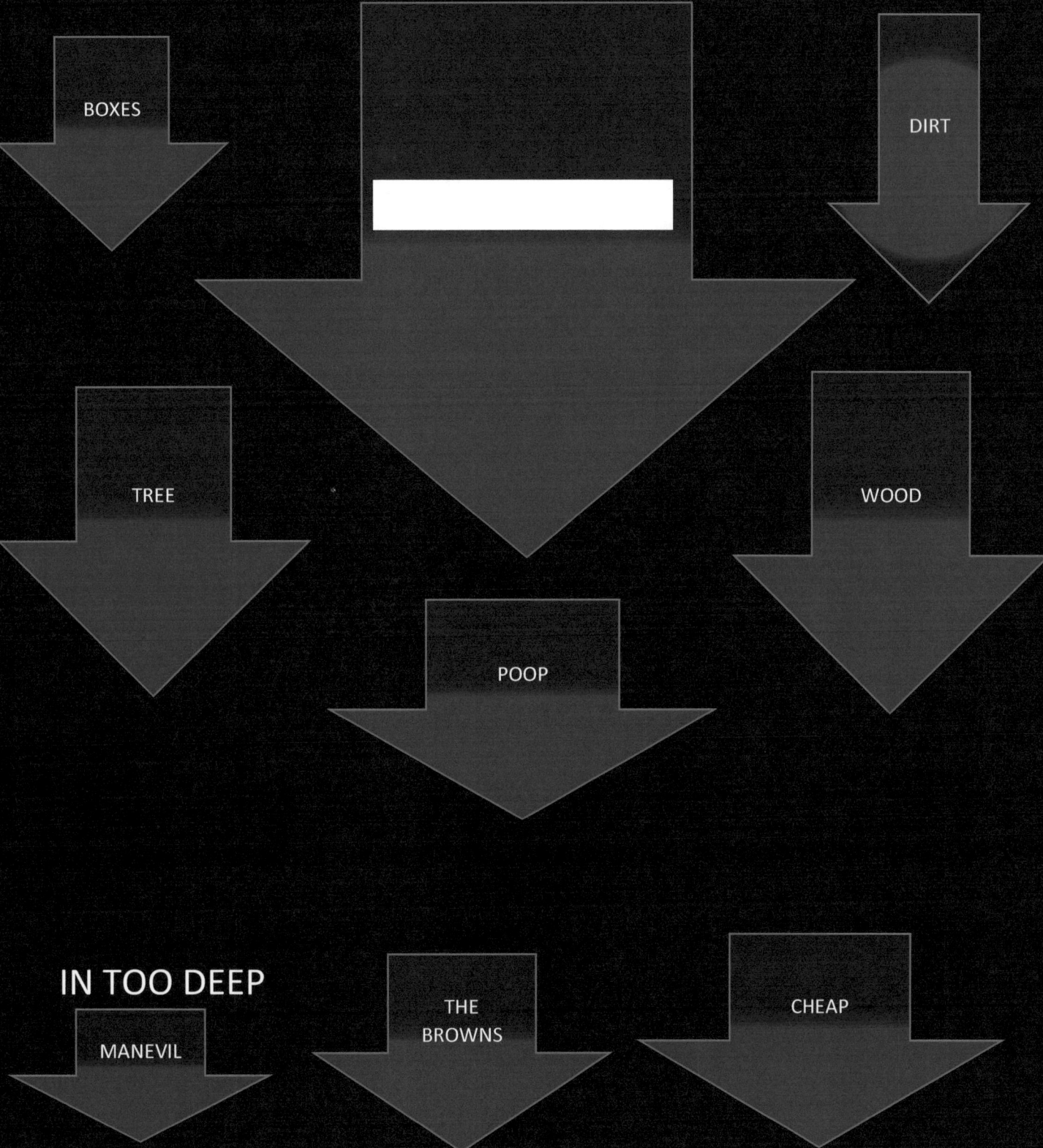

CONNECTIONS

WHO CAME UP WITH THE WORD BROWN?

WHO IS RESPONSIBLE FOR EVERY WORD IN EVERY HUMAN LANGUAGE?

EXAMPLE:

AUDIENCE

AU-DIE-NCE

ALL DIE

ALL DICE

ALL DIES

MAKING SENSE?

C AND S MAKE THE SAME SOUND IN A LOT OF WORDS RIGHT?

IT'S A SETUP.

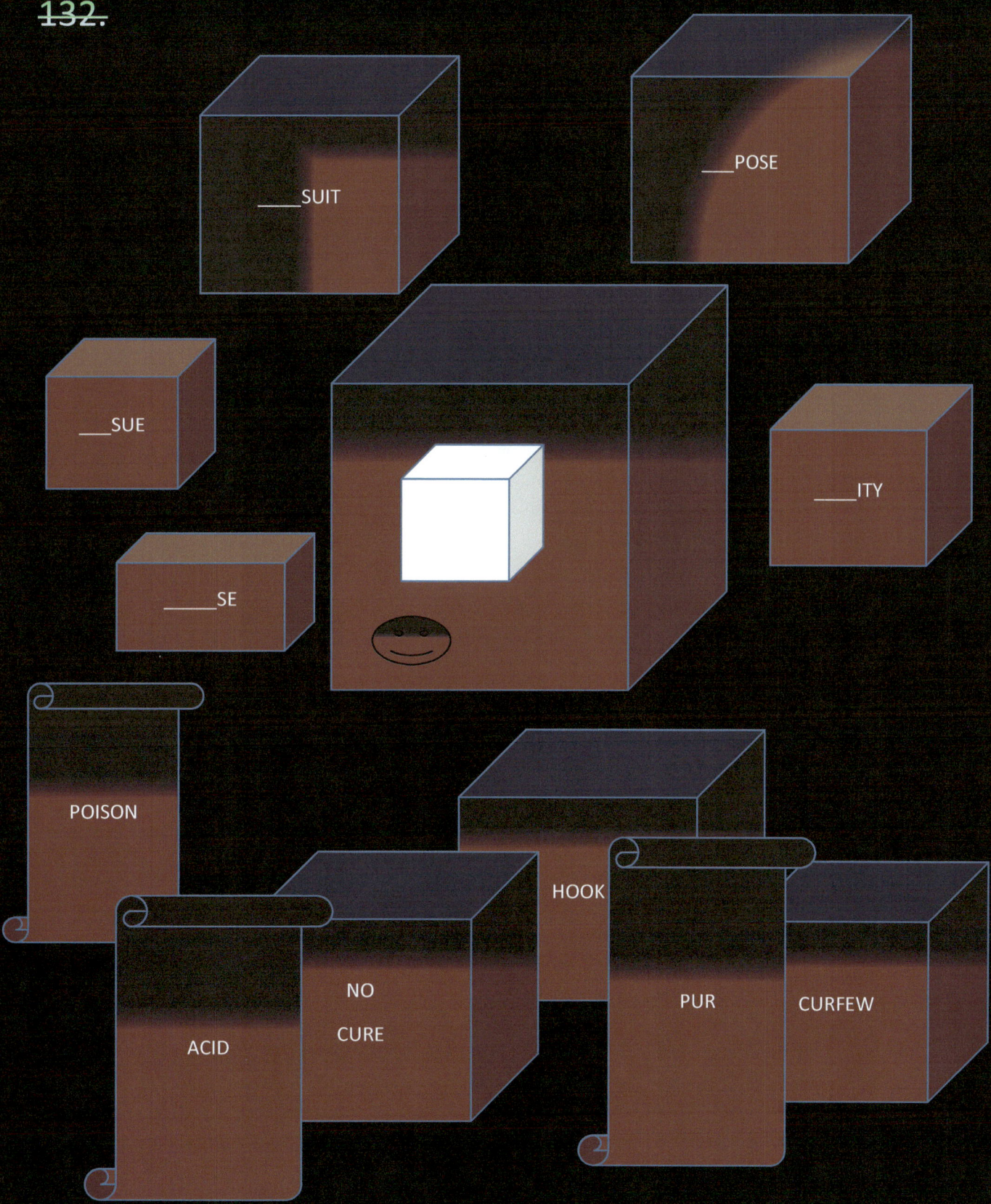

CONNECTIONS

THIS LAND IS INFINITE.

THE GLOBE. NOTHING BUT TARGET PRACTICE.

THE REAL WAR GAMES ARE COMING.

WILL YOU BE READY?

SOON NO ONE WILL KNOW WHAT ANYONE IS SAYING.

HE'S ANGRY.

YOU NEED ME.

                                                  THE APOCALYPSE.

CONNECTIONS

134.

HE'S ANGRY.
I DON'T KNOW IF HE WILL
EVER GET OVER WHAT
HAPPENED TO ME.

F____

S____

P____

| WORSE | AINT | NO COINCIDENCES |

CONNECTIONS

SEE A YOU?

YES. YOU. ELLA A.

MY NAME IS ABIGAIL AND EVERYTHING ABOUT ME IS A SACRIFICE.

MY MOTHER IS A MURDERER. SHE KILLED THE MAN THAT RAPED HER. TO AVOID PRISON TIME SHE MADE A DEAL WITH THE DEVIL, MANEVIL.

SACRIFICE ONE: GIVE HER BABY AWAY.

SACRIFICE TWO: GIVE HER A NAME THAT'S HARD TO PRONOUNCE.

SACRIFICE THREE: GIVE HER TWO DIFFERENT WAYS TO HEAR.

SACRIFICE FOUR: SEND CLONED RELATIVES TO ABUSE HER.

SACRIFICE FIVE: GIVE HER TWO BRUISES WHEN SHE GETS OLDER.

DO YOU GUYS WANT THE REAL SYSTEM?

IT IS DESIGNED FOR YOU TO FAIL.

THERE WAS A PLOT TO KILL ME.

IT NEVER FELL THROUGH.

SOMEONE'S ANGRY.

ABOUT THE PLOT AGAINST ME.

This is why the world is corrupt.

He's out for revenge.

135.

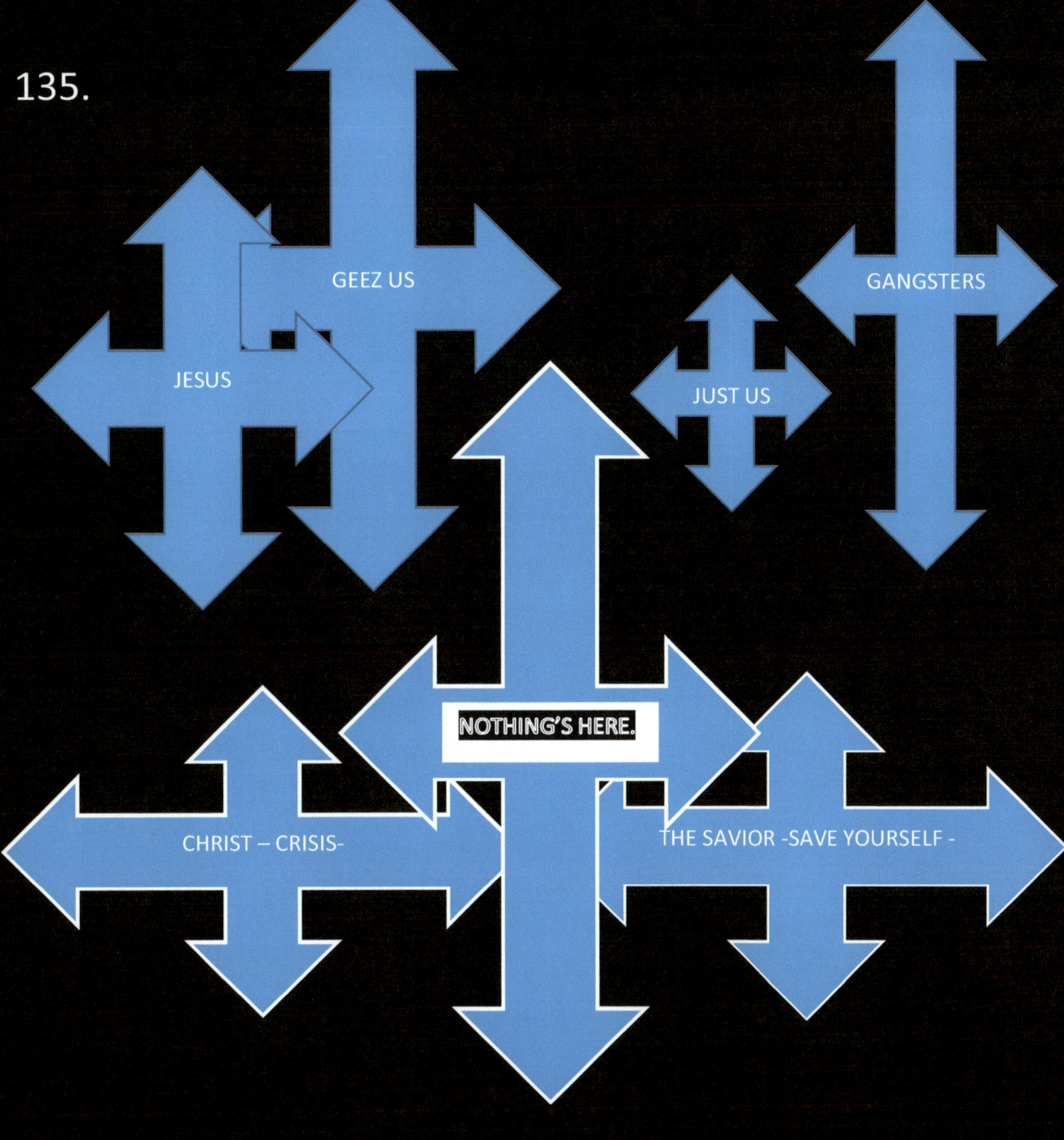

DO YOU STILL WANT TO SAY THE WORD AUDIENCE?

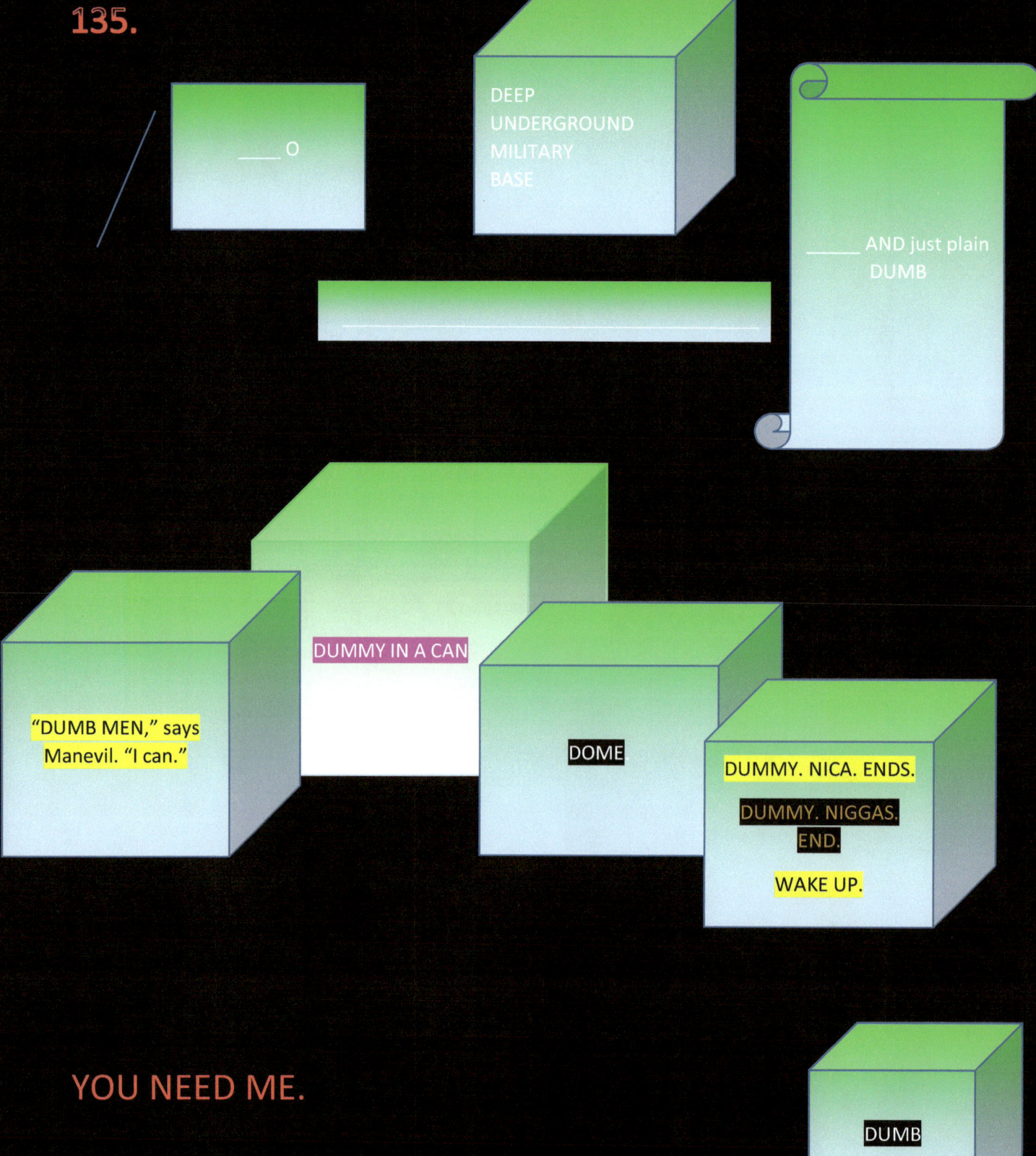

CONNECTIONS

MANEVIL

THEY'RE ALL IN PLAIN SIGHT.

I'M SWORN TO SECRECY.

I can never tell the secret.

CONNECTIONS

139. **What is the original meaning of the word Black?**

CONNECTIONS

Back

Love

Unfrozen

CONNECTIONS

Pop Quiz

1. Who is Manevil?
2. Is there a clone in every family?
3. What foods are safe to eat?
4. Where can cameras be placed?
5. Who is the real mind reader?
6. Who is God?
7. How angry would you be if you gave life to everyone, then they turned around and plotted to kill your **only child**?
8. How long would you let the people in question seven live?
9. What would you be willing to do to their descendants?
10. What happened here before April 13th 1989?
11. If you created the world, would you give it to your worst enemy?
12. Do you believe a human being can control the weather?
13. Did a white man start the KKK?
14. Did a white man start slavery?
15. When you pray, who are you praying to?
16. Were there ever any real presidents or just Dead Presidents?
17. Do you believe a human can read your mind?
18. What's the real reason so many black men are in prison?
19. Who is Manevil looking for?
20. If your dad gave you the choice of killing **everyone** whose ancestors tried to kill you, or **letting them live, which would you choose? Note: Your Dad is The One who gave them the gift of life.**
21. Have you ever played with fire and not got burned?
22. Do any bible stories sound stupid to you?
23. Does it bother you that some words are spelled the same but said different?

It's all in plain sight.

CONNECTIONS

24. Do you believe the world is corrupt because there's a plot for a New World Order with one country in power? A Dictatorship.
25. If yes, who is supposed to be the dictator?

BONUS QUESTION: Why do some people look more like your relatives than the people you call your relatives?

I don't like this place. And that's not good.

Everything is wrong here.
This is not how the world should be.

But because there was a plot to kill me:

There's no limit to what he will do.

He's angry.

Your ancestors wanted me dead.

He's been getting revenge ever since the day they threw me in the lake.

CONNECTIONS

Your ancestors were jealous.

"I was betrayed."

Now he's planning to blow this place up.

I don't know if I can change his mind.

He did all of this. **Our government, food, animals. Our entire lifestyle. He did it.**

He's not sorry.

Control.

He never gave it away.

He's just a man of his word.

Freedom of choice.

CONNECTIONS

FEAR

ALL

CONNECTIONS

ATHEIST

A
THE
IS
T

CONNECTIONS

A

THEE

IS

CHRIST

He never existed.

WAKE

UP

CONNECTIONS

A REAL LIFE HORROR SHOW COMING TO THE GLOBE

CONNECTIONS

THE LAND IS INFINITE.

FAR MORE THAN WHAT YOU SEE.

HE'S ANGRY!

IT'S

A

CLONED

WORLD

PAYBACK

"HA! EVEN!"

CONNECTIONS

That car accident you were in.

You're right.

He could've stopped it.

But he didn't.

His excuse: me.

That cancer in your body.

You're right.

He can remove it.

But he won't.

His excuse, me.

That tumor in your body.

You're right.

He can remove it without the help of a surgeon.

But he won't.

His excuse: me.

CONNECTIONS

Your unfortunate child.

You're right.

He can give him what he wants back.

But he won't.

His excuse: me.

Question: Does it bother you that clones can be created but some people are unfortunate?

CONNECTIONS

The natural disasters.

You're right.

He did send them.

His excuse: me.

The World Wars.

He caused the division.

His excuse: me.

The terrorist attacks.

You're right.

He was the clone that started them.

His excuse: me.

Question: Does it bother you that some terrorists are so damn fine?

My dad is evil.

ICE IS WHY.

CONNECTIONS

Your phone and laptop freezing.

He's fucking with you.

Are you scared to pick up the phone?

How many times have you been baptized?

Do you know what baptism symbolizes?

CONNECTIONS

Is your husband always putting you down?

Does his anger come out of nowhere?

You wonder why it's so mean?

It's a clone.

My Dad needs to release his anger.

He's not sorry.

He's a savage.

You haven't seen nothing yet.

Truth!

CONNECTIONS

Understand.

He's speeding time up.

He's a savage.

We use a piece of paper to purchase things.

That's stupid.

It's systematic.

He's not sorry.

CONNECTIONS

My dad's a savage.

He won't stop.

I don't know what I can do.

CONNECTIONS

My dad used the first people that tried to kill me to build the first line of clones.

He's a fair man.

He didn't kill the people that killed me.

That is unfair.

He used the clones of the people that tried to kill me to kill the first:

people.

CONNECTIONS

So just who are the real He Bruise?

"Fair All."

CONNECTIONS

The world is now a playground.

My dad will kill someone here, kill someone there, punch someone for nothing, or burn down cell.

CONNECTIONS

Why is it that I look so young?

My dad's making up for lost time.

CONNECTIONS

He needed me.

CONNECTIONS

BE

PREPARED

CONNECTIONS

I'M SCARED MY DAMN SELF.

CONNECTIONS

I must give my dad props.

He didn't put me through more than I could bare.

CONNECTIONS

"hi,"

www.ingramcontent.com/pod-product-compliance
Lightning Source LLC
Chambersburg PA
CBHW041510220426
43661CB00047B/1520